Perfect
Quilts *for*
Precut Fabrics

Perfect Quilts *for* Precut Fabrics

64 Patterns for Fat Quarters, Charm Squares, Jelly Rolls, and Layer Cakes

Martingale®
Create with Confidence

Perfect Quilts for Precut Fabrics: 64 Patterns for Fat Quarters, Charm Squares, Jelly Rolls, and Layer Cakes
© 2014 by Martingale & Company®

Martingale
19021 120th Ave. NE, Ste. 102
Bothell, WA 98011-9511 USA
ShopMartingale.com

Printed in China

19 18 17   8 7 6 5 4

Library of Congress Cataloging-in-Publication Data is available upon request.

ISBN: 978-1-60468-413-1

MISSION STATEMENT

Dedicated to providing quality products and service to inspire creativity.

CREDITS

PRESIDENT AND CEO: Tom Wierzbicki

EDITOR IN CHIEF: Mary V. Green

DESIGN DIRECTOR: Paula Schlosser

MANAGING EDITOR: Karen Costello Soltys

ACQUISITIONS EDITOR: Karen M. Burns

COPY EDITOR: Sheila Chapman Ryan

PRODUCTION MANAGER: Regina Girard

COVER AND INTERIOR DESIGNER: Paula Schlosser

TEXT LAYOUT: Dianna Logan / DBS

PHOTOGRAPHER: Brent Kane

ILLUSTRATORS: Christine Erikson, Lisa Lauch, Rose Sheifer, Missy Shepler, Adrienne Smitke, Laurel Strand, and Robin Strobel

CONTENTS

INTRODUCTION

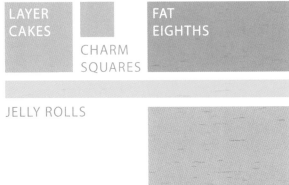

Fat quarter, Jelly Roll, Layer Cake, charm! It sounds a little like a schoolyard rhyme, doesn't it? And that's fitting, since all those different sizes of precut fabrics make quilting as easy and fun as skipping rope.

What's your favorite precut? Is it the generously sized fat quarter that allows you to cut a wide variety of sizes and shapes? Maybe the Jelly Roll is your go-to cut; those 2½"-wide ribbons of color and print make piecing a breeze. Charm squares are ideal for scrap quilts, while Layer Cakes offer terrific versatility. And the fat eighth, a relative newcomer, is quickly growing in popularity. Whatever precuts fill your stash, you'll find the perfect patterns for them here.

We gathered some of the most popular projects from our best-selling books and sorted them into sections according to the precut used. That means the next time you come home from your local quilt shop with a Jelly Roll you just couldn't resist, you can simply open to the Jelly Roll section of the book and choose from one of the 14 patterns there. What could be easier?

Large and small, traditional and modern, pieced and appliquéd—you'll find them all here, along with valuable tips for successfully working with precut fabrics. So go ahead: unwrap that bundle, pick a pattern, and start stitching. It's child's play!

TIPS FOR WORKING WITH PRECUTS

Using precut fabric bundles can make quick work of piecing a quilt top, since so much of the cutting has already been done for you. Plus, buying a precut bundle allows you to have a little bit of each different print and colorway in any given fabric line, so you can incorporate all of them into one quilt if you like.

If you're new to using precut fabrics, there are a few things that will be helpful for you to know.

What's in a Name?

Let's start with the terminology. Different companies may call their precut fabrics by different names, but here are the basics.

Moda Jelly Roll. Bundle of 2½"-wide strips, cut across the width of the fabric. It generally contains 40 strips.

Moda Honey Bun. Bundle of 1½"-wide strips, cut across the width of the fabric. It generally contains 40 strips.

Moda Layer Cake. Packet of 10" squares, 40 per packet.

Charm pack. Packet of 5" squares, usually 35 to 40 per packet, but the number can vary from 22 to more than 50.

Moda Turnover. Packet of 6" half-square triangles; each packet contains two triangles each of 40 fabrics for a total of 80 triangles.

Moda Dessert Roll. Roll of 5"-wide strips, cut across the width of the fabric. There are 10 fabrics per roll.

Fat quarter. Half of a half-yard of fabric; generally measures 18" x 21". Fat quarters may be purchased individually, or in bundles of various numbers, from four coordinating fat quarters to 35 or 40—a full fabric line.

Fat eighth. Half of a quarter-yard of fabric; generally measures 9" x 21". Fat eighths are usually sold in bundles, but some shops may sell them individually.

Tips for Success

Now that you know your options, we'd like to share some of our favorite tips discovered from working with precut fabrics.

Unwrapping Jelly Rolls and Honey Buns

To keep your long strips from tangling, gently ease the roll open and clip or secure the strips at one end. Pin the ends of the strips to your ironing board to hold them in place, and then fan them apart and choose the strips you want by easing them away from the rest.

Don't Prewash!

If you prefer to prewash your fabrics before cutting and sewing, learn to resist the temptation to wash or even rinse your precut fabrics. Washing could cause the fabric to fray, ravel, or shrink, resulting in pieces that are no longer accurately cut. If you're worried about fabrics bleeding when it comes time to wash your finished quilt, use this trick from Carrie Nelson of Miss Rosie's Quilt Company: Toss a Shout Color Catcher sheet in the washing machine. These sheets resemble fabric-softener dryer sheets, but they're made to catch any dyes that may run out of fabric during the wash cycle and prevent them from bleeding onto other parts of your quilt.

Working with Pinked Edges

Don't trim the pinked edges off any of the precut fabrics; you won't have enough fabric to make the quilt if you do. When aligning your fabrics for subcutting or sewing, use the outer points of the pinked edges as the edge of the fabrics so that your ¼" seam allowances will be accurate.

Presort Your Precuts

When you purchase a package of precut strips, squares, or even fat quarters, they all "go together" because they're from the same fabric line. But you'll have to do a bit of planning to determine which fabrics will best work together in your quilt. Many of the projects in this book explain how to sort the fabrics prior to cutting, whether it's merely separating darks from lights, or making pairs or groups of three or four fabrics that will work nicely together in individual blocks.

Undoubtedly, you won't be able to find exactly the same fabrics that were used for the quilts in this book (unless you already have the same fabric line in your stash). So, when you select your favorite Jelly Roll, Layer Cake, or charm pack, just follow the guidelines on sorting the fabrics to make sure your collection of fabrics will work for the pattern you want to make.

Use It Up

If your project ends up looking a bit on the scrappy side, consider making the binding scrappy, too. A Jelly Roll's 2½"-wide precut strips are just the right width for making double-fold binding. However, your set may have just one strip of each print per colorway. So to use up the leftover strips (full-length or partial strips), consider stitching them together end to end using a diagonal seam to make the perfect scrappy ending to your quilt.

Folded Corners

When you're working exclusively with uniform-width strips, such as 2½"-wide Jelly Roll strips, making triangle shapes that finish to the same dimensions as square or rectangular pieces won't work if you cut them traditionally. But, if you use one of the cleverest tricks around—the folded corner—you can make accurate 45° angles that work perfectly without having to cut triangles.

Several of the projects in this book use the folded-corner technique. If you're not familiar with it, here's how to do it. In this example, we'll show a rectangle with contrasting corners, but you can also use the technique for strips and squares.

1 Draw a diagonal line from corner to corner on the wrong side of a 2½" square (or other size as specified in the project directions).

2 Position the square right sides together on one corner of the rectangle as shown so that the diagonal line goes from top edge to side edge, not from the corner to the interior of the rectangle.

3 Stitch on the marked line. Press to set the stitches, and then trim away the excess fabric in the corner, leaving a ¼"-wide seam allowance. Press the remaining triangle of fabric open.

4 Continue as described in your project's instructions, using the folded-corner technique to either add squares to the remaining corners of the rectangle or add squares to the ends of strips.

Need More Help?

For useful information on quiltmaking, from rotary cutting, pressing, and sewing to binding your finished quilt, go to ShopMartingale.com/HowtoQuilt to download illustrated tutorials. They're free!

PART 1

Layer Cakes

10" SQUARES

Nash

According to Carrie, this is what happens when you try to make a quilt using a piece of string, a gum wrapper, and a plastic bag. OK, not really, but she does like to ask herself, "What can I make from the pieces I have that lets me use them in a way that's different?" Here's what you can make.

"Nash," designed and pieced by Carrie Nelson; machine quilted by LeAnne Olson

FINISHED QUILT: 70½" x 70½" • FINISHED BLOCK: 14¼" x 14¼"

Materials

Yardage is based on 42"-wide fabric, except where noted.

1¾ yards of light print for blocks and inner border*
64 assorted 10" squares for blocks and outer border
¾ yard of fabric for binding
4¾ yards of fabric for backing
79" x 79" piece of batting

*If you want to use a variety of light prints, you'll need 16 assorted light 10" squares for blocks and ½ yard of a light print for inner border.

Cutting

From the light print, cut:
4 strips, 10" x 42"; crosscut into 16 squares, 10" x 10".
 Cut each square into quarters diagonally to yield
 64 triangles.
6 strips, 2½" x 42"

From *each of 31* of the assorted squares, cut:
1 strip, 5" x 10" (31 total; 1 is extra)
1 strip, 4" x 10"; crosscut into 2 squares, 4" x 4"
 (62 total)

From *1* of the assorted squares, cut:
1 strip, 4" x 10"; crosscut into 2 squares, 4" x 4"
4 squares, 2½" x 2½"

From *each* of the remaining 32 assorted squares, cut:
3 strips, 3¼" x 10" (96 total)

From the binding fabric, cut:
300" of 2"-wide bias strips

Piecing the Blocks

For each block, you'll need the following pieces:

- **Four-patch unit:** four different 4" squares
- **Inner triangles:** four light quarter-square triangles
- **Outer triangles:** four different strip-pieced triangles

Use a scant ¼"-wide seam allowance throughout. After sewing each seam, press the seam allowances in the direction indicated by the arrows (or press them open).

1 Lay out four 4" squares as shown. Sew the squares together in pairs, and then sew the pairs together to make a four-patch unit. Make 16 four-patch units, each measuring 7½" square. Use a seam ripper to remove several stitches in the seam allowance. Open the seam allowance and reposition the fabrics in a clockwise or counterclockwise direction. Press the seam allowances in opposite directions so that the center lies flat.

Make 16.

2 Sew light quarter-square triangles to the sides of the four-patch units from step 1 as shown. Make 16 units and trim them to 10½" square.

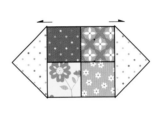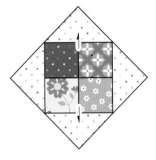

Make 16.

3 Sew three 3¼" x 10" strips together along their long edges to make a strip-pieced rectangle. Make 32 rectangles, each measuring 8¾" x 10".

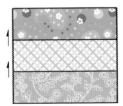

Make 32.

4 Trim each strip-pieced rectangle to make an 8¾" square. Cut each strip-pieced square in half diagonally to make two half-square triangles. Cut a total of 64 triangles, taking care to have all the squares aligned in the same direction as shown. The direction of the strips in the triangles does matter!

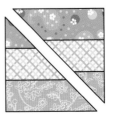

Cut 64 triangles.

5 Fold each triangle in half and finger-crease to mark the center on the long side. Stitch triangles to opposite sides of the unit from step 2, matching the center crease to the crossed seams. Sew triangles to the remaining sides of the unit as shown to complete the block. Repeat to make a total of 16 blocks.

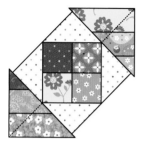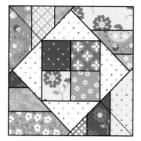

Make 16.

6 Using a large square ruler, trim each block to measure 14¾" square. To properly align the ruler, align the 7⅜" lines on the ruler with the outermost points of the light triangles as shown. Make sure that both points are lined up before trimming; that way the points will match when the blocks are sewn together. There will likely be a ⅜" seam allowance between the outer edge of the block and the outermost points of the light triangles. Carrie chose to trim less off the block to keep the strips a uniform size. You're welcome to trim a lot or a little. The most important thing is that the blocks are all trimmed to the same size and that you have at least ¼" seam allowance.

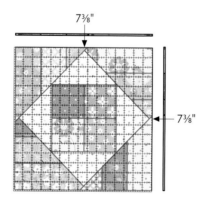

Assembling the Quilt Top

1 Lay out the blocks in four rows of four blocks each as shown in the quilt assembly diagram on page 15.

2 Sew the blocks together into rows, pressing the seam allowances in opposite directions from row to row (or press them open). Then sew the rows together and press. The quilt top should measure 57½" x 57½".

3 For the inner border, sew the light 2½"-wide strips together end to end. From the strip, cut four 57½"-long strips. Sew two strips to the sides of the quilt top and press the seam allowances toward the borders.

4 Sew assorted 2½" squares to both ends of the two remaining border strips and press. Sew these borders to the top and bottom of the quilt top and press the seam allowances toward the borders.

5 For the outer border, sort the assorted 5" x 10" strips into the following groups:

- **Side borders:** two groups of seven strips each
- **Top and bottom borders:** two groups of eight strips each

Join each group of rectangles end to end to make four long strips. Press the seam allowances in one direction (or press them open). For the side borders, trim the two shorter strips to measure 5" x 61½". For the top and bottom borders, trim the two longer strips to measure 5" x 70½".

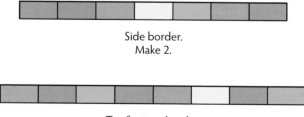

Side border.
Make 2.

Top/bottom border.

6 Sew the border strips to the sides, and then the top and bottom of the quilt top, keeping the pinked edges on the outside. Press the seam allowances toward the outer border.

Finishing the Quilt

For help with any of the finishing steps, go to ShopMartingale.com/HowtoQuilt for free downloadable information.

1 Layer, baste, and quilt your quilt, or take it to your favorite long-arm quilter for finishing.

2 Using the 2"-wide binding strips, make and attach binding.

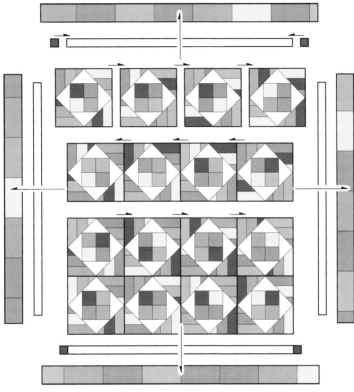

Quilt assembly

Roundabout

Loops, hoops, circles, cycles, and rings—Carrie loves round things, circle-y things, things with a curve. Donuts. Hoop earrings. Ferris wheels. Soap bubbles. Life Savers. Bowls. Cookies—they're mostly round, or really round if you use a scoop to make them. So what's not to love about a block that looks a bit like a circle or the letter O?

"Roundabout," designed by Carrie Nelson; pieced and machine quilted by Darlene Johannis

FINISHED QUILT: 73½" x 73½" • FINISHED BLOCK: 12" x 12"

Materials

Yardage is based on 42"-wide fabric, except where noted.

2⅞ yards of light fabric for block backgrounds and inner border

50 assorted 10" squares for blocks

23 assorted 10" squares for outer border

¾ yard of fabric for binding

7 yards of fabric for backing

82" x 82" piece of batting

Cutting

From the light fabric, cut:

16 strips, 4½" x 42"; crosscut into 125 squares, 4½" x 4½"

7 strips, 2½" x 42"

From *each* of the 50 assorted squares for blocks, cut:

2 rectangles, 4½" x 8½" (100 total)

From *each of 22* assorted squares for outer border, cut:

3 strips, 2½" x 10" (66 total; 2 are extra)

From the remaining square for outer border, cut:

4 squares, 5" x 5"

From the binding fabric, cut:

306" of 2"-wide bias strips

Piecing the Blocks

For each block, you'll need the following pieces:

- Four different 4½" x 8½" rectangles
- Five 4½" squares

Use a scant ¼"-wide seam allowance throughout. After sewing each seam, press the seam allowances in the direction indicated by the arrows (or press them open).

1 Draw a diagonal line from corner to corner on the wrong side of four of the background squares. Place a marked square on one end of rectangle, making sure the square is positioned exactly as shown. Sew along the marked line and trim, leaving a ¼" seam allowance. Repeat to make a total of four pieced rectangles.

 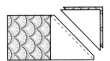

Make 4.

2 Lay out the four pieced rectangles and the remaining background square as shown.

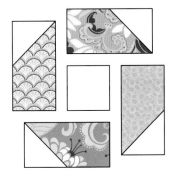

3 Sew a rectangle to the top of the background square, stitching a little more than halfway as shown. Press the unit open as indicated.

4 Sew the next rectangle to the left edge of the unit from step 3.

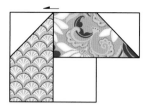

5 Sew a third rectangle to the bottom of the unit, and then sew the last rectangle to the right edge of the unit as shown.

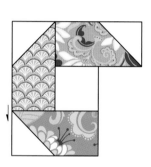 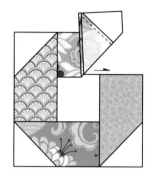

6 Complete the partial seam stitched in step 3. You can start where you stopped stitching and sew toward the outside raw edge, or you can start at the outside edge and sew toward the center square, whichever you prefer. The block should measure 12½" square. Repeat to make a total of 25 blocks.

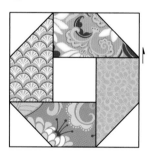

Make 25.

Assembling the Quilt Top

1 Lay out the blocks in five rows of five blocks each as shown in the quilt assembly diagram on page 19. Sew the blocks together in rows. Press the seam allowances in opposite directions from row to row (or press them open).

2 Sew the rows together and press the seam allowances in one direction (or press them open). The quilt center should measure 60½" x 60½".

3 For the inner border, sew the light 2½"-wide strips together end to end. From the long strip, cut two 60½"-long strips and sew them to the sides of the quilt top. Cut two 64½"-long strips and sew them to the top and bottom of the quilt top. Press the seam allowances toward the inner border.

4 For the outer border, sort the assorted 2½" x 10" strips to make two sets of 32 strips each. Select one set of strips and sort it into four groups of eight strips each. Join each group of eight strips side by side as shown. Press the seam allowances in one direction (or press them open). Make four pieced sections each measuring 10" x 16½". Repeat to make a second set of four pieced sections.

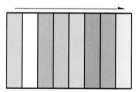

Make 8.

5 Cut each pieced section in half lengthwise to make 16 pieced outer-border strips, and then sort them into two groups of two matching sets.

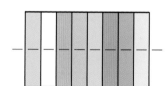 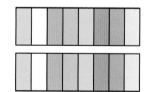

6 Join one set of strips to make a 5" x 64½" pieced outer-border strip, keeping the pinked edges on the same side. Press the seam allowances in one direction (or press them open). Repeat to make a total of four pieced outer-border strips.

7 Sew an outer-border strip to each side of the quilt top, keeping the pinked edges on the outside. Press the seam allowances toward the outer border.

8 Join 5" squares to the ends of the two remaining outer-border strips. Press the seam allowances toward the border strip. Sew these borders to the top and bottom of the quilt top and press the seam allowances toward the outer border.

Finishing the Quilt

For help with any of the finishing steps, go to ShopMartingale.com/HowtoQuilt for free downloadable information.

1 Layer, baste, and quilt your quilt, or take it to your favorite long-arm quilter for finishing.

2 Using the 2"-wide binding strips, make and attach binding.

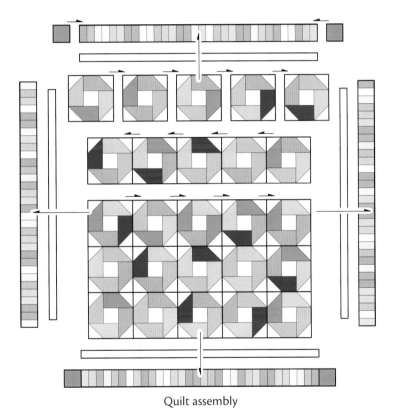

Quilt assembly

Rebecca

The design team behind Me and My Sister Quilts named this pretty
project after their niece Rebecca. (She must be a lucky girl!)

"Rebecca," designed and pieced by Mary Jacobson and Barbara Groves

FINISHED QUILT: 71" x 85" • FINISHED BLOCK: 9" x 9"

Materials

Yardage is based on 42"-wide fabric, except where noted.

50 coordinating 10" squares for blocks

2¼ yards of pink print for inner and outer borders and binding

2 yards of white solid for blocks, sashing, and middle border

5½ yards of fabric for backing

79" x 93" piece of batting

Cutting

From the white solid, cut:

4 strips, 2½" x 42"; crosscut into 64 squares, 2½" x 2½"

10 strips, 1½" x 42"; crosscut into 38 rectangles, 1½" x 9½"

23 strips, 1½" x 42"

From the pink print, cut:

15 strips, 3½" x 42"

9 strips, 2¼" x 42"

Making the Four Patch Flip Blocks

Choose 32 of the 10" squares for the blocks. The remaining 18 squares will be used for the setting blocks on the sides and corners.

1 Draw a diagonal line on the wrong side of the white 2½" squares.

2 Place a white 2½" square on each corner of a 10" square. Stitch on the drawn lines. Trim the seam allowance to ¼", flip, and press. Make 16.

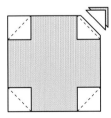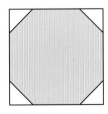

Make 16.

3 Layer one block from step 2 and one 10" square right sides together. Using a ¼" seam allowance, stitch along two opposite sides of the squares as shown.

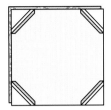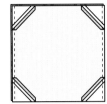

4 Cut through the vertical center of the squares as shown and press the seam allowances open. Make 32 units.

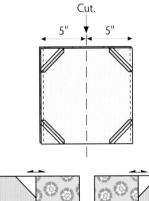

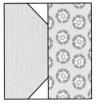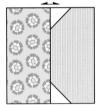

Make 32.

5 Divide the 32 units from step 4 into 16 new pairs of contrasting colors or values. With right sides together, layer each pair, aligning the seams. Make sure that the white corners are opposite each other as shown. Using a ¼" seam allowance, stitch along two opposite sides, making sure to stitch across the previous seam lines as shown.

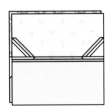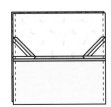

6 Cut through the vertical center of the sewn units as shown and press the seam allowances open. The blocks should measure 9½" x 9½". Make a total of 32 Four Patch Flip blocks.

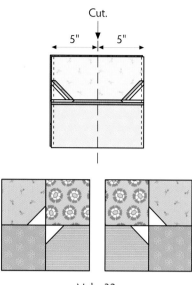

Make 32.

Making Blocks for Setting Triangles

1 Divide the 18 remaining 10" squares into nine pairs, combining two contrasting colors or contrasting values (light and dark).

2 Layer each pair of squares right sides together. Using a ¼" seam allowance, stitch along two opposite sides of the squares as shown.

3 Cut through the vertical center of the squares as shown and press the seam allowances open. Make a total of 18 two-patch units.

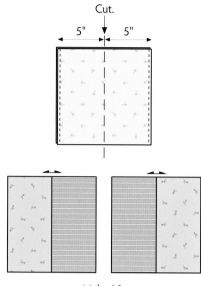

Make 18.

4 Divide the 18 two-patch units from step 3 into nine new combinations of contrasting pairs. With right sides together, layer a pair of two-patch units, aligning the seams. Using a ¼" seam allowance, stitch along two opposite sides, making sure to stitch across the previous seam lines as shown. Repeat for all pairs.

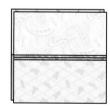 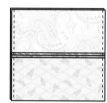

5 Cut through the vertical center of the sewn units as shown and press the seam allowances open. Make a total of 18 Four Patch blocks. The blocks

should measure 9½" x 9½". These blocks will be cut later for the side and corner setting blocks. Adding some spray starch when pressing will give them extra stability.

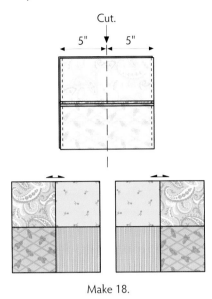

Make 18.

6 Select *four* of the blocks from step 5 and cut them diagonally as shown, aligning the ¼" line of your ruler with opposite corners of the block. These will be the corner setting triangles; the cut-off pieces will not be used.

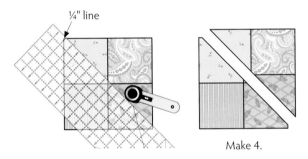

Make 4.

Assembling the Quilt Top

1 Sew 15 of the white 1½" x 42" strips together end to end for the sashing. From the pieced strip, cut:

- 2 strips, 1½" x 29½"
- 2 strips, 1½" x 31½"
- 2 strips, 1½" x 49½"
- 2 strips, 1½" x 69½"
- 3 strips, 1½" x 79½"

2 Referring to the quilt assembly diagram below, arrange the blocks and sashing strips into diagonal rows. The side setting blocks will be trimmed later. Sew the blocks and 1½" x 9½" sashing strips into rows. Press the seam allowances toward the sashing strips.

3 Working from the center outward, sew the block rows and sashing strips together. Press the seam allowances toward the sashing strips. Add the corner blocks last, aligning the center seam with the center seam of the Four Patch Flip block in the adjacent rows.

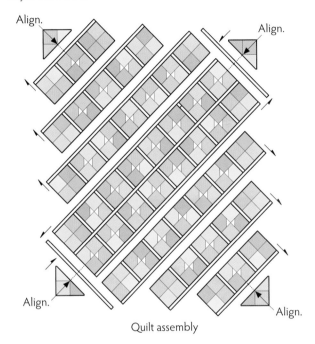

Quilt assembly

4 Trim the sides and square up the corners of the quilt as shown, cutting ¼" from the center points of the side setting blocks.

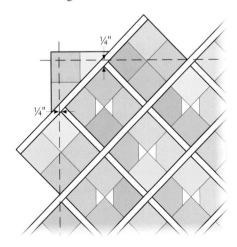

Rebecca ■ 23

Adding the Borders

1 Join seven of the pink 3½" x 42" strips end to end for the inner border.

2 Measure the quilt from top to bottom through the middle to determine the length of the side borders. From the pieced strip, cut side borders to the needed length and attach them to the sides of the quilt.

3 Measure the quilt from side to side through the middle, including the side borders, to determine the length of the top and bottom borders. From the pieced strip, cut the top and bottom borders to the needed length and attach them to the quilt. Sew carefully, as the edges of the quilt are cut on the bias and will stretch easily. Using a walking foot will help feed the layers evenly.

4 Join the remaining eight white 1½" x 42" strips end to end for the middle border. Repeat the measuring and cutting process as you did for the inner border to add the white borders to your quilt.

5 Join the remaining eight pink 3½" x 42" strips end to end for the outer border. Repeat the measuring and cutting process and add the outer pink borders to the quilt.

Finishing the Quilt

For help with any of the finishing steps, go to ShopMartingale.com/HowtoQuilt for free downloadable information.

1 Layer, baste, and quilt your quilt, or take it to your favorite long-arm quilter for finishing.

2 Using the pink 2¼"-wide print strips, make and attach binding.

Spin City

From firecrackers to amusement-park rides, things that spin, twirl, or go round and round signify fun. This quilt block looks like it's spinning, is made entirely from strips, and you don't have to decide until the last couple of seams where you want the light and dark parts.

"Spin City," designed by Carrie Nelson; pieced by Debbie Outlaw; quilted by Maggi Honeyman

FINISHED QUILT: 72" x 72" • FINISHED BLOCK: 15" x 15"

Materials

Yardage is based on 42"-wide fabric, except where noted.

32 matching pairs of assorted 10" squares for blocks (64 total)

16 assorted 10" squares for outer border

½ yard of white print for inner border

⅝ yard of fabric for binding

4½ yards of fabric for backing

77" x 77" piece of batting

Template plastic

Permanent pen

Cutting

From *each* of the assorted squares for blocks, cut:

3 strips, 3" x 10" (6 matching strips; 192 total)

From the white print, cut:

8 strips, 1¾" x 42"

From 1 medium or dark square for outer border, cut:

1 strip, 1¾" x 10"; crosscut into 4 squares, 1¾" x 1¾"

From *each* of the remaining 15 squares for outer border, cut:

2 border strips, 5" x 10" (30 total)

From the binding fabric, cut:

300" of 2"-wide bias strips

Piecing the Blocks

For each block, you'll need the following pieces:

- **Fabric 1:** six matching 3" x 10" strips
- **Fabric 2:** six matching 3" x 10" strips

Use a scant ¼"-wide seam allowance throughout. Directions are for making one block. Repeat to make a total of 16 blocks. After sewing each seam, press the seam allowances in the direction indicated by the arrows.

1 From the template plastic, cut a 3" x 10" rectangle. On the right side of the template, use a permanent pen to mark a point 3½" from the top as shown. On the left side of the template, mark a point 6½" from the top. Draw a diagonal line connecting

the two points. The template must look exactly like the one shown in the diagram. Using a rotary cutter and ruler, cut the rectangle apart on the drawn line to make a cutting-guide template.

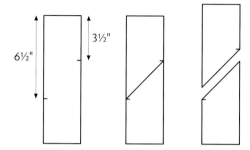

2 Use a piece of clear tape to affix the template to the underneath side of a small ruler with the diagonal edge of the template along the outer edge of the ruler as shown below. This template is used as a guide only to make trimming the strips easier.

3 Using the template/ruler and two 3" x 10" strips of each fabric, trim the strips exactly as shown. If you have stacked your strips, make sure that all of the strips are right side up before cutting! It's important that the pieces match the diagram or you'll need more 10" squares.

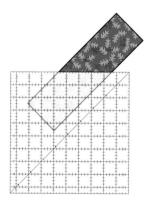

4 Join two pieces from step 3 to make a strip, off-setting the ends as shown. Again, the pieced strip must match the diagram. Press the seam allowances open. Repeat to make four matching pieced strips.

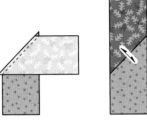

Make 4.

5 Trim the pieced strips to measure 3" x 8". After trimming, the seam line on the right edge should be 2½" from the top and the seam on the left edge should be 5½" from the top as shown. Trim the eight remaining strips (four of each fabric) to measure 3" x 8".

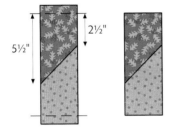

6 Lay out three strips side by side, placing the pieced strip in the center as shown. Sew the strips together. Make four matching units.

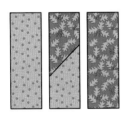 

Make 4.

7 Lay out the units in a four-patch arrangement, rotating the units as shown. Before stitching, lay out the same units in reverse order. Which way do you prefer? (Carrie likes to vary the placement of the light and dark fabrics so that not all of the blocks have a light background.)

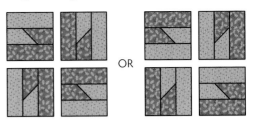

OR

8 Sew the units together in rows, and then sew the rows together to complete a block, taking care to match the seam intersection in the center of the block. Don't press the center seam just yet. Repeat to make a total of 16 blocks.

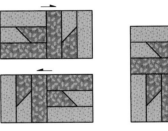

Make 16.

9 Use a seam ripper to remove two or three stitches from the seam allowances on both sides of the center seam as shown. On the wrong side of each block, gently reposition the seam allowances to evenly distribute the fabric. Press the seam allowances in opposite directions, opening the seam so that the center lies flat. When you look at the wrong side of the block, the seam allowances should be going in a counterclockwise direction around the center. Each block should measure 15½" square.

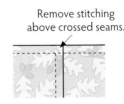
Remove stitching above crossed seams.

Assembling the Quilt Top

1 Lay out the blocks in four rows of four blocks each as shown in the quilt assembly diagram at right.

2 Sew the blocks together into rows, pressing the seam allowances in opposite directions from one row to the next (or press them open). Then sew the rows together and press. The quilt top should measure 60½" x 60½".

3 Piece the white 1¾"-wide strips together end to end. From the strip, cut four strips, 60½" long. Sew two inner-border strips to the sides of the quilt top and press the seam allowances toward the border.

4 Sew a 1¾" square to both ends of the two remaining inner-border strips and press. Sew these strips to the top and bottom of the quilt top and press the seam allowances toward the border.

5 For the outer border, sort the 5" x 10" border strips into the following groups:

- **Side borders:** two groups of seven strips each
- **Top and bottom borders:** two groups of eight strips each

Join each group of strips end to end to make four long strips. Press the seam allowances in one direction (or press them open). For the side borders, trim the two shorter strips to measure 5" x 63". For the top and bottom borders, trim the two longer strips to measure 5" x 72".

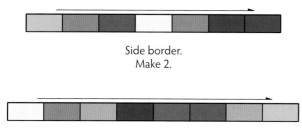

Side border.
Make 2.

Top/bottom border.

6 Sew the border strips to the sides, and then the top and bottom of the quilt top as shown in the layout diagram, keeping the pinked edges on the outside. Press the seam allowances toward the outer border.

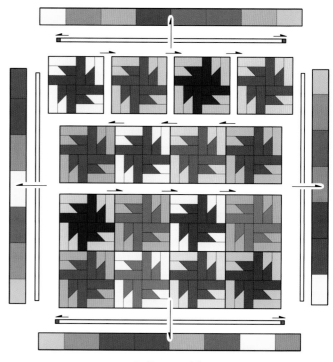

Quilt assembly

Finishing the Quilt

For help with any of the finishing steps, go to ShopMartingale.com/HowtoQuilt for free downloadable information.

1 Layer, baste, and quilt your quilt, or take it to your favorite long-arm quilter for finishing.

2 Using the 2"-wide binding strips, make and attach binding.

Red-Letter Day

A sophisticated, modern quilt, this is a project that comes together quickly. The blocks are simple and bold, surrounded by white, but this quilt would look equally stunning with a gray or black background.

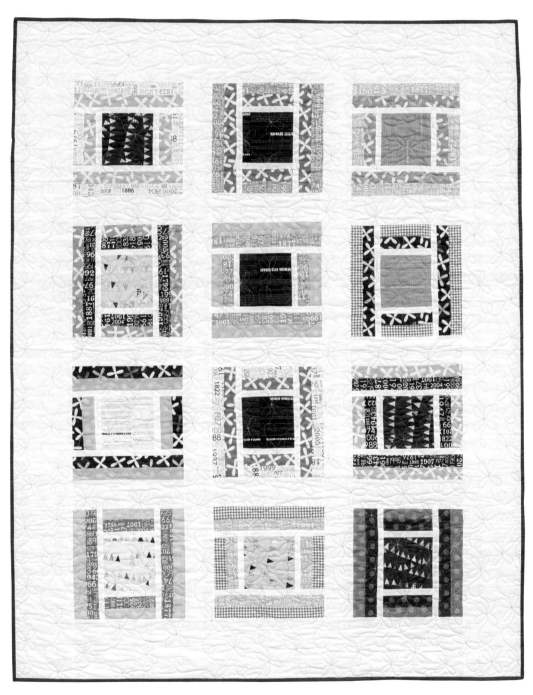

"Red-Letter Day," designed by Sue Pfau; pieced by Abby Sisk; quilted by Jennifer Krohn

FINISHED QUILT: 45" x 57" • FINISHED BLOCK: 9½" x 9½"

Materials

Yardage is based on 42"-wide fabric, except where noted.

18 to 20 assorted 10" squares for blocks
1⅞ yards of white fabric for blocks, sashing, and border
½ yard of fabric for binding
3¼ yards of fabric for backing
53" x 65" piece of batting

Cutting

From *each of 6* of the 10" squares, cut:
2 squares, 5" x 5" (12 total)
From the remaining 10" squares, cut:
24 matching sets of 3 strips, 1½" x 10" (72 total)
From the white fabric, cut:
5 strips, 6" x 42"
3 strips, 3" x 42"; crosscut into 9 strips, 3" x 10"
3 strips, 3" x 42"
12 strips, 1" x 42"
From the binding fabric, cut:
6 strips, 2½" x 42"

If Bigger Is Better

This quilt can easily be made bigger. For each additional block, you'll need one 5" square and two sets of three matching 1½" x 10" strips. You'll also need additional white fabric.

Piecing the Blocks

1 Choose two complementary sets of three 1½" x 10" strips. Sew them together lengthwise to make three identical strip sets. Press the seam allowances toward the darker fabric.

Make 3.

2 Sew the 10" strip sets lengthwise to a white 1" x 42" strip. Press the seam allowances toward the darker fabric. Cut through the white strip to make three 10" segments. Cut one of the segments into two segments, 5" wide. Keep the other two segments intact.

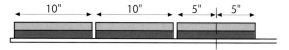

3 Sew the two 5"-wide segments to opposite sides of a 5" square, placing the white strip next to the square. Press the seam allowances toward the square.

4 Sew the 10"-long segments to opposite sides of the unit from step 3, placing the white strip next to the center unit. Press the seam allowances toward the block center. Repeat the steps to make 12 blocks.

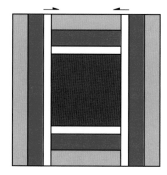

Make 12.

Assembling the Quilt Top

1 Arrange the blocks in three vertical rows of four blocks each, referring to the quilt assembly diagram on page 31. Alternate each block so that the longer white strips are horizontal in one and vertical in the next.

2 Sew a white 3" x 10" strip to the bottom of the top three blocks in each vertical row. Press the seam allowances toward the blocks.

3 Sew the blocks together into three vertical rows, pressing the seam allowances toward the blocks.

4 Join the white 3" x 42" strips end to end using diagonal seams. Measure the length of the vertical rows and cut two strips to this length. Sew the vertical rows together with the sashing strips. Press the seam allowances toward the blocks.

5 Measure the width of the quilt through the center and cut two white 6" x 42" strips to this length. Sew to the top and bottom of the quilt. Press the seam allowances toward the quilt center.

6 Join the three remaining white 6" x 42" strips end to end using diagonal seams. Measure the length

of the quilt through the center and cut two strips to this length. Sew to the sides of the quilt. Press the seam allowances toward the quilt center.

Finishing the Quilt

For help with any of the finishing steps, go to ShopMartingale.com/HowtoQuilt for free downloadable information.

1 Layer, baste, and quilt your quilt, or take it to your favorite long-arm quilter for finishing.

2 Using the 2½"-wide binding strips, make and attach binding.

Quilt assembly

Little Red

Carrie designed this quilt after seeing a similar antique version, but that one required templates to make it. Her updated pattern is template-free. A small version—in red—is on page 62. Maybe this one should be "Big Cream-Peach-Aqua-Green." Or maybe not!

"Little Red," designed by Carrie Nelson; pieced by Judy Adams; quilted by Diane Tricka

FINISHED QUILT: 66¾" x 66¾" • FINISHED BLOCK: 8⅞" x 8⅞"

Materials

Yardage is based on 42"-wide fabric, except where noted.

36 assorted light 10" squares for blocks
36 assorted medium or dark 10" squares for blocks
2 yards of floral for outer border and binding
½ yard of white print for inner border
4¼ yards of fabric for backing
72" x 72" piece of batting

Cutting

From *each of 18* light squares, cut:
1 square, 9¾" x 9¾" (18 total)

From *each* of the remaining 18 light squares, cut:
1 strip, 4⅛" x 10"; crosscut into 2 squares, 4⅛" x 4⅛"
    (36 total)
1 strip, 3¾" x 10"; crosscut into 2 squares, 3¾" x 3¾"
    (36 total)

From *each of 18* medium or dark squares, cut:
1 square, 9¾" x 9¾" (18 total)

From *each* of the remaining 18 medium or dark squares, cut:
1 strip, 4⅛" x 10"; crosscut into 2 squares, 4⅛" x 4⅛"
    (36 total)
1 strip, 3¾" x 10"; crosscut into 2 squares, 3¾" x 3¾"
    (36 total)

From the white print, cut:
6 strips, 2" x 42"

From the floral, cut:
4 border strips, 5½" x 72", from the lengthwise
    grain*
280" of 2"-wide bias strips

*If you prefer crosswise-grain strips, cut 8 border strips, 5½" x 42".

Piecing the Blocks

For each block, you'll need the following pieces:

   • Two different 9¾" squares (one light and one
      medium or dark)
   • Four different 4⅛" squares (two light and two
      medium or dark)
   • Four different 3¾" squares (two light and two
      medium or dark)

Use a scant ¼"-wide seam allowance throughout. After sewing each seam, press the seam allowances in the direction indicated by the arrows.

1 Draw a diagonal line from corner to corner on the wrong side of the 4⅛" and 3¾" squares. Place medium or dark 4⅛" squares on diagonally opposite corners of a light 9¾" square. Sew along the marked line and trim, leaving a ¼" seam allowance.

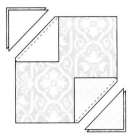 

2 In the same manner, place marked light 4⅛" squares on diagonally opposite corners of a medium or dark 9¾" square. Sew and trim.

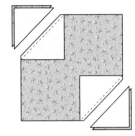 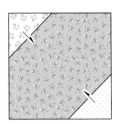

3 Repeat step 1, sewing the marked medium or dark 3¾" squares to the remaining corners of the light squares as shown. Make 18 light Snowball blocks. And yes, the snowballs are a little lopsided, but that's on purpose so that step 5 will work.

Make 18.

4 In the same manner, sew the marked light 3¾" squares to the remaining corners of the medium or dark squares. Make 18 dark Snowball blocks.

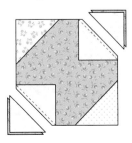 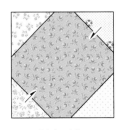

Make 18.

5 On the wrong side of the light Snowball blocks, draw a diagonal line from corner to corner across the larger triangles, as shown below. Layer a marked Snowball block right sides together with a dark Snowball block, making sure that the snowball corners match the facing corners according to size. The triangles should nestle into each other with the seam allowances abutting. Sew a scant ¼" on both sides of the marked line. Cut the squares apart on the line to make two blocks. Press the seam allowances toward the darker side of the block (or press open). Repeat to make a total of 36 blocks. The blocks should measure 9⅜" square.

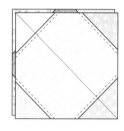

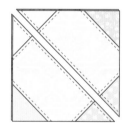

 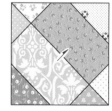

Make 36.

Assembling the Quilt Top

1 Lay out the blocks in six rows of six blocks each, rotating every other block 90° as shown in the quilt assembly diagram above right.

2 Sew the blocks together in rows, pressing the seam allowances in opposite directions from one row to the next (or press them open). Then sew the rows together and press. The quilt top should measure 53¾" x 53¾".

3 Piece the white 2"-wide strips together end to end. From the strips, cut two strips, 53¾" long, and sew them to opposite sides of the quilt top. Press the seam allowances toward the border. Cut two strips, 56¾" long, and sew them to the top and bottom of the quilt top; press.

4 Trim two of the floral 5½"-wide strips to measure 56¾" long. Sew the strips to opposite sides of the quilt top and press the seam allowances toward the outer border. Trim the remaining two strips to measure 66¾" long. Sew these strips to the top and bottom of the quilt top and press.

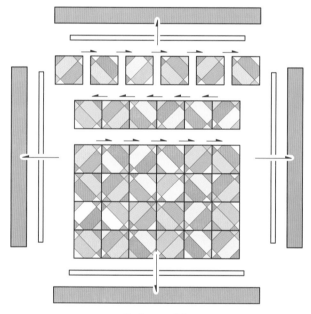

Quilt assembly

Finishing the Quilt

For help with any of the finishing steps, go to ShopMartingale.com/HowtoQuilt for free downloadable information.

1 Layer, baste, and quilt your quilt, or take it to your favorite long-arm quilter for finishing.

2 Using the 2"-wide binding strips, make and attach binding.

Snow in June

Snowball and Nine Patch blocks go together like peanut butter and jelly. This block combination has proven itself through the test of time. It's classic yet fun and works well in any combination of colors or fabric styles.

"Snow in June," designed and made by Rebecca Silbaugh
FINISHED QUILT: 68½" x 68½" • FINISHED BLOCK: 6" x 6"

Materials

Yardage is based on 42"-wide fabric, except where noted.

42 assorted 10" squares for blocks
2¼ yards of light fabric for Snowball blocks
⅞ yard of floral for side and corner setting triangles
⅝ yard of fabric for binding
4½ yards of fabric for backing
76" x 76" piece of batting

Cutting

From *each* of the assorted squares, cut:

4 strips, 2½" x 10" (168 total; 1 is extra); crosscut 56 of the strips into 4 squares, 2½" x 2½" (224 total)

From the light fabric, cut:

11 strips, 6½" x 42"; crosscut into 64 squares, 6½" x 6½"

From the floral, cut:

7 squares, 10" x 10"; cut into quarters diagonally to yield 28 side setting triangles

2 squares, 5½" x 5½"; cut in half diagonally to yield 4 corner setting triangles

From the binding fabric, cut:

8 strips, 2¼" x 42"

Piecing the Blocks

1 Randomly select three of the 2½"-wide strips and sew them together side by side along their long edges. Press the seam allowances to one side. Make 37 strip sets. Cut each strip set into four segments, 2½" wide (148 total).

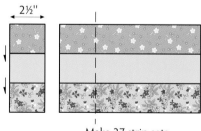

Make 37 strip sets.
Cut 148 segments.

2 Randomly select three segments from step 1 and arrange them so the seam allowances alternate directions as shown. Sew the segments together and

press the seam allowances toward the outer segments. Make 49 Nine Patch blocks, each measuring 6½" x 6½". You'll have one extra segment.

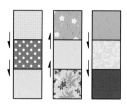 

Nine Patch block.
Make 49.

3 Mark a diagonal line from corner to corner on the wrong side of each 2½" square. Place a marked square on one corner of a light 6½" square as shown, right sides together. Sew on the marked line. Trim the excess fabric from the small square only, leaving a ¼" seam allowance. Press the resulting triangle toward the corner. Repeat on the remaining corners of the background square. Make 36 Snowball blocks, each measuring 6½" x 6½".

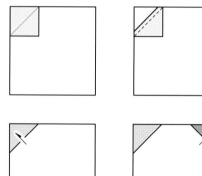

Snowball block.
Make 36.

4 Refer to step 3 to sew 2½" squares to three corners of a light 6½" square. Make 24 partial Snowball blocks.

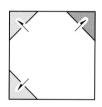

Partial Snowball block.
Make 24.

5 Refer to step 3 to sew 2½" squares to two adjacent corners of the remaining four light 6½" squares. Make four corner Snowball blocks.

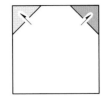

Corner Snowball block.
Make 4.

Assembling the Quilt Top

1 Refer to the quilt assembly diagram below to lay out the blocks in diagonal rows as shown, alternating the Nine Patch and Snowball blocks in each row and from row to row. Place the partial blocks at the ends of each row and the corner blocks in each corner. Review your layout. Once you're satisfied with the color and value placement, sew the blocks in each row together, matching seam intersections. Press the seam allowances in alternating directions from row to row.

2 Onto the end of each sewn row, stitch a floral side setting triangle. Make sure you are sewing the short side of the triangle to the blocks and that the bottom edges of the blocks and triangles are aligned. Press the seam allowances in the same direction as the others in the row.

3 Join the rows. Press the seam allowances away from the center.

4 Find and pin-mark the midpoint of each corner block's raw edge and the midpoint of each corner setting triangle's long edge. Matching the midpoints, sew a corner setting triangle to each corner of the quilt top. Press the seam allowances toward the triangles.

5 Trim the quilt edges ¼" from the block points.

Finishing the Quilt

For help with any of the finishing steps, go to ShopMartingale.com/HowtoQuilt for free downloadable information.

1 Layer, baste, and quilt your quilt, or take it to your favorite long-arm quilter for finishing.

2 Using the 2¼"-wide binding strips, make and attach binding.

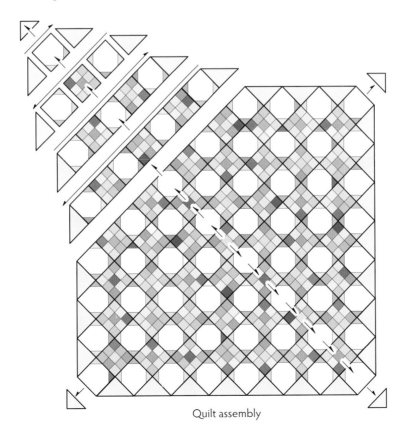

Quilt assembly

Bennington

Bennington is a lovely little town in Kansas that is home to Lynne Hagemeir, a fabric designer for Moda and the creative mind behind Kansas Troubles patterns. Carrie made the little Bennington quilt (see page 104) while she was "retreating" there.

"Bennington," designed by Carrie Nelson; pieced by Nicole Reed; quilted by Debbie Thornton

FINISHED QUILT: 63½" x 63½" • FINISHED BLOCK: 8½" x 8½"

Materials

Yardage is based on 42"-wide fabric, except where noted.

18 assorted light 10" squares for blocks
47 assorted medium or dark 10" squares for blocks and outer border
½ yard of cream print for inner border
⅝ yard of fabric for binding
4 yards of fabric for backing
68" x 68" piece of batting

Cutting

From *each* of the 18 light squares, cut:
2 strips, 4¾" x 10"; crosscut into 4 squares, 4¾" x 4¾" (72 total)

From *each* of 36 medium or dark squares, cut:
1 strip, 4¾" x 10"; crosscut into 2 squares, 4¾" x 4¾" (72 total)
1 strip, 2½" x 10"; crosscut into 2 squares, 2½" x 2½" (72 total)
1 border strip, 2" x 10" (36 total)

From *1* medium or dark square, cut:
4 border squares, 5" x 5"

From *each* of the remaining 10 medium or dark squares, cut:
4 border strips, 2" x 10" (40 total)

From the cream print, cut:
6 strips, 2" x 42"

From the binding fabric, cut:
270" of 2"-wide bias strips

Piecing the Blocks

For each Bow Tie block, you'll need the following pieces:

- **Background squares:** two matching light 4¾" squares
- **Bow Tie squares:** two matching medium or dark 4¾" squares
- **Snowball corners:** two matching medium or dark 2½" squares

Use a scant ¼"-wide seam allowance throughout. After sewing each seam, press the seam allowances in the direction indicated by the arrows.

1 Draw a diagonal line from corner to corner on the wrong side of the 72 medium or dark 2½" squares.

2 Lay a marked square on the corner of each light 4¾" square, right sides together and raw edges aligned. Stitch along the drawn line and trim away the excess fabric, leaving a ¼" seam allowance.

3 Lay out the pieces for each block in a four-patch arrangement as shown. Sew the pieces together in rows, and then sew the rows together to complete a Bow Tie block. Don't press the center seam just yet. Repeat to make a total of 36 blocks.

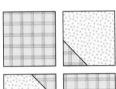
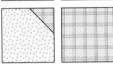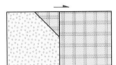

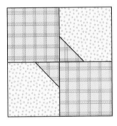

Make 36.

4 Use a seam ripper to remove two or three stitches from the seam allowance on both sides of the center seam as shown.

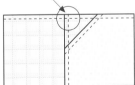

Remove stitching above crossed seams.

5 On the wrong side of the block, gently reposition the seam allowance to evenly distribute the fabric. Press the seam allowances in opposite directions, opening the seam allowances so that the center lies flat. When you look at the wrong side of the block,

the seam allowances should be going in a counter-clockwise direction around the center. The block should measure 9" square.

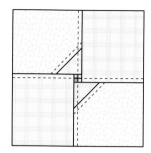

Assembling the Quilt Top

1 Lay out the blocks in six rows of six blocks each as shown in the quilt assembly diagram at right.

2 Sew the blocks together into rows, pressing the seam allowances in opposite directions from one row to the next (or press them open). Then sew the rows together and press. The quilt top should measure 51½" x 51½".

3 Sew the cream 2"-wide strips together end to end. From the strip, cut four strips, 51½" long.

4 Sew two inner-border strips to the sides of the quilt top and press the seam allowances toward the borders.

5 Select one 2" x 10" border strip and cut it into four 2" squares.

6 Sew 2" squares from step 5 to both ends of the two remaining inner-border strips and press. Sew these borders to the top and bottom of the quilt top and press the seam allowances toward the borders.

7 Select 72 of the 2" x 10" border strips (you'll have three extra strips). Divide the strips into two sets of 36 strips each. Join the strips in one set as shown and press the seam allowances in one direction (or press them open). The pieced strip should measure 10" x 54½". Repeat to make a second pieced strip.

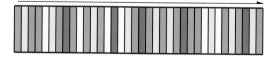

Make 2.

8 Cut each pieced strip in half lengthwise to make a total of four pieced border strips, each measuring 5" x 54½".

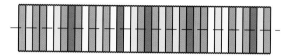

9 Sew two border strips to the sides of the quilt top, keeping the pinked edges on the outside. Press the seam allowances toward the outer borders.

10 Sew 5" border squares to both ends of the two remaining border strips, keeping the pinked edges on the outside, and press. Sew these borders to the top and bottom of the quilt top and press the seam allowances toward the borders.

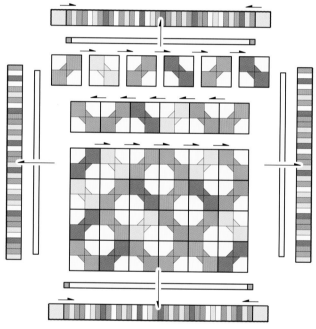

Quilt assembly

Finishing the Quilt

For help with any of the finishing steps, go to ShopMartingale.com/HowtoQuilt for free downloadable information.

1 Layer, baste, and quilt your quilt, or take it to your favorite long-arm quilter for finishing.

2 Using the 2"-wide binding strips, make and attach binding.

Claire's Asters

Both Claudia and Le Ann are avid readers who especially enjoy historical fiction. While making this quilt, they were both reading the Outlander series by Diana Gabaldon, and named this quilt after Claire, the main character, who enjoys picking flowers in the Scottish Highlands and in the North Carolina mountains. You, too, can have a pretty bouquet with this pieced and appliquéd project.

"Claire's Asters," pieced by Claudia Plett; designed, machine appliquéd, and machine quilted by Le Ann Weaver

FINISHED QUILT: 67¼" x 81" • FINISHED BLOCK: 12" x 12"

Materials

Yardage is based on 42"-wide fabric, except where noted. This quilt uses not only 10" squares, but also 5" squares and fat quarters (18" x 21").

10" Squares

31 assorted medium-green print squares for blocks
20 assorted light-green print squares for blocks
9 assorted blue and purple print squares for blocks

5" Squares

32 assorted light-blue and light-purple print squares (or eight 10" squares) for appliqué
8 assorted green print squares for appliqué (or use scraps from blocks)
4 assorted yellow print squares for sashing cornerstones
3 assorted yellow print squares for appliqué

Fat Quarters

10 assorted blue and purple prints for sashing and outer border
4 assorted cream prints for blocks

Additional Fabric and Supplies

1⅛ yards of green print for inner border and binding
5 yards of fabric for backing
72" x 85" piece of batting
1½ yards of 16"-wide fusible web for machine appliqué

Cutting

From the assorted light-green 10" squares, cut:
80 squares, 3½" x 3½"
From the assorted medium-green 10" squares, cut:
80 squares, 3½" x 3½"
80 squares, 3" x 3"
20 squares, 2½" x 2½"
From the assorted blue and purple 10" squares, cut:
80 squares, 3" x 3"
From the assorted cream print fat quarters, cut:
80 rectangles, 2½" x 5½"

From the assorted blue and purple fat quarters, cut:*
18 rectangles, 5½" x 15"
31 rectangles, 2¼" x 12½"
4 squares, 5½" x 5½"
From the assorted yellow 5" squares, cut:
12 squares, 2¼" x 2¼"
From the green print for inner border and binding, cut:
15 strips, 2¼" x 42"

*Refer to the cutting diagram for the most efficient cutting of your fat quarters. Be sure to cut across the 18" length rather than the 20" or 21" length. To get a total of 31 rectangles, 2¼" x 12½", cut 4 from one fat quarter and 3 each from the remaining fat quarters.

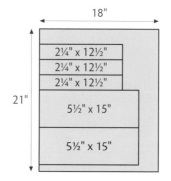

Cutting guide for assorted blue and purple print fat quarters

Piecing the Blocks

1 Mark a diagonal line on the wrong side of the light-green 3½" squares. Layer each light-green square right sides together with a medium-green 3½" square and stitch ¼" on each side of the marked lines. Cut the squares apart on the marked lines and press the seam allowances toward the medium-green print. Trim these units to 3" x 3". Make a total of 160 light-green/medium-green half-square-triangle units.

Make 160.

2 Using the half-square-triangle units from step 1, the blue and purple 3" squares, and the medium-green 3" squares, make four-patch units as shown.

Press the seam allowances toward the squares. Make 80 four-patch units.

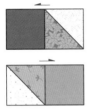

Make 80.

3 Combine four of the four-patch units with four cream print 2½" x 5½" rectangles and a medium-green 2½" square to make a block as shown. Press the seam allowances toward the cream print fabrics. Your block should measure 12½" x 12½". Make 20 blocks.

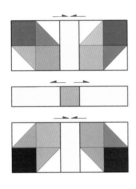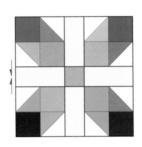

Make 20.

Assembling the Quilt Top

1 Make four sashing units as shown using 16 of the blue and purple 2¼" x 12½" strips and the 12 yellow print 2¼" squares. Press the seam allowances toward the rectangles.

Make 4.

2 Join four blocks and three blue and purple 2¼" x 12½" strips into a row as shown. Press the seam allowances toward the rectangles. Make five rows.

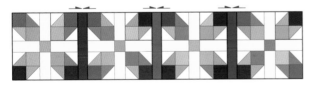

Make 5.

3 Matching the seam intersections, sew the block rows together with the sashing rows to form the quilt center. Press toward the sashing.

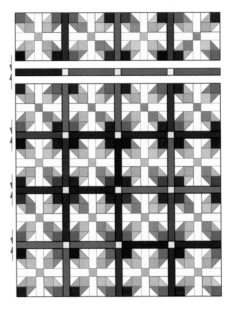

4 For the inner border, stitch seven of the green print 2¼" strips together end to end. Measure the length of your quilt and cut two strips this length for the sides of the quilt. Add the side border strips and press the seam allowances toward the borders. Then measure and cut two strips for the top and bottom. Sew to the quilt and press.

5 Using the patterns on pages 45 and 46 and the light-blue and light-purple print 5" squares, prepare the appliqué shapes for fusing.

6 Appliqué four asters to each of 10 blue and
purple 5½" x 15" rectangles and one large aster
to two 5½" squares using the placement guides
with the patterns. Fuse the yellow flower centers
after fusing and stitching the flower petals. You may
want to use a blanket stitch for securing the edges
of the appliqué.

Make 2.

Make 10.

7 Make two side borders, each using three appliquéd rectangles and two plain blue or purple
rectangles as shown. Press the seam allowances open
to reduce bulk. Measure the quilt top from top to
bottom and trim the plain blue end so the strip measures the correct length.

Make 2.

8 Sew the borders from step 7 to the sides of the
quilt and press the seam allowances toward the
inner border.

9 Make the top and bottom borders, each using
two appliquéd rectangles, two plain blue print
rectangles, one appliquéd square, and one plain blue
or purple 5½" square. Press the seam allowances
open. Measure the width of the quilt top and trim
the plain blue end so that the strip measures the correct length.

Make 2.

10 Sew the top and bottom borders to the quilt.
Press toward the inner border.

Finishing the Quilt

For help with any of the finishing steps, go to
ShopMartingale.com/HowtoQuilt for free downloadable information.

1 Layer, baste, and quilt your quilt, or take it to
your favorite long-arm quilter for finishing.

2 Using the remaining green print 2¼"-wide strips,
make and attach binding.

Appliqué placement guide
Corner block

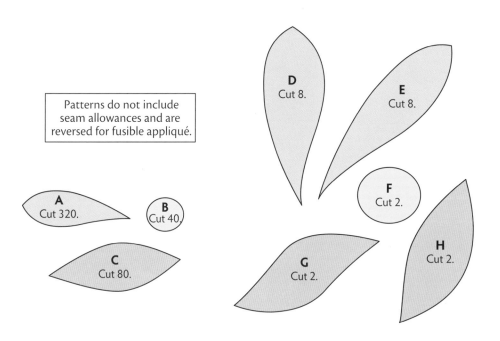

Patterns do not include seam allowances and are reversed for fusible appliqué.

A
Cut 320.

B
Cut 40.

C
Cut 80.

D
Cut 8.

E
Cut 8.

F
Cut 2.

G
Cut 2.

H
Cut 2.

Center of block

Appliqué placement guide
Rectangle block

PART

2

Charm Squares

5" SQUARES

Tiny Bits

If you're like many quilters, you'd love to make a handmade gift for each friend or family member who is expecting a baby. This quilt is both simple and quick to stitch, so you have a good chance of actually getting the gift wrapped and ready to go before the baby arrives!

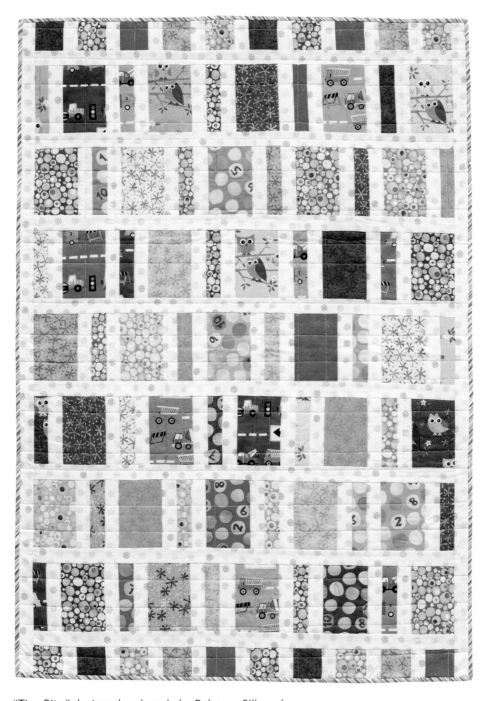

"Tiny Bits," designed and made by Rebecca Silbaugh

FINISHED QUILT: 31½" x 44" • FINISHED BLOCK: 5" x 4½"

Materials

Yardage is based on 42"-wide fabric, except where noted.

1 yard of light print for blocks, sashing, and border
40 assorted 5" squares for blocks and border
⅓ yard of fabric for binding
1⅔ yards of fabric for backing
36" x 50" piece of batting

Doing Laundry

Before cutting anything, do some laundry! Don't *wash* your fabrics, but do break apart the pack of charm squares and throw them into your dryer. Turn on the dryer without heat for just a few minutes. The tumbling action will automatically mix the colors and prints for you like magic! Take the squares out of the dryer and restack them before heading to your cutting mat.

Cutting

From *each of 35* assorted 5" squares, cut:
1 rectangle, 1½" x 5" (35 total)
1 rectangle, 3½" x 5" (35 total; this piece will automatically be left after cutting the previous piece, so you don't really have to cut anything)
From *each* of the remaining 5 assorted 5" squares, cut:
4 squares, 2½" x 2½" (20 total)
From the light print, cut:
20 strips, 1½" x 42"; crosscut *10 of the strips* into:
   63 rectangles, 1½" x 5"
   22 rectangles, 1½" x 2½"
From the binding fabric, cut:
4 strips, 2¼" x 42"

Piecing the Blocks

1 Sew a light 1½" x 5" rectangle to each assorted 1½" x 5" rectangle along the long edges. Press the seam allowances toward the assorted rectangle. Make 35.

Make 35.

2 Sew an assorted 3½" x 5" rectangle of a different print to each unit from step 1. Press the seam allowances toward the large rectangle. Make 35 blocks, each measuring 5½" x 5".

Make 35.

Assembling the Quilt Top

1 Refer to the quilt assembly diagram on page 50 to lay out the blocks in seven rows of five blocks and four light 1½" x 5" rectangles each, rotating the blocks so the large and small assorted rectangles alternate from row to row. Rearrange the blocks as needed until you are satisfied with the color placement. Sew the blocks and rectangles in each row together. Press the seam allowances toward the blocks.

2 Measure the length of the pieced rows; determine the average of these measurements and trim eight light 1½" x 42" strips to the average length. Alternately sew the light sashing strips and block rows together, beginning and ending with a sashing strip. Press the seam allowances toward the sashing strips.

3 Measure the length of the quilt top through the middle and near both edges; determine the average of these measurements and trim the two remaining light 1½"-wide strips to the average length. Sew the side border strips to the sides of the quilt top. Press the seam allowances toward the quilt center.

4 Sew a light 1½" x 2½" rectangle to one edge of each assorted 2½" square. Press the seam allowances toward the assorted fabrics. Make 20.

Make 20.

5 Sew 10 of the units from step 4 together end to end, alternating the light and assorted fabrics. Add a light 1½" x 2½" rectangle to the square end of the row. Make two pieced border strips.

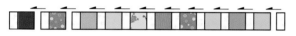

Make 2.

6 Sew the pieced border strips to the top and bottom of the quilt top. Press the seam allowances toward the quilt center.

Finishing the Quilt

For help with any of the finishing steps, go to ShopMartingale.com/HowtoQuilt for free downloadable information.

1 Layer, baste, and quilt your quilt, or take it to your favorite long-arm quilter for finishing.

2 Using the 2¼"-wide binding strips, make and attach binding.

Making Gifts

Do you have a friend that you'd really like to make a gift for but whose taste in fabrics is worlds apart from yours? Would you rather pull out your hair than select fabrics for her? Save your hair! Instead, grab a precut pack that fits her style and make a small project. Choosing a precut bundle reduces the anxiety of picking out individual fabrics. Plus, a small project will be manageable and over before you know it!

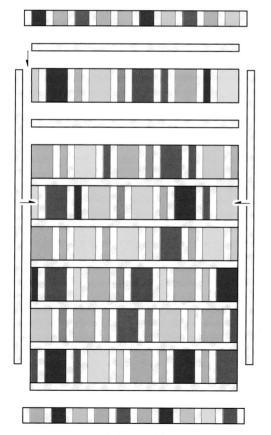

Quilt assembly

Confetti

This quilt starts with Four Patch blocks—lots of them! Because Barb and Mary were using their favorite bright colors, they found it hard to stop sewing. Once they placed the Four Patch blocks on point with a crisp white background, they both shouted, "Confetti!"

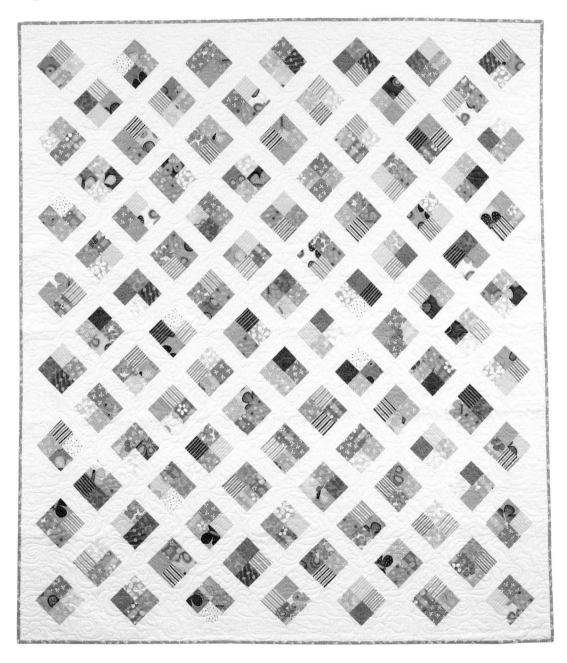

"Confetti," designed and pieced by Mary Jacobson and Barbara Groves

FINISHED QUILT: 60½" x 69" • FINISHED BLOCK: 4" x 4"

Materials

Yardage is based on 42"-wide fabric, except where noted.

98 assorted 5" squares for blocks

3¾ yards of white solid for sashing and setting triangles

⅝ yard of pink print for binding

4½ yards of fabric for backing

69" x 77" piece of batting

Cutting

From the white solid, cut:

11 strips, 2½" x 42"; crosscut into 86 rectangles, 2½" x 4½"

13 strips, 2½" x 42"

4 strips, 14" x 42"; crosscut into 7 squares, 14" x 14". Cut each square into quarters diagonally to yield 28 side setting triangles (2 are extra).*

1 strip, 8" x 42"; crosscut into 2 squares, 8" x 8". Cut each square in half diagonally to yield 4 corner setting triangles.*

From the pink print, cut:

7 strips, 2¼" x 42"

Setting triangles are cut larger than needed and will extend beyond the blocks.

Piecing the Blocks

1 Divide the 98 assorted 5" squares into 49 pairs, combining two contrasting colors or contrasting values (light and dark).

2 Layer each pair of squares right sides together and, using a ¼" seam allowance, stitch along two opposite sides of the squares as shown.

3 Cut through the vertical center of the squares as shown and press the seam allowances open. Make a total of 98 two-patch units.

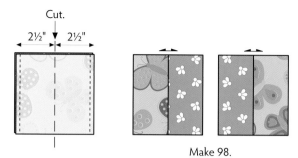

2½" 2½" Cut.

Make 98.

4 Divide the 98 two-patch units from step 3 into 49 new combinations of contrasting pairs. With right sides together, layer the two-patch units, aligning the seams. Using a ¼" seam allowance, stitch along two opposite sides, making sure to stitch across the previous seam lines as shown.

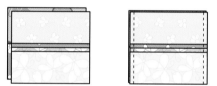

5 Cut through the center of the sewn units as shown and press the seam allowances open. Make a total of 98 Four Patch blocks. The blocks should measure 4½" x 4½".

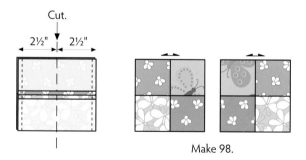

Cut.

2½" 2½"

Make 98.

Assembling the Quilt Top

1 Arrange and sew Four Patch blocks and white 2½" x 4½" sashing rectangles together into rows. Make two of each as shown. Each row begins and ends with a Four Patch block. Begin with a row of 3 Four Patch blocks, then 5, 7, 9, 11, and 12. Press the seam allowances toward the sashing rectangles.

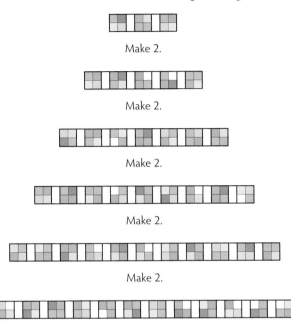

Make 2.

Make 2.

Make 2.

Make 2.

Make 2.

Make 2.

2 Sew the 13 white 2½" x 42" sashing strips together end to end. From the pieced strip, cut the following lengths. Measure your rows first and make adjustments if needed.

- 2 strips, 2½" x 16½"
- 2 strips, 2½" x 28½"
- 2 strips, 2½" x 40½"
- 2 strips, 2½" x 52½"
- 2 strips, 2½" x 64½"
- 1 strip, 2½" x 70½"

3 Attach the corresponding sashing strip to each row as shown, except for the two longest rows (center rows) with 12 blocks each. Press the seam allowances toward the white strips.

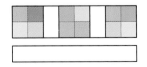 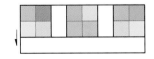

4 Sew the 2½" x 70½" sashing strip between the two center rows.

5 Arrange one Four Patch block, one white 2½" x 4½" sashing piece, and two white side setting triangles as shown. Sew and trim the triangles. Add the white corner triangle. Make four. The corner triangles will be trimmed later.

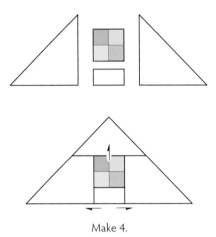

Make 4.

6 Lay out the rows, side setting triangles, and corner units in a diagonal setting on a design wall or flat surface. Sew the setting triangles to the ends of the rows. The triangles were cut oversized and the points will extend beyond the blocks. Trim the setting triangles even with the top edge of each row.

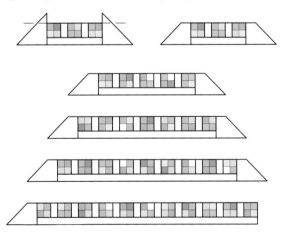

7 Referring to the assembly diagram, arrange and sew the rows together. Start with the center unit and work outward. Attach the corner units last.

8 Trim the sides and square up the corners of the quilt as shown, cutting 2" beyond the points of the Four Patch blocks. The quilt should measure 60½" x 69".

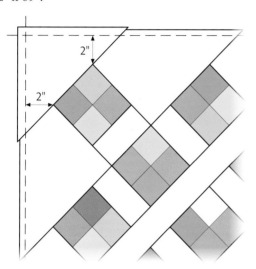

Finishing the Quilt

For help with any of the finishing steps, go to ShopMartingale.com/HowtoQuilt for free downloadable information.

1 Layer, baste, and quilt your quilt, or take it to your favorite long-arm quilter for finishing.

2 Using the pink 2¼"-wide strips, make and attach binding.

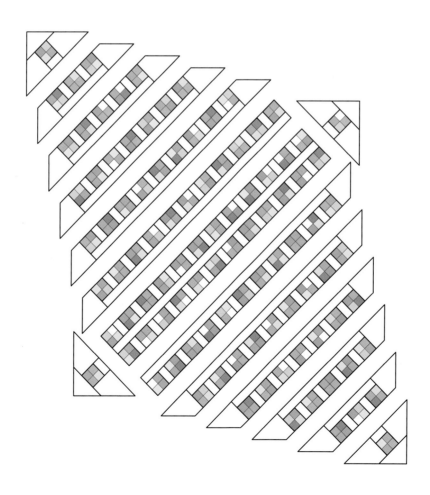

Down the Drain

The blocks create a lot of motion in this stunning quilt made with water-themed 5" squares. What a great kid's quilt or wall hanging!

"Down the Drain," designed and pieced by Claudia Plett; machine quilted by Le Ann Weaver

FINISHED QUILT: 53" x 53" • FINISHED BLOCK: 7½" x 7½"

Materials

Yardage is based on 42"-wide fabric, except where noted.

112 assorted light-blue print 5" squares for blocks and borders (or 10 fat quarters)

123 assorted dark-blue print 5" squares for blocks and borders (or 11 fat quarters)

½ yard of light-blue print for binding

3½ yards of fabric for backing

57" x 57" piece of batting

Cutting

From *32* of the light-blue squares, cut:
4 squares, 2⅜" x 2⅜" (128 total)

From *26* of the light-blue squares, cut:
1 square, 2¾" x 2¾" (26 total)

From *18* of the light-blue squares, cut:
1 square, 5" x 5"; cut into quarters diagonally to yield 4 A triangles (72 total)

From *36* of the light-blue squares, cut:
1 square, 4⅝" x 4⅝"; cut in half diagonally to yield 2 B triangles (72 total)

From *43* of the dark-blue squares, cut:
4 squares, 2⅜" x 2⅜" (172 total)

From *26* of the dark-blue squares, cut:
1 square, 2¾" x 2¾" (26 total)

From *18* of the dark-blue squares, cut:
1 square, 5" x 5"; cut into quarters diagonally to yield 4 A triangles (72 total)

From *36* of the dark-blue squares, cut:
1 square, 4⅝" x 4⅝"; cut in half diagonally to yield 2 B triangles (72 total)

From the light-blue binding fabric, cut:
6 strips, 2¼" x 42"

Piecing the Blocks

1 Randomly select two light-blue and two dark-blue 2⅜" squares and sew them together to make a four-patch unit as shown. Press as indicated. Make 36 units, each measuring 4¼" x 4¼".

Make 36.

2 Making sure to position all of the four-patch units as shown with the light-blue squares on the upper right and lower left, sew two different light-blue A triangles to opposite sides of the unit. Press the seam allowances toward the triangles. Sew two different dark-blue A triangles to the remaining sides and press.

3 Again making sure the light-blue squares are positioned as shown, sew two different light-blue B triangles to the unit from step 2. Press the seam allowances toward the just-added triangles. Sew two different dark-blue B triangles to the remaining sides to complete the block; press. Your blocks should each measure 8" x 8". Make 36 blocks.

Make 36.

Assembling the Quilt Top

1 For easy assembly, sew the blocks in units of four blocks each, rotating the blocks so that four dark-blue B triangles meet in the center as shown. (See the "Design Wall" tip on page 57.) Press as indicated. Make nine units.

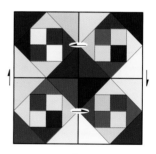

Make 9.

2 Sew the four-block units into three rows of three units each. Press the seam allowances in opposite directions from one row to the next. Then stitch the rows together.

Design Wall

Try using a design wall to position your blocks to keep identical fabrics from touching each other. Have fun rotating them—but don't get dizzy!

3 For the side inner border, sew together 24 dark-blue 2⅜" squares. Press the seam allowances in one direction. Make two and sew them to the sides of your quilt center. Press the seam allowances toward the inner border.

4 Make two more inner borders using 26 dark-blue 2⅜" squares for each border. Sew these borders the top and bottom of your quilt center. Press the seam allowances toward the inner border.

5 Using the 26 dark-blue and 26 light-blue 2¾" squares, make 52 half-square-triangle units by marking a diagonal line on the wrong side of the light-blue squares from corner to corner. Place a dark- and light-blue square right sides together and stitch ¼" from each side of the line. Cut apart on the marked line and press the seam allowances toward the dark-blue triangle. Repeat for all units. Your units should measure 2⅜" x 2⅜".

6 Sew 13 half-square-triangle units and 13 light-blue 2⅜" squares together to make an outer-border unit. Press the seam allowances toward the light-blue squares. Make four outer-border units.

Make 4.

7 Sew two borders to the sides of your quilt top. Press the seam allowances toward the inner border. Add a light-blue 2⅜" square to each end of the two remaining border units, and then sew them to the top and bottom of your quilt as shown. Press the seam allowances toward the inner border.

Finishing the Quilt

For help with any of the finishing steps, go to ShopMartingale.com/HowtoQuilt for free downloadable information.

1 Layer, baste, and quilt your quilt, or take it to your favorite long-arm quilter for finishing.

2 Using the light-blue 2¼"-wide strips, make and attach binding.

BFF

BFF: best friends forever! Pinwheel and Four Patch blocks are longtime favorites of quiltmakers everywhere, and together they're fabulous. Me and My Sister Designs is known for using brightly colored fabrics, so creating a quilt with black fabric was a first for this design team. But the border fabric had so many appealing colors in it, they couldn't resist. Make this fun quilt with your BFF!

"BFF," designed and pieced by Barbara Groves and Mary Jacobson

FINISHED QUILT: 64" x 80" • FINISHED BLOCK: 8" x 8"

Materials

Yardage is based on 42"-wide fabric, except where noted.

96 assorted print 5" squares for Four Patch blocks

2⅜ yards of black print for Pinwheel blocks and outer border

1 yard of white-with-red polka dot for Pinwheel blocks

1 yard of black-with-white polka dot for inner border and binding

5¼ yards of fabric for backing

72" x 88" piece of batting

Cutting

From the white-with-red polka dot, cut:

6 strips, 4⅞" x 42"; crosscut into 48 squares, 4⅞" x 4⅞"

From the black print, cut:

6 strips, 4⅞" x 42"; crosscut into 48 squares, 4⅞" x 4⅞"

7 strips, 6¾" x 42"

From the black-with-white polka dot, cut:

6 strips, 2" x 42"

8 strips, 2¼" x 42"

Making the Pinwheel Blocks

1 Draw a diagonal line on the wrong side of each white-with-red polka dot 4⅞" square. Layer each marked square right sides together on top of a black print 4⅞" square. Stitch ¼" from each side of the drawn line, cut apart on the drawn line, and press. The half-square-triangle units should measure 4½" x 4½". Make 96.

Make 96.

2 Arrange and sew four half-square-triangle units together to make a Pinwheel block as shown. Make 24 Pinwheel blocks. The blocks should measure 8½" x 8½".

Make 24.

Making the Four Patch Blocks

1 Divide the 96 coordinating 5" squares into 48 pairs, combining two contrasting colors or contrasting values (light and dark).

2 Layer each pair of squares right sides together, and using ¼" seam allowance, stitch along two opposite sides of the squares as shown.

3 Cut through the vertical center of the squares as shown and press the seam allowances open. Make a total of 96 two-patch units.

Cut.

2½" 2½"

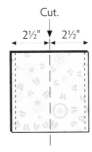 

Make 96.

4 Divide the 96 two-patch units from step 3 into 48 new combinations of contrasting pairs. With right sides together, layer the two-patch units, aligning the seams. Using a ¼" seam allowance, stitch along two opposite sides, making sure to stitch across the previous seam lines as shown.

5 Cut through the center of the sewn units as shown and press the seam allowances open. Make a total of 96 Four Patch blocks.

Cut.

2½"   2½"

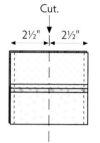

Make 96.

6 Arrange and sew four of the Four Patch blocks together into a Sixteen Patch block as shown. Make 24 Sixteen Patch blocks. The Sixteen Patch blocks should measure 8½" x 8½".

Make 24.

Assembling the Quilt Top

1 Referring to the quilt assembly diagram, arrange the blocks in eight rows of six blocks each, alternating them as shown. Sew the blocks into rows.

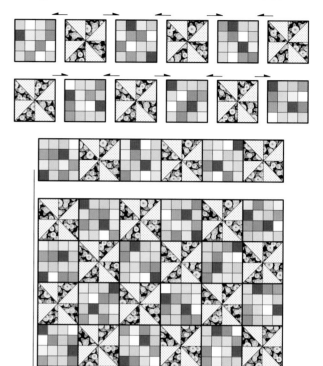

Quilt assembly

2 Sew the rows together. The quilt should now measure 48½" x 64½".

Adding the Borders

1 Sew the six black-with-white polka dot 2" x 42" inner-border strips together end to end.

2 Measure the quilt from top to bottom through the middle to determine the length of the side borders. From the pieced strip, cut the side borders to the needed length and attach them to the sides of the quilt.

3 Measure the quilt from side to side through the middle, including the side borders, to determine the length of the top and bottom borders. From the pieced strip, cut the top and bottom borders to the needed length and attach them to the top and bottom of the quilt. The quilt should now measure 51½" x 67½".

4 Piece the seven black print 6¾" x 42" outer-border strips end to end.

5 Repeat the measuring and cutting process as you did for the inner borders. Add the black outer borders. The quilt should now measure 64" x 80".

Finishing the Quilt

For help with any of the finishing steps, go to ShopMartingale.com/HowtoQuilt for free downloadable information.

1 Layer, baste, and quilt your quilt, or take it to your favorite long-arm quilter for finishing.

2 Using the black-with-white polka dot 2¼"-wide binding strips, make and attach binding.

Little Red, Small

This is the small version of the 66¾" square quilt shown on page 32. Make one or both—in matching fabrics or in a whole new color palette, as shown here.

"Little Red, Small," designed and pieced by Carrie Nelson; quilted by Louise Haley

FINISHED QUILT: 29¼" x 37" • FINISHED BLOCK: 3⅞" x 3⅞"

Materials

Yardage is based on 42"-wide fabric, except where noted.

48 assorted light 5" squares for blocks
48 assorted medium or dark 5" squares for blocks
⅜ yard of medium or dark print for outer border
¼ yard of light print for inner border
⅓ yard of fabric for binding
1¼ yards of fabric for backing
34" x 42" piece of batting

Cutting

From *each of 24* light squares, cut:
1 square, 4¾" x 4¾" (24 total)
From *each* of the remaining 24 light squares, cut:
1 strip, 2¼" x 5"; crosscut into 2 squares, 2¼" x 2¼" (48 total)
1 strip, 1⅞" x 5"; crosscut into 2 squares, 1⅞" x 1⅞" (48 total)
From *each of 24* medium or dark squares, cut:
1 square, 4¾" x 4¾" (24 total)
From *each* of the remaining 24 medium or dark squares, cut:
1 strip, 2¼" x 5"; crosscut into 2 squares, 2¼" x 2¼" (48 total)
1 strip, 1⅞" x 5"; crosscut into 2 squares, 1⅞" x 1⅞" (48 total)
From the light print, cut:
2 strips, 1¼" x 31½"
2 strips, 1¼" x 25¼"
From the medium or dark print, cut:
2 strips, 2½" x 33"
2 strips, 2½" x 29¼"
From the binding fabric, cut:
150" of 2"-wide bias strips

Piecing the Blocks

For each pair of blocks, you'll need the following pieces:

- Two different 4¾" squares (one light and one medium or dark)
- Four different 2¼" squares (two light and two medium or dark)
- Four different 1⅞" squares (two light and two medium or dark)

Use a scant ¼"-wide seam allowance throughout. After sewing each seam, press the seam allowances in the direction indicated by the arrows.

1 Refer to "Folded Corners" on page 10 to draw a diagonal line from corner to corner on the wrong side of the 2¼" and 1⅞" squares. Sew marked medium or dark 2¼" squares on diagonally opposite corners of a light 4¾" square.

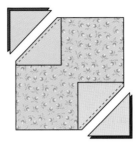 

2 In the same manner, sew marked light 2¼" squares on diagonally opposite corners of a medium or dark 4¾" square.

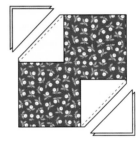 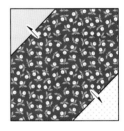

3 Repeat step 1, sewing the marked medium or dark 1⅞" squares to the remaining corners of the light squares. Make 24 light Snowball blocks.

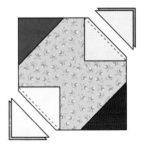 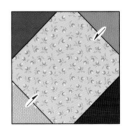

Make 24.

4 In the same manner, sew the marked light 1⅞" squares to the remaining corners of the medium or dark squares. Make 24 dark Snowball blocks.

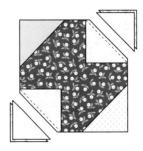 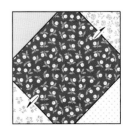

Make 24.

5 On the wrong side of the light Snowball blocks, draw a diagonal line from corner to corner across the larger triangles. Layer a marked Snowball block right sides together with a dark Snowball block, making sure that the snowball corners match the facing corners according to size. The triangles should nestle into each other with the seam allowances abutting. Sew a scant ¼" on both sides of the marked line. Cut the squares apart on the line to make two blocks. Press the seam allowances toward the darker side of the block (or press open). Repeat to make a total of 48 blocks. The blocks should each measure 4⅜" square.

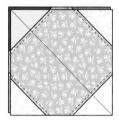

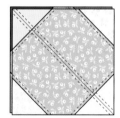

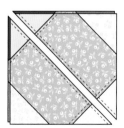

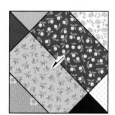 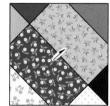

Make 48.

Assembling the Quilt Top

1 Lay out the blocks in eight rows of six blocks each; rotate every other block 90° as shown in the quilt assembly diagram above right.

2 Sew the blocks together into rows, pressing the seam allowances in opposite directions from one row to the next (or press them open). Then sew the rows together and press. The quilt top should measure 23¾" x 31½".

3 Sew the light 31½"-long strips to opposite sides of the quilt top and press the seam allowances toward the border. Sew the light 25¼"-long strips to the top and bottom of the quilt top and press.

4 Sew the medium or dark 33"-long strips to opposite sides of the quilt top and press the seam allowances toward the outer border. Sew the medium or dark 29¼"-long strips to the top and bottom of the quilt top and press.

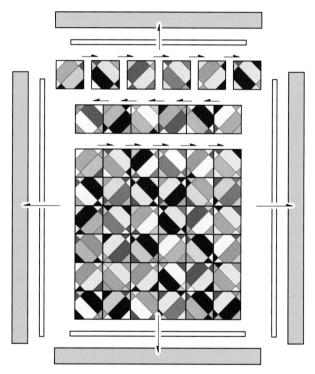

Quilt assembly

Finishing the Quilt

For help with any of the finishing steps, go to ShopMartingale.com/HowtoQuilt for free downloadable information.

1 Layer, baste, and quilt your quilt, or take it to your favorite long-arm quilter for finishing.

2 Using the 2"-wide binding strips, make and attach binding.

Happy Ending

This quilt goes together quickly and results in a fun vertical zigzag to showcase beautiful quilting designs or your favorite fabrics. Just be sure you have adequate contrast between your charm squares and the background fabric.

"Happy Ending," designed and made by Lesley Chaisson

FINISHED QUILT: 81½" x 105½"

Materials

Yardage is based on 42"-wide fabric, except where noted.

96 assorted print 5" squares for patchwork

7¼ yards of sage-green solid for background and border

⅞ yard of red print for binding

8 yards of fabric for backing

86" x 110" piece of batting

Cutting

From the sage-green solid, cut:

12 strips, 5" x 42"; crosscut into 96 squares, 5" x 5"

15 strips, 8½" x 42"; crosscut into:

    2 rectangles, 4½" x 8½"

    19 squares, 8½" x 8½"

    20 rectangles, 8½" x 16½"

9 border strips, 5" x 42"

From the red print, cut:

10 strips, 2½" x 42"

Assembling the Quilt Top

1 On the wrong side of each green 5" square, mark a diagonal line from corner to corner. Layer each marked square right sides together with a print square. Sew ¼" from each side of the marked lines; cut the squares apart on the marked lines to make 192 half-square-triangle units. Press the seam allowances toward the green solid. Trim the units so that they measure 4½" x 4½".

2 Sew the triangle squares together in pairs to form 48 rectangles with angles slanting to the left and 48 with angles slanting to the right. Press as indicated.

Make 48 of each.

3 Sew a left-slanting and a right-slanting rectangle together so that the assorted prints form a point. Press the seam allowances as shown and repeat to make 46 pieced squares. (You will have two left-slanting and two right-slanting units left over for step 8.) The squares should measure 8½" x 8½".

Make 46.

4 Sew together 2 square units from step 3 to make 10 rectangles with points touching. Press the seam allowances to one side.

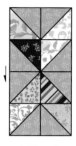

Make 10.

5 Sew two green 8½" x 16½" rectangles to opposite sides each unit from step 4 as shown. Press the seam allowances toward the green fabric.

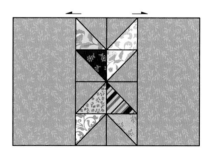

Make 10.

6 Sew pieced squares from step 3 to opposite sides of a green 8½" square, making sure the points are oriented away from the center square. Repeat to make 11 of these units.

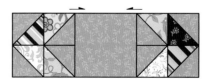

Make 11.

7 Sew green 8½" squares to opposite sides of the remaining four pieced squares from step 3. Make four.

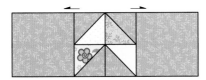

Make 4.

8 Using the remaining pieced rectangles from step 2, sew a left-slanting rectangle to one end of a green 4½" x 8½" rectangle and a right-slanting rectangle to the other end as shown. Make two units.

Make 2.

9 Following the quilt assembly diagram below, arrange the units to form three vertical rows. Press the seam allowances in opposite directions, and then sew the rows together.

10 Sew eight of the green 5"-wide strips together end to end in pairs. Cut the remaining strip in half and add a half strip to two of the long border strips for the sides. Measure the length of the quilt top and cut two border strips to this length. Sew the borders to the sides of the quilt top and press the seam allowances toward the border strips. Repeat, measuring the width of the quilt top, and then cutting and sewing the top and bottom borders.

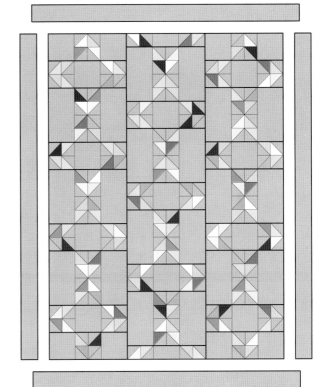

Finishing the Quilt

For help with any of the finishing steps, go to ShopMartingale.com/HowtoQuilt for free downloadable information.

1 Layer, baste, and quilt your quilt, or take it to your favorite long-arm quilter for finishing.

2 Using the red print 2½"-wide strips, make and attach binding.

Christmas Bonus

Here's a beautiful yet easy quilt to create for the holidays—or any other time of the year! This quilt features pale-pink prints in the background, but you can easily make the same design using a light-blue or traditional cream background. Just add three darker colors and voilà!

"Christmas Bonus," designed and pieced by Claudia Plett; machine quilted by Le Ann Weaver

FINISHED QUILT: 72½" x 88½" • FINISHED BLOCK: 8" x 8"

Materials

Yardage is based on 42"-wide fabric, except where noted.

224 pale-pink 5" squares for block backgrounds and border

60 red 5" squares for blocks

72 green 5" squares for blocks

40 blue 5" squares for blocks

1 yard of red print for bias binding (or ⅔ yard for straight-grain binding)

5¾ yards of fabric for backing

77" x 93" piece of batting

Cutting

From *74* of the pale-pink 5" squares, cut:

74 squares, 4½" x 4½"

From the red print, cut:

1½" bias strips to total 350" for single-fold bias binding *OR* 9 strips, 2¼" x 42", for double-fold straight-grain binding

Piecing the Blocks

1 Pair two 5" squares right sides together, mark a diagonal line from corner to corner on the wrong side of the lighter square, and sew ¼" on each side of the marked line to make the following sets of half-square-triangle units.

- Use 48 red squares and 48 pink squares to make 96 of half-square-triangle unit A as shown. Press the seam allowances toward the red triangles.
- Use 60 green squares and 60 pink squares to make 120 of half-square-triangle unit B as shown. Press the seam allowances toward the green triangles.
- Use 40 blue squares and 40 pink squares to make 80 of half-square-triangle unit C as shown. Press the seam allowances toward the blue triangles.

- Use 12 red squares and 12 green squares to make 24 of half-square-triangle unit D as shown. Press the seam allowances toward the green triangles.

Unit A.
Make 96.

Unit B.
Make 120.

Unit C.
Make 80.

Unit D.
Make 24.

2 Trim all of the half-square-triangle units to measure 4½" x 4½".

3 Sew the units together as shown, and press the seam allowances as indicated by the arrows.

- Sew three A units and one C unit together to make block E. Make a total of 32.
- Sew three B units and one C unit together to make block F. Make a total of 24.
- Sew two B units, one C unit, and one D unit together to make block G. Make a total of 24. All of the blocks should measure 8½" x 8½".

Block E.
Make 32.

Block F.
Make 24.

Block G.
Make 24.

Assembling the Quilt Top

1 Lay out the blocks in 10 rows of eight blocks each, referring to the diagram for block placement and rotating the blocks as shown. Sew the blocks together in rows and press the seam allowances in opposite directions from row to row.

2 Sew the rows together and press the seam allowances in one direction to complete the quilt center.

Adding the Border

This quilt features a notched border. If you choose to use a straight-edged border instead, trim the remaining pink 5" squares to 4½" and use a total of 76 pink 4½" squares. If you choose to use the notched border, follow these steps:

1 Measuring 1" from the corner of a pink 4½" square and using a ruler marked with a 45° line, trim away the corner at a 45° angle as shown. Trim 22 of the 4½" pink squares.

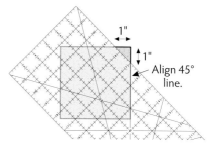

Trim corner.

2 Sew the notched squares in pairs as shown.

3 Cut the remaining pink 5" square in half diagonally to make two half-square triangles for the corners on the bottom border. (The top border doesn't have notches.)

4 For the side borders, sew 12 pink 4½" squares and four notched pairs together as shown to make a border strip. Make two and sew them to the sides of your quilt top. (If you're making a straight-edged border, sew 20 squares together for each side border.)

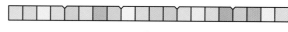

Make 2.

5 For the bottom border, sew 10 pink 4½" squares and three notched pairs together to make a border strip. Add a corner triangle to each end as shown. Sew the border to the bottom of your quilt.

Make 1.

6 For the top border, sew 18 pink 4½" squares together to make a border strip. Sew the border to the top of your quilt.

Finishing the Quilt

For help with any of the finishing steps, go to ShopMartingale.com/HowtoQuilt for free downloadable information.

1 Layer, baste, and quilt your quilt, or take it to your favorite long-arm quilter for finishing.

2 Using the red print strips, make and attach single-fold bias binding. (For a straight-edged quilt, make and attach double-fold binding.)

Spin City, Small

This petite version of "Spin City" is half the size of the one on page 25, and is made using 5" charm squares rather than 10" Layer Cake squares.

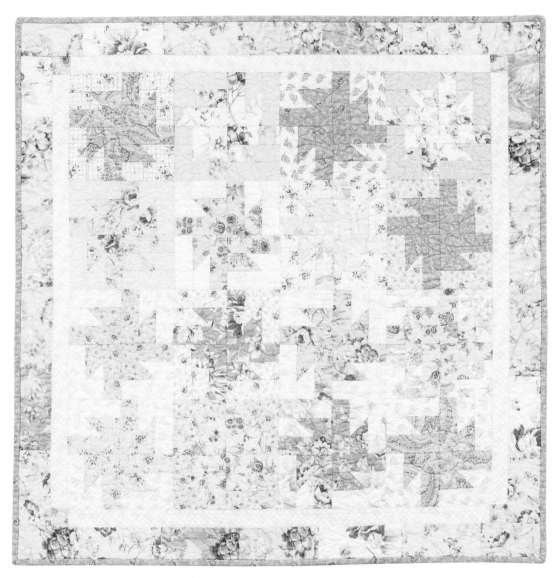

"Spin City, Small," designed and pieced by Carrie Nelson; quilted by Louise Haley

FINISHED QUILT: 30½" x 30½" • FINISHED BLOCK: 6" x 6"

Materials

Yardage is based on 42"-wide fabric, except where noted.

32 matching pairs of assorted 5" squares for blocks (64 total)
14 assorted 5" squares for outer border
¼ yard of white print for inner border
⅓ yard of fabric for binding
1⅛ yards of fabric for backing
36" x 36" piece of batting
Template plastic
Permanent pen

Cutting

From *each* of the assorted squares for blocks, cut:
3 strips, 1½" x 5" (6 matching strips; 192 total)
From the white print, cut:
4 strips, 1½" x 24½"
From *1 square* for outer border, cut:
4 squares, 1½" x 1½"
From *each* of the remaining 13 assorted squares for outer border, cut:
2 border strips, 2½" x 5" (26 total; don't worry about the pinked edges)
From the binding fabric, cut:
135" of 2"-wide bias strips

Piecing the Blocks

For each block, you'll need the following pieces:

- Fabric 1: six matching 1½" x 5" strips
- Fabric 2: six matching 1½" x 5" strips

Use a scant ¼"-wide seam allowance throughout. Directions are for making one block. Repeat to make a total of 16 blocks.

1 From the template plastic, cut a 1½" x 5" rectangle. On the right side of the template, mark a point 1¾" from the top. On the left side of the template, mark a point 3¼" from the top. Draw a diagonal line connecting the two points. Cut the rectangle apart on the drawn line to make a cutting-guide template.

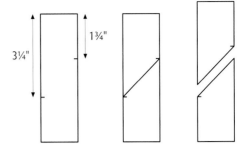

2 Use a piece of clear tape to affix the template to the underneath side of a small ruler with the template's diagonal edge along the outer edge of the ruler as shown below. Using the template/ruler and two 1½" x 5" strips of each fabric, trim the strips exactly as shown, making sure all of the strips are right side facing up before cutting.

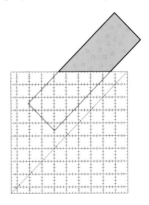

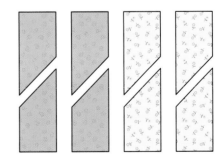

3 Using two different pieces from step 2, sew the pieces together to make a strip. Press the seam allowances open. Repeat to make four matching pieced strips.

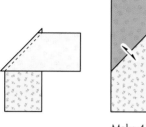

Make 4.

4 Trim the pieced strips to measure 1½" x 3½". After trimming, the seam line on the right edge should be 1" from the top and the seam on the left edge should be 2½" from the top as shown. Trim the eight remaining strips (four of each fabric) to measure 1½" x 3½".

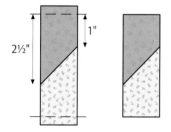

5 Lay out three strips side by side, placing the pieced strip in the center as shown. Sew the strips together. Make four matching units.

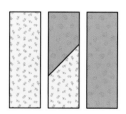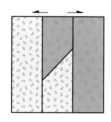

Make 4.

6 Lay out the units in a four-patch arrangement, rotating the units as shown. Before stitching, lay out the same units in reverse order, and decide which arrangement you prefer.

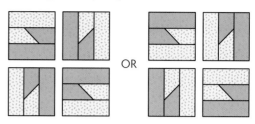

OR

7 Sew the units together in rows, and then sew the rows together to complete a block, taking care to match the seam intersection in the center of the block. Don't press the center seam just yet. Repeat to make a total of 16 blocks.

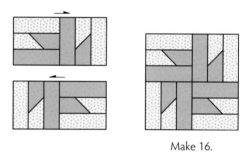

Make 16.

8 Use a seam ripper to remove two or three stitches from the seam allowances on *both* sides of the center seam as shown. On the wrong side of each block, gently reposition the seam allowances to evenly distribute the fabric. Press the seam allowances in opposite directions, opening the seam so that the center lies flat. When you look at the wrong side of the block, the seam allowances should be going in a counterclockwise direction around the center. Each block should measure 6½" square.

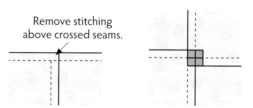

Remove stitching above crossed seams.

Assembling the Quilt Top

1 Lay out the blocks in four rows of four blocks each as shown in the quilt assembly diagram at right. Sew the blocks together into rows, pressing the seam allowances in opposite directions from one row to the next (or press them open). Then sew the rows together and press. The quilt top should measure 24½" x 24½".

2 Sew two white print 1½"-wide strips to the sides of the quilt top and press the seam allowances toward the borders.

3 Sew a 1½" square to each end of the two remaining white strips and press. Sew these borders to the top and bottom of the quilt top and press the seam allowances toward the borders.

4 For the outer border, sort 2½" x 5" border strips into the following groups:

- **Side borders:** two groups of six strips each
- **Top and bottom borders:** two groups of seven strips each

Join each group of strips end to end to make four long strips. Press the seam allowances in one direction (or press them open). For the side borders, trim the two shorter strips to measure 2½" x 26½". For the top and bottom borders, trim the two longer strips to measure 2½" x 30½".

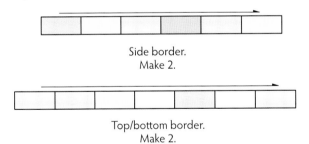

Side border.
Make 2.

Top/bottom border.
Make 2.

5 Sew the border strips to the sides, and then the top and bottom of the quilt top, keeping the pinked edges on the outside. Press the seam allowances toward the outer borders.

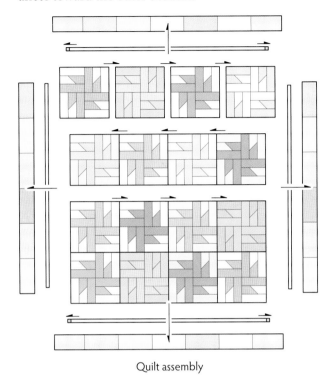

Quilt assembly

Finishing the Quilt

For help with any of the finishing steps, go to ShopMartingale.com/HowtoQuilt for free downloadable information.

1 Layer, baste, and quilt your quilt, or take it to your favorite long-arm quilter for finishing.

2 Using the 2"-wide binding strips, make and attach binding.

Cobblestone Nickels and Dimes

Here's a wonderful way for you to use your 5" and 10" squares along with fat quarters! By using appliquéd setting squares in a diagonal block setting, you can create a very impressive and "charming" quilt that looks more difficult than it is. The appliqué is optional if you're looking for a quicker project.

"Cobblestone Nickels and Dimes," designed, pieced, and appliquéd by Claudia Plett; machine quilted by Le Ann Weaver

FINISHED QUILT: 79½" x 91" • FINISHED BLOCK: 4" x 4"

Materials

Yardage is based on 42"-wide fabric, except where noted. Fat quarters are 18" x 21".

210 assorted light print 5" squares for blocks

210 assorted dark print 5" squares for blocks

14 cream print 10" squares OR 1⅓ yards of cream print for appliqué block backgrounds

6 light- or medium-red print 10" squares for appliqué (optional)

4 dark-red print 10" squares for appliqué (optional)

1 yellow print 10" square for appliqué (optional)

7 fat quarters of assorted cream prints for setting triangles

⅔ yard of medium-green print for binding

7 yards of fabric for backing

84" x 95" piece of batting

2 skeins of green embroidery floss for appliqué blocks (optional)

Cutting

From *each of 42* assorted light print 5" squares, cut:

4 squares, 2½" x 2½" (168 total)

From *each of 42* assorted dark print 5" squares, cut:

4 squares, 2½" x 2½" (168 total)

From *each* of the remaining 168 assorted light print 5" squares, cut:

3 strips, 1½" x 5"; cut into 2 rectangles, 1½" x 2½", and 2 rectangles, 1½" x 4½"*

From *each* of the remaining 168 assorted dark print 5" squares, cut:

3 strips, 1½" x 5"; cut into 2 rectangles, 1½" x 2½", and 2 rectangles, 1½" x 4½"*

Refer to the cutting diagram below; keep light and dark fabrics in separate stacks.

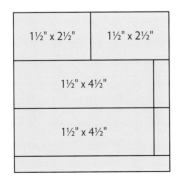

Cutting guide for nickels

From the cream print fat quarters, cut a total of:

7 squares, 13" x 13"; cut each square into quarters diagonally to yield 28 triangles (2 are extra)

2 squares, 7" x 7"; cut each square in half diagonally to yield 4 triangles

From the yellow print 10" square, cut:

82 squares, 1" x 1"

From the medium-green print for binding, cut:

9 strips, 2¼" x 42"

Piecing the Blocks

The pieced blocks are simply squares with a border; for each block you will need one center 2½" square and one set of four side pieces for the borders. Combine light centers with dark borders for block A and dark centers with light borders for block B.

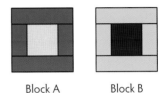

Block A   Block B

1 To make block A, stitch matching dark 1½" x 2½" rectangles to opposite sides of a light center square. Press the seam allowances away from the square. Add the matching 1½" x 4½" dark pieces to the top and bottom. Press. Repeat to make 168 of block A. The blocks should measure 4½" x 4½".

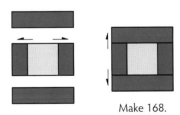

Make 168.

2 To make block B, repeat step 1, sewing light rectangles to dark center squares. Make 168 of block B.

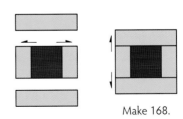

Make 168.

Making the Appliqué Blocks

If you are electing not to appliqué, skip to step 5.

1 Using the appliqué placement guide on page 80, lightly mark positioning lines as shown on 10 of the cream 10" squares (set aside the remaining four). Mark 26 cream triangles cut from the 13" squares in the same manner, omitting the middle flower and stem.

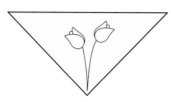

2 Embroider the stem lines on all marked blocks using a stem stitch.

3 Make templates for the tulip petals using the patterns on page 80. Cut 46 A and 36 A reversed from the light- or medium-red 10" squares. Add seam allowances if you're using hand appliqué. For fusible appliqué, reverse the templates when tracing the shapes onto paper-backed fusible web. Cut 46 of B and 36 of B reversed from the dark-red 10" squares.

4 For each center block, you'll need three yellow 1" squares, two A pieces, one A reversed piece, two B pieces, and one B reversed piece. Fold the yellow squares in half horizontally and vertically and pin in place for the tulip centers. Stitch or fuse the B piece, and then the A piece, making sure to sew through all layers to secure the flower centers. Appliqué 10 center blocks and 26 side triangles.

5 Trim the 10 appliquéd blocks to 8½" x 8½" by trimming two sides as shown. Trim the four remaining cream 10" squares you set aside earlier so that they also measure 8½" x 8½". If you didn't do the appliqué, simply trim all 14 cream 10" squares to measure 8½" square.

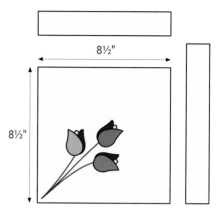

Assembling the Quilt Top

1 For easy quilt assembly, join the Cobblestone blocks in units of four blocks each, alternating two A blocks and two B blocks and positioning the blocks exactly as shown so that seam allowances don't butt up to one another. Press as indicated by the arrows. Make 84 four-block units. Try to arrange the blocks so that you don't have like colors next to each other, and try to have different center colors in each of the four grouped blocks.

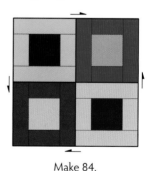

Make 84.

2 Assemble two corner sections as shown, using one four-block unit, one corner background triangle, and two side setting triangles for each. Press the seam allowances toward the triangles.

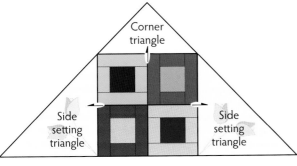

Make 2.

3 Following the assembly diagram, arrange the block units in diagonal rows, rotating the appliquéd blocks so the stems all point toward the center as shown. Sew the blocks together in rows and press the seam allowances in opposite directions from row to row. Sew the rows together and press.

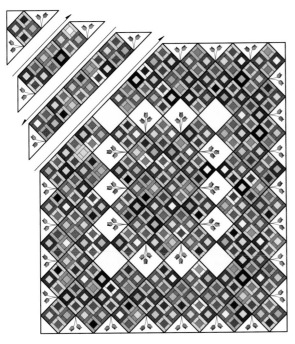

Quilt assembly

4 Trim and square up the outside edges of the quilt, making sure to leave ¼" beyond the block corners.

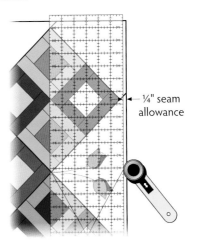

¼" seam allowance

Finishing the Quilt

For help with any of the finishing steps, go to ShopMartingale.com/HowtoQuilt for free downloadable information.

1 Layer, baste, and quilt your quilt, or take it to your favorite long-arm quilter for finishing.

2 Using the medium-green 2¼"-wide strips, make and attach binding.

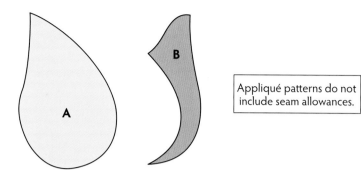

Appliqué patterns do not
include seam allowances.

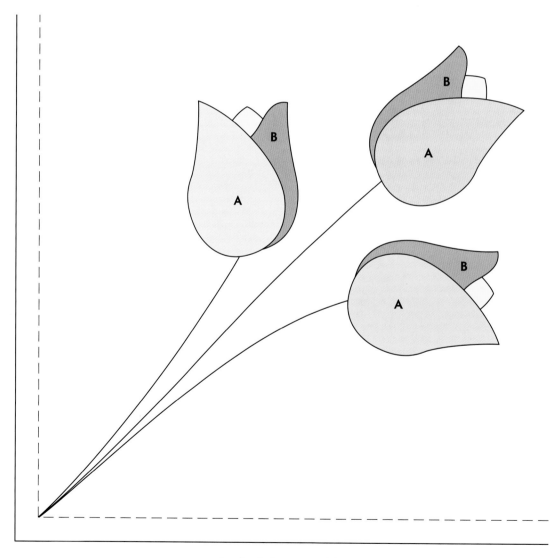

Appliqué placement guide

Pretty in Pink

What could be prettier than pink, besides lots of it? If you don't "think pink," this ultrafeminine quilt would be just as lovely in your favorite color.

"Pretty in Pink," designed and made by Jodi Crowell

FINISHED QUILT: 69" x 69" • FINISHED BLOCK: 9" x 9"

Materials

Yardage is based on 42"-wide fabric, unless otherwise noted. Each charm square needs to measure at least 3½" x 3½".

334 assorted pink 5" squares for blocks

3⅛ yards of small-scale white print for blocks

1 yard of medium-green print for vine, stem, bud, and leaf appliqués

Scraps of dark-green prints for leaf and bud appliqués

Scraps of assorted pink prints for heart, flower, and bud appliqués

Scraps of assorted yellow prints for flower center appliqués

¾ yard of pink fabric for binding

4½ yards of fabric for backing

75" x 75" piece of batting

¼"-wide bias bar

Cutting

All measurements include a ¼"-wide seam allowance. The template pattern for piece C is on page 84.

From the assorted pink 5" squares, cut:

294 squares, 3½" x 3½"

40 C pieces

From the white print, cut:

27 strips, 3½" x 42"; crosscut into 297 squares, 3½" x 3½"

16 C pieces

From the medium-green print, cut:

670" of 1"-wide bias strips

From the pink binding fabric, cut:

370" of 2"-wide bias strips

Piecing the Blocks

1 Make freezer-paper templates of the A and B shapes by tracing the patterns on page 84. Make 104 A templates and 16 B templates.

2 Using the pink 3½" squares and the templates from step 1, mark and cut out 68 A shapes and 8 B shapes, adding a ¼"-wide seam allowance to the curved edge only. Fold the seam allowance under and baste. Pin each shape to a white 3½" square, aligning the straight edges as shown. Hand stitch along the curved edge with matching thread. Repeat using the remaining white 3½" squares to make 36 A shapes and 8 B shapes. Pin and stitch each white shape to a 3½" pink square.

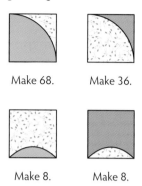

Make 68.   Make 36.

Make 8.   Make 8.

3 Referring to the illustrations below and the photo on page 81 for placement, arrange the A and B units from step 2, pink and/or white 3½" squares, and the pink and/or white C pieces to make the specified number of each unit shown. Stitch the pieces in each row together; press the seams in alternate directions from row to row. Then stitch the rows together to complete the block. Make the number of blocks indicated for each combination of pieces.

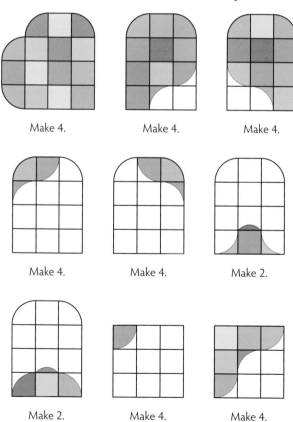

Make 4.   Make 4.   Make 4.

Make 4.   Make 4.   Make 2.

Make 2.   Make 4.   Make 4.

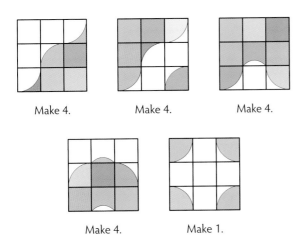

Make 4.   Make 4.   Make 4.

Make 4.   Make 1.

Assembling the Quilt Top

1 Refer to the assembly diagram below to arrange the blocks into seven horizontal rows of seven blocks each.

2 Sew the blocks in each row together; press the seam allowances in alternate directions from row to row. Sew the rows together; press the seam allowances in one direction.

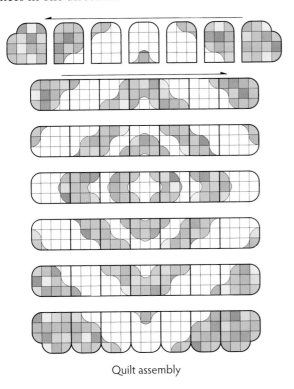

Quilt assembly

Adding the Appliqués

1 Make freezer-paper templates for the heart, flower, flower center, leaf, inner bud, and outer bud, using the patterns on page 84. For hand appliqué, add a ¼" seam allowance to each piece when you cut it out. For fusible appliqué, no seam allowance is needed.

2 Stitch the medium-green 1" bias strips together to make one long strip. Fold the strip in half, wrong sides together, and stitch a scant ¼" from the long raw edges. Insert the ¼"-wide bias bar into the tube, rotating the seam to be along the center of one side, and press flat. From the long tube, cut 48 stems, each 6" in length. For the vines, cut the remaining tube into four 54" lengths and four 28" lengths. Referring to the photo, stitch the stems and vines in place using matching thread.

3 Referring to the photo for placement, arrange the prepared heart, flower, flower center, leaf, inner bud, and outer bud appliqués on the quilt top. Stitch them in place using matching thread.

4 After all the appliqué work is complete, gently press the quilt top.

Finishing the Quilt

For help with any of the finishing steps, go to ShopMartingale.com/HowtoQuilt for free downloadable information.

1 Layer, baste, and quilt your quilt, or take it to your favorite long-arm quilter for finishing. Below is the quilting motif used for the pink squares in the quilt shown.

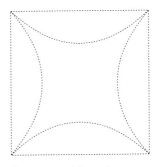

Quilting motif for pink squares

2 Using the pink 2"-wide bias strips, make and attach binding.

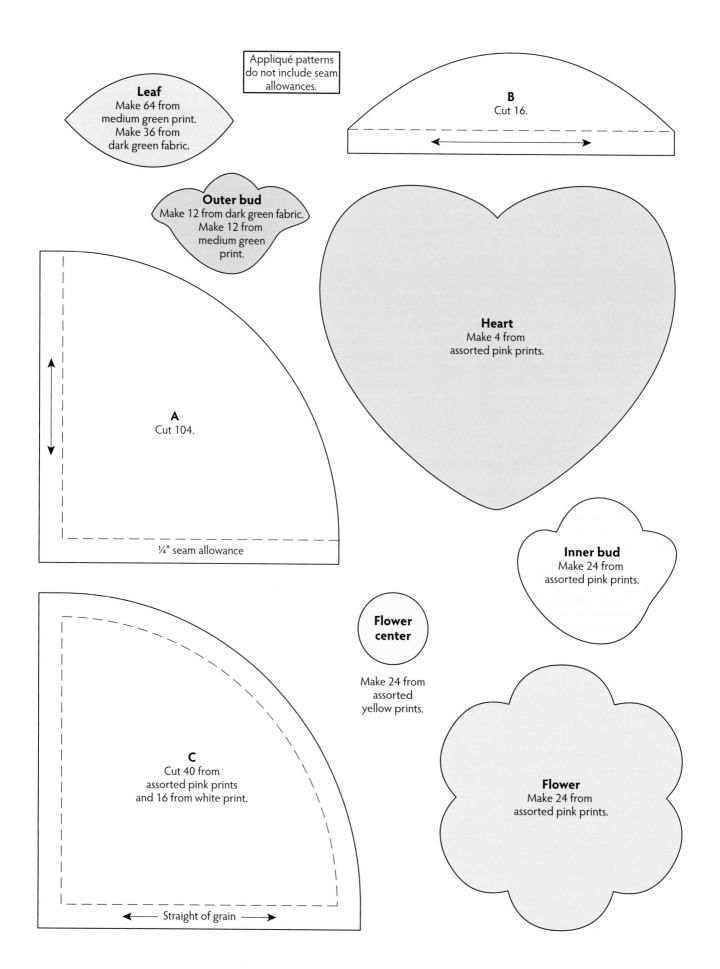

Leaf
Make 64 from
medium green print.
Make 36 from
dark green fabric.

Appliqué patterns
do not include seam
allowances.

B
Cut 16.

Outer bud
Make 12 from dark green fabric.
Make 12 from
medium green
print.

Heart
Make 4 from
assorted pink prints.

A
Cut 104.

¼" seam allowance

Inner bud
Make 24 from
assorted pink prints.

**Flower
center**

Make 24 from
assorted
yellow prints.

C
Cut 40 from
assorted pink prints
and 16 from white print.

Flower
Make 24 from
assorted pink prints.

Straight of grain

People Will Find You Interesting

If you're shy talking to people you don't know, ask them questions about themselves. Or show off this quilt—it can spark a conversation. Plus it's a perfect project to practice your points.

"People Will Find You Interesting," designed by Mary Etherington and Connie Tesene of Country Threads

FINISHED QUILT: 15" x 19" • FINISHED BLOCK: 3" x 3"

Materials

Yardage is based on 42"-wide fabric, except where noted.

30 assorted medium- to dark-value 5" squares for blocks and pieced border

18 assorted light- to medium-value 5" squares for block backgrounds

¼ yard of pink print for side and corner triangles

¼ yard of brown print for binding

⅝ yard of fabric for backing

20" x 24" piece of batting

Cutting

All measurements include ¼"-wide seam allowances.

From *each of 18* medium- to dark-value 5" squares, cut:

1 square, 2⅞" x 2⅞"; cut each square in half diagonally to make 2 triangles (36 total)

3 squares, 1⅞" x 1⅞"; cut each square in half diagonally to make 2 triangles (108 total)

From the remaining 12 medium- to dark-value 5" squares, cut:

4 squares, 1⅞" x 1⅞"; cut each square in half diagonally to make 2 triangles (96 total; 4 are extra)

From each of the light- to medium-value 5" squares, cut:

2 squares, 1⅞" x 1⅞"; cut each square in half diagonally to make 2 triangles (72 total)

1 square, 1½" x 1½" (18 total)

From the pink print, cut:

3 squares, 6" x 6"; cut each square into quarters diagonally to make 4 triangles (12 total; 2 are extra)

2 squares, 4½" x 4½"; cut each square in half diagonally to make 2 triangles (4 total)

From the brown print, cut:

2 strips, 2¼" x 42"

Making Do

If you don't have a set of precut charm squares, you'll need one fat eighth (9" x 21") *each* of nine assorted medium- to dark-value fabrics. Cut two 2⅞" squares and eleven 1⅞" squares from each fabric; you may need a couple of additional small squares for the border. You'll also need one fat eighth *each* of six assorted light- to medium-value fabrics for the backgrounds. Cut six 1⅞" squares and three 1½" squares from each fabric.

Making the Quilt Top

Each block is made from two medium/dark 2⅞" triangles, four medium/dark 1⅞" triangles, four light/medium 1⅞" triangles, and one light/medium 1½" square. Many (but not all) of the blocks have matching light/medium pieces.

1 Sew two different 2⅞" triangles together, being careful not to stretch the bias edges. Press the seam allowances in one direction. Repeat with all the 2⅞" triangles to make 18 half-square-triangle units.

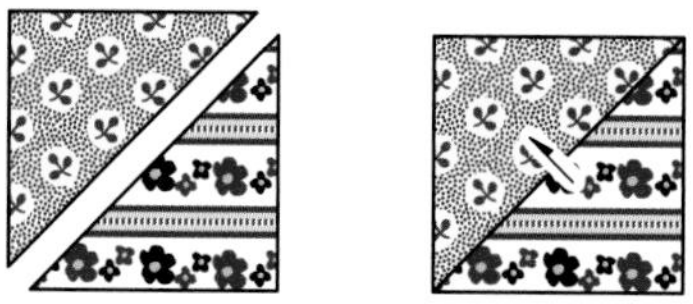

Make 18.

2 Pair four matching light/medium 1⅞" triangles and four assorted medium/dark triangles. Sew the triangle pairs together and press the seam allowances in one direction. Make 72 half-square-triangle units for the blocks. Repeat with the remaining 1⅞" triangles to make approximately 64 additional units for the borders.

Make 72 for blocks. Make 64 for borders.

3 Sew a unit from step 1, four half-square-triangle units from step 2, and a light/medium 1½" square together to make a block. Press as indicated. Make 18 blocks. Many (but not all) of the blocks have the same light/medium background fabric to help the individual blocks show more clearly.

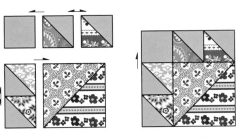

Make 18.

4 Arrange the blocks, side triangles, and corner triangles as shown. Sew the blocks and side triangles into diagonal rows. The pink triangles are cut oversized and will extend beyond the pieced blocks. Sew the rows together and add the pink 4½" triangles on each corner. Trim the quilt top ¼" outside the block corners.

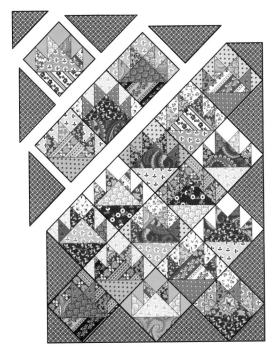

5 Sew 13 half-square-triangle units together, orienting the triangles in the same direction. Make two units and sew one to the top and one to the bottom of the quilt. Sew 19 half-square-triangle units together for each side border. With this many seams, it can be difficult to make the borders exactly the same size as the quilt center. Connie and Mary suggest you go for the "make do" look: if it's too long, cut if off. If it's too short, add more triangle units! You can also adjust the lengths by taking a little larger or smaller seam allowance between some of the triangle squares. Can you see which of these methods they used?

Finishing the Quilt

For help with any of the finishing steps, go to ShopMartingale.com/HowtoQuilt for free downloadable information.

1 Layer, baste, and quilt your quilt, or take it to your favorite long-arm quilter for finishing.

2 Using the brown 2¼"-wide strips, make and attach binding.

Nickel Bricks

Here's a marvelous way to use those charm squares you've been saving for a special project! Why not choose a theme for your print fabrics, such as food, animals, sports, or even bold stripes or polka dots? Or you could experiment with different background colors—perhaps red or bright blue. Use your creative energy to build your brick quilt!

"Nickel Bricks," designed and pieced by Claudia Plett; machine quilted by Mary M. Covey

FINISHED QUILT: 66½" x 75½" • FINISHED BLOCK: 4½" x 4½"

Materials

Yardage is based on 42"-wide fabric, except where noted.

168 assorted 5" squares for blocks and outer border
3¾ yards of black tone on tone for blocks, borders, and binding
4 yards of fabric for backing
71" x 80" piece of batting

Cutting

From the black tone on tone, cut:
42 strips, 1½" x 42"
18 strips, 2" x 42"
7 strips, 2¼" x 42"
4 squares, 5" x 5"
From *each* of the 5" squares, cut:
1 rectangle, 3" x 5" (168 total)
1 rectangle, 2" x 5" (168 total)

Making the Quilt Bigger

For a different-sized quilt, you'll need one black 1½" x 42" strip for every four blocks. Cut all strips in advance for quick strip piecing.

Piecing the Blocks

You will strip piece 168 Brick blocks using the assorted 3" x 5" rectangles and black 1½" strips. Set aside 82 of the 2" x 5" rectangles for the outer border. You will have 86 left over to use in another project.

1. Stitch the 3" x 5" rectangles, right sides together, to black 1½" strips along the 5" edges as shown, leaving just a small space between each rectangle. Stitch eight rectangles to one strip. Make 21 strips. Do not cut the pieces apart yet. (You may cut the threads between strips; just don't cut the strips yet.)

2. In the same manner, sew a black strip to the opposite side of each strip of rectangles.

3. Press the seam allowances toward the black strips. Cut apart the bricks by trimming the black strips even with the edges of the 3" x 5" rectangles as shown. Your Brick blocks should measure 5" x 5".

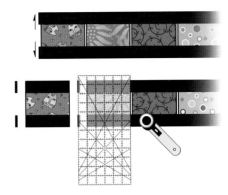

Assembling the Quilt Top

1. For easy assembly, group your blocks in units of four, rotating them as shown. Sew each group of four together and press all seam allowances toward the black strips.

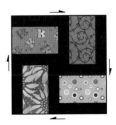

Make 42.

2. Stitch the four-block units into seven rows of six units each. Press the seam allowances to one side, alternating the direction from row to row. Then stitch the rows together and press.

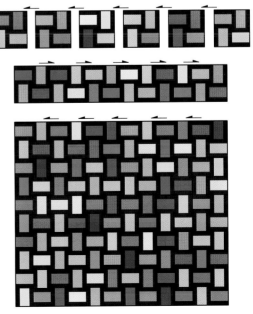

Adding the Borders

1 Piece seven of the black 2" strips together end to end. From this long strip, cut two side inner-border strips, 63½" long. Stitch these strips to the sides of your quilt top. Press the seam allowances toward the inner border.

2 Cut two 57½"-long inner-border strips and sew them to the top and bottom of your quilt top. Press the seam allowances toward the inner border. Your quilt center should measure 57½" x 66½".

3 Using the 2" x 5" rectangles you set aside earlier and the remaining black 2" strips, chain piece 82 rectangles along only one 5" side in the same manner as for the Brick blocks. Press the seam allowances toward the black strips; trim apart to create 82 border units, 3½" x 5".

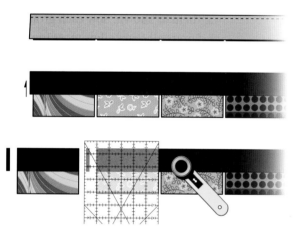

4 Create two side borders of 22 border units each. Join these to the sides of your quilt center. Press toward the inner border.

5 Create two borders of 19 units each for the top and bottom. Sew a black 5" square on each end of these borders. Join to the top and bottom of your quilt. Press the seam allowances toward the inner border.

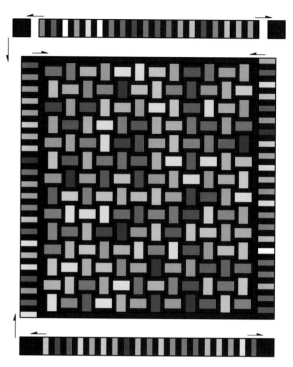

Finishing the Quilt

For help with any of the finishing steps, go to ShopMartingale.com/HowtoQuilt for free downloadable information.

1 Layer, baste, and quilt your quilt, or take it to your favorite long-arm quilter for finishing.

2 Using the black 2¼"-wide strips, make and attach binding.

Interlocking Squares

Is there a special man in your life who deserves a quilt of his own? This quilt has a distinctly masculine feel, but if blue gives you the "blues," experiment with charm squares in shades of your favorite color. Or make it scrappy, playing close attention to the placement of dark and light prints.

"Interlocking Squares," designed and made by Jodi Crowell

FINISHED QUILT: 80½" x 89"

Materials

Yardage is based on 42"-wide fabric, except where noted.

190 assorted light-blue 5" squares for blocks
206 assorted dark-blue 5" squares for blocks
5⅛ yards of white-and-blue print for blocks, side triangles, and corner triangles
⅝ yard of dark-blue fabric for binding
8 yards of fabric for backing
87" x 95" piece of batting

Cutting

All measurements include a ¼"-wide seam allowance. Cut all strips across the width of fabric (selvage to selvage).

From the dark-blue 5" squares, cut:
206 squares, 3½" x 3½"
From the light-blue 5" squares, cut:
190 squares, 3½" x 3½"
From the white-and-blue print, cut:
43 strips, 3½" x 42"; crosscut into 463 squares, 3½" x 3½"
19 squares, 5½" x 5½"; cut into quarters diagonally to yield 76 triangles
2 squares, 3" x 3"; cut in half diagonally to yield 4 triangles
From the dark-blue binding fabric, cut:
9 strips, 2" x 42"

Making the Quarter-Circle Units

1 Make 100 freezer-paper templates of the quarter-circle shape on page 93.

2 Prepare and cut out 52 dark-blue quarter circles and 48 light-blue quarter circles, adding a ¼"-wide seam allowance to the curved edge only. Fold the seam allowance under and baste. Pin each quarter circle to a white-and-blue 3½" square, aligning the straight edges. Hand stitch along the curved edge with matching thread.

Make 52.   Make 48.

Assembling the Quilt Top

1 Refer to the quilt assembly diagram below to arrange the quarter-circle blocks, dark-blue squares, light-blue squares, white-and-blue squares, and 5½" triangles into diagonal rows as shown.

2 Sew the pieces in each row together; press the seam allowances in alternate directions from row to row. Sew the rows together; press the seam allowances in one direction. Add the white-and-blue 3" triangles to each corner.

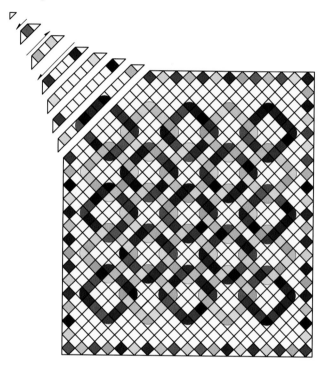

Quilt assembly

Finishing the Quilt

For help with any of the finishing steps, go to ShopMartingale.com/HowtoQuilt for free downloadable information.

1 Layer, baste, and quilt your quilt, or take it to your favorite long-arm quilter for finishing.

2 Using the dark-blue 2"-wide strips, make and attach binding.

Keeping Track

When sewing so many smaller individual pieces into rows, instead of larger pieced blocks, it's extremely easy to miscount and lose track of where you are, especially when dealing with hundreds of squares. To help keep track of the pieces and completed rows, photocopy the diagram below and use a highlighter to mark off each piece as you stitch.

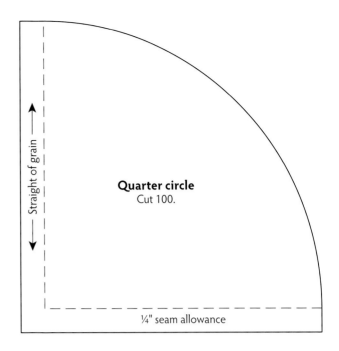

Straight of grain

Quarter circle
Cut 100.

¼" seam allowance

Roundabout, Small

Just like its bigger sister, "Roundabout" on page 16, this little quilt features pieced rectangles sewn around a center square. This fun pattern uses the Big O block, which creates lots of movement in the finished design.

"Roundabout, Small," designed and pieced by Carrie Nelson; machine quilted by Louise Haley

FINISHED QUILT: 32½" x 32½" • FINISHED BLOCK: 5¼" x 5¼"

Materials

Yardage is based on 42"-wide fabric, except where noted.

⅞ yard of light fabric for block backgrounds and inner border

50 assorted print 5" squares for blocks

17 assorted print 5" squares for outer border

⅜ yard of fabric for binding

1¼ yards of fabric for backing

38" x 38" piece of batting

Cutting

From the light fabric, cut:

8 strips, 2¼" x 42"; crosscut into 125 squares, 2¼" x 2¼"

2 strips, 1⅜" x 28½"

2 strips, 1⅜" x 26¾"

From *each* of the 50 assorted-print squares for blocks, cut:

2 rectangles, 2¼" x 4" (100 total)

From *each of 16* assorted-print squares for outer border, cut:

2 rectangles, 2¼" x 5" (32 total)

From the remaining assorted-print square, cut:

4 squares, 2½" x 2½"

From the binding fabric, cut:

145" of 2"-wide bias binding

Piecing the Blocks

For each block, you'll need the following pieces:

- **Print squares:** four different 2¼" x 4" rectangles
- **Background:** five 2¼" squares

Use a scant ¼"-wide seam allowance throughout. After sewing each seam, press the seam allowances in the direction indicated by the arrows (or press them open).

1 Draw a diagonal line from corner to corner on the wrong side of four of the background squares. Place a marked square on one end of a print rectangle, making sure the square is positioned exactly as shown. Sew along the marked line and trim, leaving a ¼" seam allowance. Repeat to make a total of four pieced rectangles.

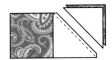

Make 4.

2 Lay out the four pieced rectangles and the remaining background square.

3 Sew a rectangle to the top of the background square, stitching a little more than halfway. Press the unit open as indicated.

4 Sew the next rectangle to the left edge of the unit from step 3.

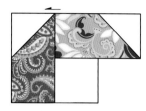

5 Sew a third rectangle to the bottom of the unit, and then sew the last rectangle to the right edge of the unit as shown.

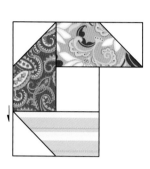 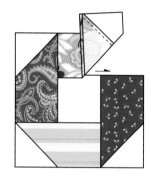

6 Complete the partial seam stitched in step 2. You can start where you stopped stitching and sew toward the outside raw edge, or you can start at the outside edge and sew toward the center square, whichever you prefer. The block should measure 5¾" square. Repeat to make a total of 25 blocks.

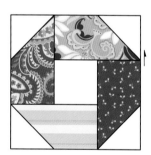

Make 25.

Assembling the Quilt Top

1 Lay out the blocks in five rows of five blocks each as shown in the quilt assembly diagram on page 97. Sew the blocks together in rows. Press the seam allowances in opposite directions from row to row (or press them open).

2 Sew the rows together and press the seam allowances in one direction (or press them open). The quilt center should measure 26¾" x 26¾".

3 For the inner border, sew the light 26¾"-long strips to opposite sides of the quilt center, and then sew the light 28½"-long strips to the top and bottom of the quilt top. Press the seam allowances toward the inner border.

4 For the outer border, sort the assorted 2¼" x 5" strips to make two sets of 16 strips each. Select one set of strips and sort it into two groups of eight strips each. Join each group of eight strips side by side. Press the seam allowances in one direction (or press them open). Make two pieced sections. Each section should measure 10" x 14½". Repeat to make a second set of two pieced sections.

Make 8.

5 Cut each pieced section in half lengthwise to make eight pieced outer-border strips, and then sort them into two groups of two matching sets.

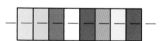 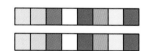

6 Join one set of strips to make a 2½" x 28½"-long pieced outer-border strip, keeping the pinked edges on the same side. Press the seam allowances in one direction (or press them open). Repeat to make a total of four pieced outer-border strips.

7 Sew two outer-border strips to the sides of the quilt top, keeping the pinked edges on the outside. Press the seam allowances toward the outer border.

8 Join 2½" squares to the ends of the two remaining outer-border strips. Press the seam allowances toward the border strips. Sew these borders to the top and bottom of the quilt top and press the seam allowances toward the outer border.

Finishing the Quilt

For help with any of the finishing steps, go to ShopMartingale.com/HowtoQuilt for free downloadable information.

1 Layer, baste, and quilt your quilt, or take it to your favorite long-arm quilter for finishing.

2 Using the 2"-wide binding strips, make and attach binding.

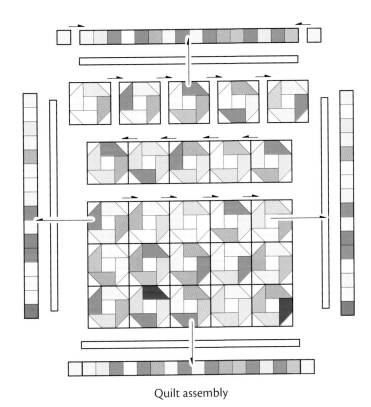

Quilt assembly

Better to Be Overdressed

Spiffy little Bow Tie blocks dress up this quilt, but its country flair gives it a down-home feel.

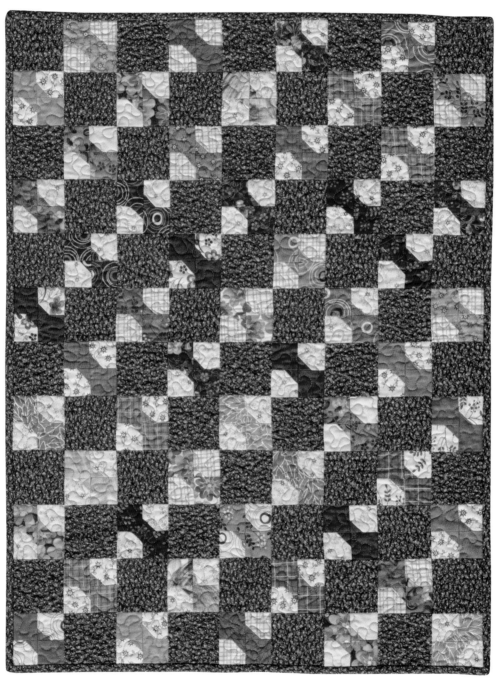

"Better to Be Overdressed," designed and made by
Mary Etherington and Connie Tesene of Country Threads

FINISHED QUILT: 22½" x 30" • FINISHED BLOCK: 2½" x 2½"

Materials

Yardage is based on 42"-wide fabric, except where noted.

27 assorted dark-value 5" squares for Bow Tie blocks
27 assorted light-value 5" squares for Bow Tie blocks
⅞ yard of dark-purple print for alternate blocks and binding
⅞ yard of fabric for backing
28" x 36" piece of batting

Cutting

All measurements include ¼"-wide seam allowances.

From each of the assorted dark-value 5" squares, cut:
4 squares, 1¾" x 1¾" (108 total)*
4 squares, 1⅛" x 1⅛" (108 total)*
From each of the assorted light-value 5" squares, cut:
4 squares, 1¾" x 1¾" (108 total)*
From the dark-purple print, cut:
5 strips, 3" x 42"; crosscut into 54 squares, 3" x 3"
4 strips, 2¼" x 42"

Keep squares of the same fabric together.

Making Do

If you don't have a set of precut charm squares, you'll need one fat eighth (9" x 21") *each* of 11 assorted dark-value prints; cut 10 squares, 1¾" x 1¾", and 10 squares, 1⅛" x 1⅛", from each. You'll also require one fat eighth *each* of nine assorted light-value prints; cut 12 squares, 1¾" x 1¾", from each. You'll have a couple squares and some leftover fabric you can use for piecing the back of the quilt.

Piecing the Blocks

Each Bow Tie block is made from four matching dark-value and two matching light-value squares.

1 Place a dark 1⅛" square on the corner of a light 1¾" square, right sides together. Stitch diagonally from corner to corner on the dark square; trim the outside corner of the small square and press the resulting triangle toward the corner. Repeat with a second set of matching dark- and light-value squares.

Make 2.

2 Arrange the two units from step 1 with two matching dark-value 1¾" charm squares and sew the units together to make a Bow Tie block.

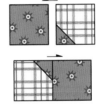 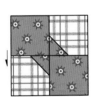

3 Repeat steps 1 and 2 to make 54 Bow Tie blocks.

Assembling the Quilt Top

Alternate the Bow Tie blocks and dark-purple 3" squares in 12 rows of nine blocks and squares in each row. In the quilt shown, (almost) all the Bow Tie blocks are oriented in the same direction, but there are many different ways to arrange them. Experiment! Sew the blocks into rows, pressing seam allowances toward the purple squares. Sew the rows together and press.

Finishing the Quilt

For help with any of the finishing steps, go to ShopMartingale.com/HowtoQuilt for free downloadable information.

1 Layer, baste, and quilt your quilt, or take it to your favorite long-arm quilter for finishing.

2 Using the dark-purple 2¼"-wide strips, make and attach binding.

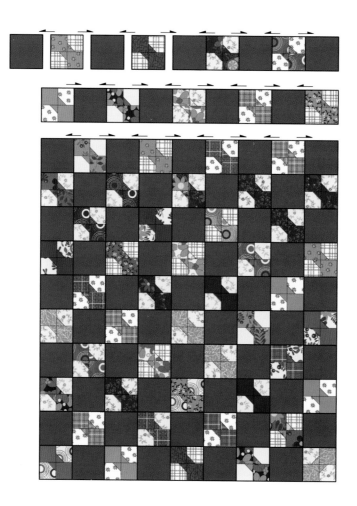

Halloween Harvest

The orange and black fabrics in this quilt practically shout, "Trick or treat!" This simple quilt is fun to sew with any of your favorite charm squares in any color combination. Add many more stars or none at all. Either way, this quilt is a treat to whip up.

"Halloween Harvest," designed and made by Lesley Chaisson

FINISHED QUILT: 73" x 82" • FINISHED BLOCK: 9" x 9"

Materials

Yardage is based on 42"-wide fabric, except where noted.

72 assorted 5" squares for blocks
2 different gold print 5" squares for stars*
3½ yards of orange fabric for background, inner border, and binding
1⅓ yards of black print for outer border
5 yards of fabric for backing
77" x 86" piece of batting
5" x 12" piece of fusible web for 2 star appliqués

One charm square is used for each star appliqué. If you want more than two stars, you'll need additional charm squares.

Cutting

All measurements include ¼"-wide seam allowances.

From the orange fabric, cut:
5 strips, 9½" x 42"; cut into 18 squares, 9½" x 9½"
10 strips, 5" x 42"
8 strips, 2½" x 42"
From the black print, cut:
8 strips, 5" x 42"

Piecing the Blocks

Sew four charm squares together to make a Four Patch block. Press the seam allowances in the direction of the arrows. Make 18 blocks.

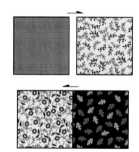

Make 18.

Assembling the Quilt Top

1 Sew one orange 9½" square to each Four Patch block. Press the seam allowances toward the orange square.

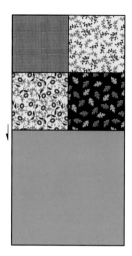

2 Sew six of the units from step 1 together, alternating the position of the orange squares. Make three rows; press.

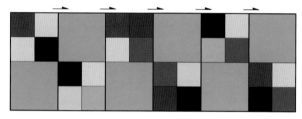

Make 3.

3 Cut one orange 5"-wide strip in half and sew a half strip to each of two orange 5" x 42" strips for sashing between rows. Measure the length of the three rows from step 2 and cut the sashing strips to the measured length. They should measure 54½". Sew the rows and sashing strips together. Press the seam allowances toward the orange fabric.

4 For the inner border, cut one orange 5" strip in half and sew a half strip to each of two orange 5" x 42" strips as before. Cut these strips to the measured length from step 3 and sew them to the top and bottom of the quilt; press.

5 Sew the remaining four orange 5" x 42" strips together in pairs for the side borders. Measure your quilt, cut the border strips to the measured length, and sew them to the sides. Press the seam allowances toward the orange border.

6 Sew the black border strips together into one long length. Repeat the measuring process and sew strips to the top and bottom first, and then sew strips to the sides. Press the seam allowances toward the black border.

7 Using the star pattern below and the two gold charm squares, make and appliqué two stars to the quilt top.

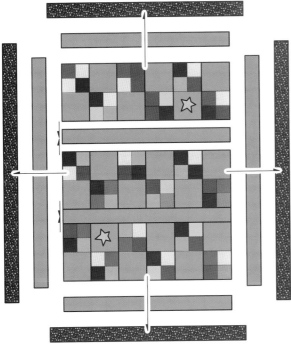

Finishing the Quilt

For help with any of the finishing steps, go to ShopMartingale.com/HowtoQuilt for free downloadable information.

1 Layer, baste, and quilt your quilt, or take it to your favorite long-arm quilter for finishing.

2 Using the orange 2½"-wide strips, make and attach binding.

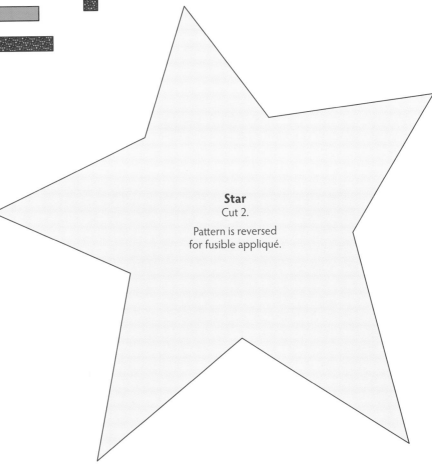

Star
Cut 2.

Pattern is reversed
for fusible appliqué.

Bennington, Small

Little Bow Tie blocks set together to form rings give this quilt plenty of impact. Make just this one, or make the big version on page 38 for an incredible pair.

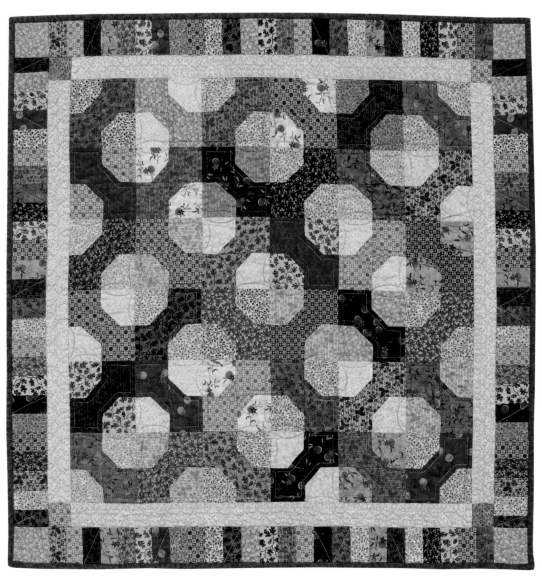

"Bennington, Small," designed and pieced by Carrie Nelson; quilted by Louise Haley

FINISHED QUILT: 29½" x 29½" • FINISHED BLOCK: 3¾" x 3¾"

Materials

Yardage is based on 42"-wide fabric, except where noted.

18 assorted light 5" squares for blocks
55 assorted medium or dark 5" squares for blocks and outer border
¼ yard of cream print for inner border
⅓ yard of fabric for binding
1 yard of fabric for backing
34" x 34" piece of batting

Cutting

From *each* of the 18 light squares, cut:
2 strips, 2⅜" x 5"; crosscut into 4 squares, 2⅜" x 2⅜" (72 total)

From *each* of 36 medium or dark squares, cut:
1 strip, 2⅜" x 5"; crosscut into 2 squares, 2⅜" x 2⅜" (72 total)
1 strip, 1½" x 5"; crosscut into 2 squares, 1½" x 1½" (72 total)

From *1* medium or dark square, cut:
2 strips, 1¾" x 5"; crosscut into 4 inner-border squares, 1¾" x 1¾"

From *1* medium or dark square, cut:
2 strips, 2½" x 5"; crosscut into 4 outer-border squares, 2½" x 2½"

From *each* of the 17 remaining medium or dark squares, cut:
3 border strips, 1½" x 5" (51 total)

From the cream print, cut:
4 strips, 1¾" x 23"

From the binding fabric, cut:
130" of 2"-wide bias binding

Piecing the Blocks

For each Bow Tie block, you will need the following pieces:

- **Background squares:** two matching light 2⅜" squares
- **Bow Tie squares:** two matching medium or dark 2⅜" squares
- **Snowball corners:** two matching medium or dark 1½" squares

Use a scant ¼"-wide seam allowance throughout. After sewing each seam, press the seam allowances in the direction indicated by the arrows.

1. Draw a diagonal line from corner to corner on the wrong side of the 72 medium or dark 1½" squares.

2. Lay a marked square on one corner of each light 2⅜" square, right sides together and raw edges aligned. Stitch along the drawn line and trim away the excess fabric, leaving a ¼" seam allowance.

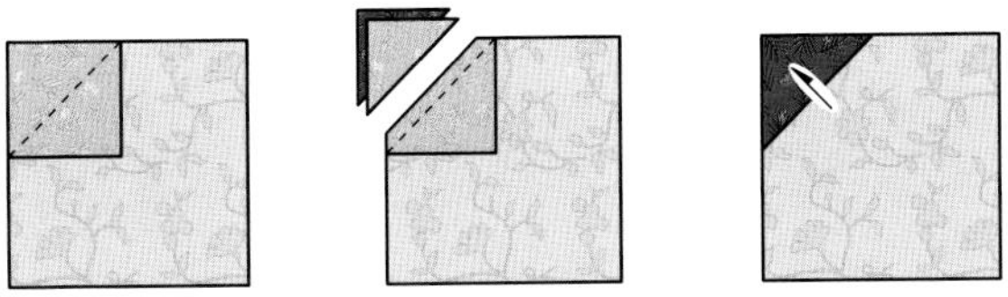

3. Lay out the pieces for each block in a four-patch arrangement. Sew the pieces together in rows, and then sew the rows together to complete a Bow Tie block. Repeat to make a total of 36 blocks measuring 4¼" square.

 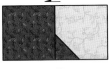
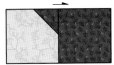

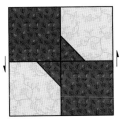

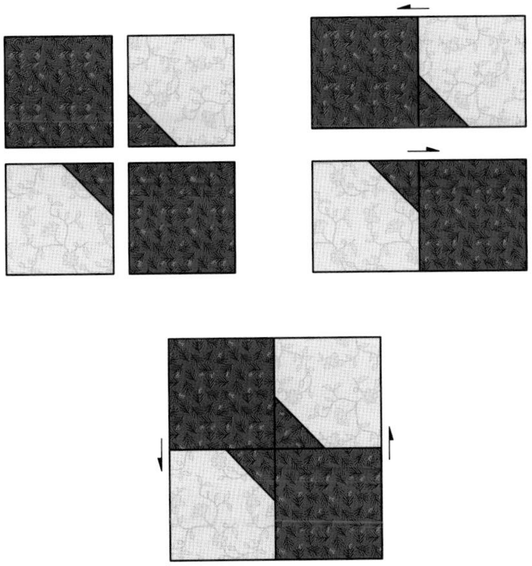

Make 36.

4. Use a seam ripper to remove two or three stitches from the seam allowance on both sides of the center seam as shown.

Remove stitching above crossed seams.

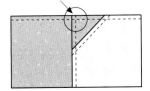

5 On the wrong side of the block, gently reposition the seam allowance to evenly distribute the fabric. Press the seam allowances in opposite directions, opening the seam allowances so that the center lies flat. When you look at the wrong side of the block, the seam allowances should be going in a counter-clockwise direction around the center.

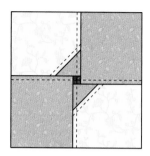

Assembling the Quilt Top

1 Lay out the blocks in six rows of six blocks each as shown in the quilt assembly diagram at right.

2 Sew the blocks together into rows, and then sew the rows together. The quilt top should measure 23" x 23".

3 Sew two of the cream 1¾"-wide strips to the sides of the quilt top and press the seam allowances toward the border.

4 Sew 1¾" squares to both ends of the two remaining cream strips and press. Sew these borders to the top and bottom of the quilt top and press the seam allowances toward the border.

5 For the outer border, select 50 of the 1½" x 5" border strips (you'll have one extra strip). Divide the strips to make two sets of 25 strips. Join the strips in one set together and press the seam allowances in one direction (or press them open). The pieced strip should measure 5" x 25½". Repeat to make a second pieced strip.

Make 2.

6 Cut each pieced strip set in half lengthwise to yield a total of four pieced border strips, each measuring 2½" x 25½".

7 Sew two pieced border strips to the sides of the quilt top, keeping the pinked edges on the outside. Press the seam allowances toward the outer border.

8 Sew 2½" outer-border squares to both ends of the two remaining outer-border strips, keeping the pinked edges on the outside, and press. Sew these borders to the top and bottom of the quilt top and press toward the outer border.

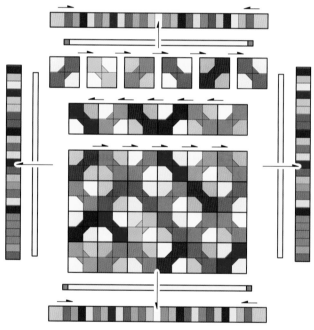

Quilt assembly

Finishing the Quilt

For help with any of the finishing steps, go to ShopMartingale.com/HowtoQuilt for free downloadable information.

1 Layer, baste, and quilt your quilt, or take it to your favorite long-arm quilter for finishing.

2 Using the 2"-wide binding strips, make and attach binding.

Hearts and Flowers

Nothing says "love" like hearts and flowers. The pieced background accentuates the appliqué perfectly, and the curved border nicely frames the project.

"Hearts and Flowers," designed and made by Jodi Crowell

FINISHED QUILT: 71" x 81½" • **FINISHED BLOCK: 10½" x 10½"**

Materials

Yardage is based on 42"-wide fabric, except where noted. If using scraps, each piece needs to measure at least 4" x 4".

324 assorted medium and/or dark 5" squares for blocks and heart, butterfly, and flower appliqués

336 assorted cream and/or beige 5" squares for blocks

½ yard of dark-green print for stem, vine, flower, and leaf appliqués

Scraps of light-green prints for flower and leaf appliqués

Scraps of assorted yellow prints for flower appliqués

¾ yard of blue fabric for bias binding

5½ yards of fabric for backing

77" x 88" piece of batting

⅜"-wide bias bar

Freezer paper

Cutting

All measurements include a ¼"-wide seam allowance. Patterns for pieces A, B, and C are on page 111.

From the assorted medium and/or dark 5" squares, cut:

126 squares, 4" x 4"

30 A pieces

26 B pieces

26 B reversed pieces

4 C pieces

From the assorted off-white and/or beige 5" squares, cut:

336 squares, 4" x 4"

From the dark-green print, cut:

235" of 1¼"-wide bias strips

From the blue fabric, cut:

375" of 2"-wide bias strips

Making the Quarter-Circle Units

Using the quarter-circle pattern on page 110, make 44 freezer-paper templates. Use the templates to prepare and cut out 44 assorted off-white or beige shapes, adding a ¼"-wide seam allowance to the curved edge only. Fold the seam allowance under and baste. Pin each quarter-circle shape to a medium or dark 4" square, aligning the straight edges. Hand stitch along the curved edge with matching thread.

Piecing the Blocks

1 Sew nine off-white and/or beige 4" squares together in rows; press. Sew the rows together as shown to make 30 Nine Patch blocks; press.

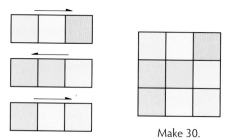

Make 30.

2 Sew three medium and/or dark 4" squares, one off-white and/or beige 4" square, two quarter-circle units, one B piece, one B reversed piece, and one A piece together in rows; press. Sew the rows together; press. Make 22 side border blocks.

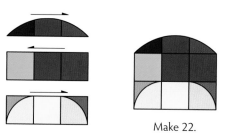

Make 22.

3 Sew four medium and/or dark 4" squares, one B piece, one B reversed piece, two A pieces, and one C piece together in rows; press. Sew the rows together; press. Make four corner blocks.

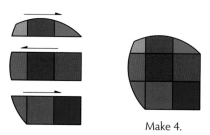

Make 4.

Adding the Appliqués

You'll be using the remaining 5" squares for the appliqués. Don't discard the scraps; they can be used for the smaller appliqué shapes.

1 Make freezer-paper appliqués for the heart, flower petal, flower center, leaf, bud center, outer bud, and butterfly using the patterns and numbers to cut on pages 110 and 111.

2 Arrange six heart shapes in the center of a Nine Patch block as shown. Stitch in place using matching thread. Make 14 blocks. (The remaining Nine Patch blocks will be used in step 1 of "Assembling the Quilt Top.")

Make 14.

Assembling the Quilt Top

1 Refer to the quilt assembly diagram below to arrange the appliquéd Nine Patch blocks, remaining Nine Patch blocks, side border blocks, and corner blocks into eight horizontal rows of seven blocks each.

2 Sew the blocks in each row together; press the seam allowances in alternate directions from row to row. Sew the rows together; press the seam allowances in one direction.

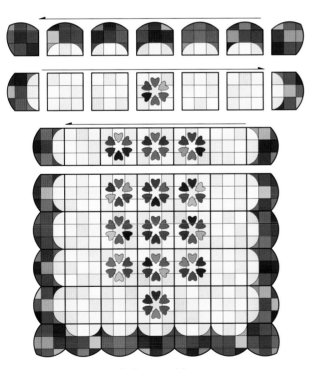

Quilt assembly

3 Referring to the quilt photo on page 107 for placement, arrange six of the heart shapes from step 1 of "Adding the Appliqués" on the left side of the quilt, centering them as shown. Stitch in place using matching thread. Repeat to stitch six heart shapes to the right side.

4 Stitch the dark-green 1¼" bias strips together to make one long strip. Fold the strip in half lengthwise, *wrong* sides together, and stitch a scant ¼" seam along the long raw edges. Insert the ⅜"-wide bias bar, centering the seam along one flat side, and press flat to make a bias tube. From the long tube, cut 16 stems, each 8" in length. For the vine, cut the remaining tube into four 26" lengths. Referring to the photo and the placement guide below, arrange the stems and vines and stitch them in place using matching thread.

Stem and vine placement guide

5 Referring to the photo for placement, arrange the appliqué shapes for the flower petals, flower centers, leaves, bud centers, outer buds, and butterfly (prepared in step 1 of "Adding the Appliqué") on the quilt top. Stitch in place using matching thread. After all the appliqué work is complete, gently press the quilt top.

Finishing the Quilt

For help with any of the finishing steps, go to ShopMartingale.com/HowtoQuilt for free downloadable information.

1 Layer, baste, and quilt your quilt, or take it to your favorite long-arm quilter for finishing.

2 Using the blue 2"-wide bias strips, make and attach binding.

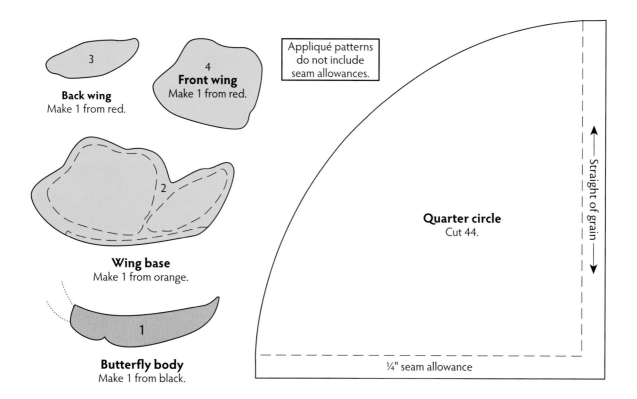

Back wing
Make 1 from red.

Front wing
Make 1 from red.

Appliqué patterns do not include seam allowances.

Wing base
Make 1 from orange.

Butterfly body
Make 1 from black.

Quarter circle
Cut 44.

Straight of grain

¼" seam allowance

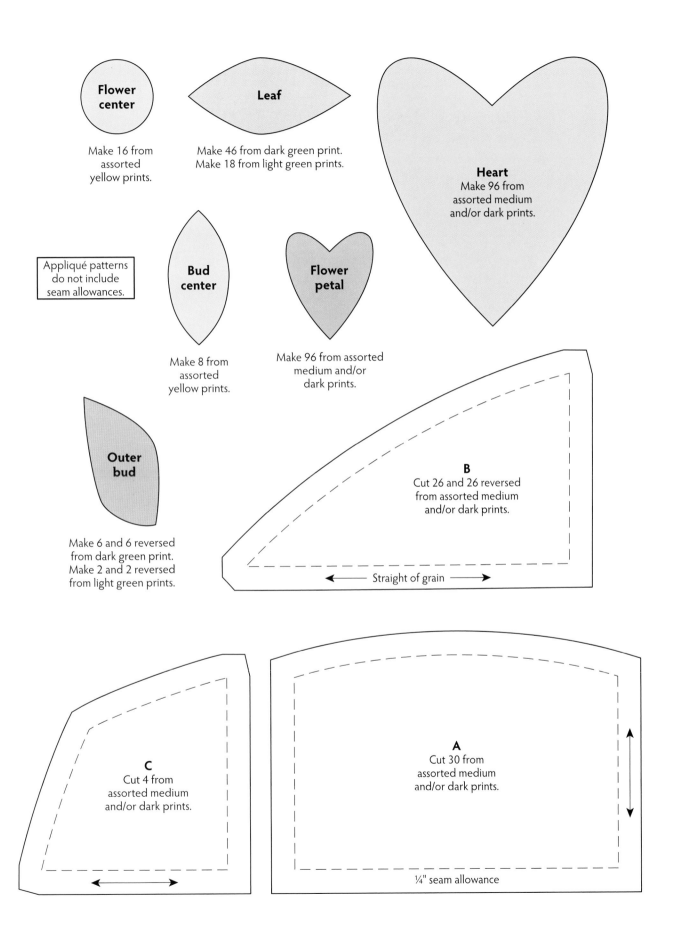

Flower center

Make 16 from assorted yellow prints.

Leaf

Make 46 from dark green print.
Make 18 from light green prints.

Heart
Make 96 from assorted medium and/or dark prints.

Appliqué patterns do not include seam allowances.

Bud center

Make 8 from assorted yellow prints.

Flower petal

Make 96 from assorted medium and/or dark prints.

Outer bud

Make 6 and 6 reversed from dark green print.
Make 2 and 2 reversed from light green prints.

B
Cut 26 and 26 reversed from assorted medium and/or dark prints.

← Straight of grain →

C
Cut 4 from assorted medium and/or dark prints.

A
Cut 30 from assorted medium and/or dark prints.

¼" seam allowance

Aunt Bea

Get the chicken frying . . . Barney's coming to dinner! This easy, nostalgic quilt is made using the popular feedsack and 1950s-style prints. One simple block is all you need to create this fun down-home quilt.

"Aunt Bea," designed and pieced by Barbara Groves and Mary Jacobson

FINISHED QUILT: 50" x 50" • FINISHED BLOCK: 8" x 8"

Materials

Yardage is based on 42"-wide fabric, except where noted.

50 coordinating 5" squares for blocks
1⅞ yards of red print for blocks and border
½ yard of plaid for binding
3¼ yards of fabric for backing
58" x 58" piece of batting
25 white buttons for embellishment
1 skein of red embroidery floss for tying buttons

Cutting

From the red print, cut:

13 strips, 2½" x 42"; crosscut into 50 rectangles,
    2½" x 8½"
5 strips, 5¼" x 42"

From the plaid, cut:

6 strips, 2¼" x 42"

Piecing the Blocks

1 Divide the 50 coordinating 5" squares into 25 pairs of contrasting colors or contrasting values (light and dark). Layer each pair of squares right sides together and, using a ¼" seam allowance, stitch along two opposite sides of the squares as shown.

2 Cut the squares in half vertically as shown and press the seam allowances open. Make a total of 50 two-patch units.

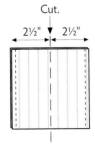  

Make 50.

3 Divide the 50 two-patch units from step 2 into 25 new combinations of contrasting pairs. With right sides together, layer the two-patch units, aligning the seams. Using a ¼" seam allowance, stitch along two opposite sides, making sure to stitch across the previous seam lines as shown.

4 Cut the units in half as shown and press the seam allowances open. Make a total of 50 Four Patch blocks.

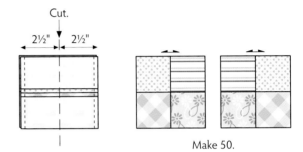

Make 50.

5 Arrange and sew two Four Patch blocks and two red print 2½" x 8½" rectangles into blocks as shown. The blocks should measure 8½" x 8½" square. Make a total of 25 blocks.

Make 25.

Assembling the Quilt Top

1 Arrange the blocks into five rows of five blocks each, alternating the orientation of the blocks as shown.

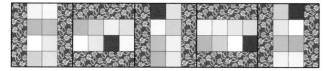

Make 3.

Make 2.

2 Sew the rows together, referring to the quilt assembly diagram below. The quilt top should measure 40½" x 40½".

3 Join the five red 5¼" x 42" border strips end to end. Measure the quilt from top to bottom through the middle to determine the length of the side borders. From the pieced strip, cut side borders to the needed length and attach them to the sides of the quilt.

4 Measure the quilt from side to side through the middle, including the side borders, to determine the length of the top and bottom borders. From the pieced strip, cut the top and bottom borders to the needed length and attach them to the top and bottom of the quilt.

Finishing the Quilt

For help with any of the finishing steps, go to ShopMartingale.com/HowtoQuilt for free downloadable information.

1 Layer, baste, and quilt your quilt, or take it to your favorite long-arm quilter for finishing.

2 Using the plaid 2¼"-wide strips, make and attach binding.

3 Decorate the quilt with your favorite buttons; tie them to the center of each block using a needle and embroidery floss.

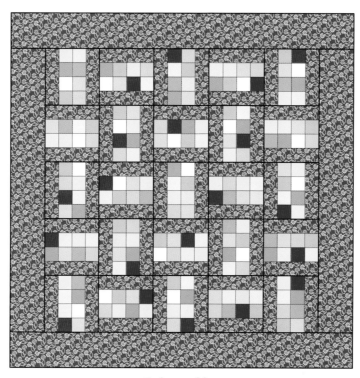

Quilt assembly

Punch Party

Arrange this lap quilt outside for a summer date on the patio. Add a glass of lemonade and a tray of freshly cut fruit—what more do you need for a perfect party?!

"Punch Party," designed and made by Lesley Chaisson

FINISHED QUILT: 62¾" x 62¾"

Materials

Yardage is based on 42"-wide fabric, except where noted.

99 assorted 5" squares*
2⅜ yards of green fabric for background
⅝ yard of peach fabric for binding
3¾ yards of fabric for backing
67" x 67" piece of batting

The instructions for this quilt use charm squares for all but the green fabric. This will result in the outer edges of the quilt being cut on the bias. If you prefer that the outer edges be on the straight grain, you will need to cut quarter-square triangles rather than half-square triangles. For this, you will need 11 squares, 7" x 7", and only 77 charm squares.

Cutting

All measurements include ¼"-wide seam allowances.

From the assorted 5" squares, cut:
99 squares in half diagonally to make 198 triangles*

From the green fabric, cut:
16 strips, 4½" x 42"; cut into:
    4 rectangles, 4½" x 24½"
    4 rectangles, 4½" x 16½"
    44 rectangles, 4½" x 8½"
    8 squares, 4½" x 4½"
2 strips, 2½" x 42"; cut into:
    2 rectangles, 2½" x 12½"
    2 rectangles, 2½" x 16½"

From the peach fabric, cut:
7 strips, 2½" x 42"

If you choose to use 11 squares, 7" x 7", cut those squares into quarters diagonally to make 44 quarter-square triangles for the side units.

Assembling the Quilt Top

1 Randomly select 154 charm triangles and sew them together in pairs to make 77 half-square-triangle units. Press and trim to 4½" x 4½".

2 Using the pieces listed as follows, sew two of every unit (except the center unit) by referring to the diagrams. Press the seam allowances in the direction indicated by the arrows.

Corner unit 1: six half-square-triangle units; 10 charm triangles; two rectangles, 4½" x 8½"; one rectangle, 4½" x 16½"; one rectangle, 4½" x 24½"

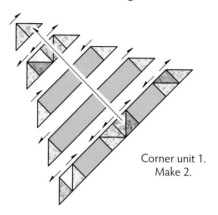

Corner unit 1.
Make 2.

Corner unit 2: two half-square-triangle units; eight charm triangles; one rectangle, 4½" x 16½"; one rectangle, 4½" x 24½"

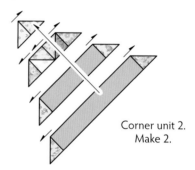

Corner unit 2.
Make 2.

Side unit 1: six half-square-triangle units; two charm triangles; one square, 4½" x 4½"; five rectangles, 4½" x 8½"

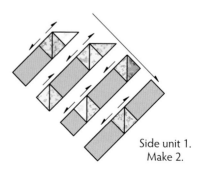

Side unit 1.
Make 2.

Rectangle unit: eight half-square-triangle units; two squares, 4½" x 4½"; five rectangles, 4½" x 8½"

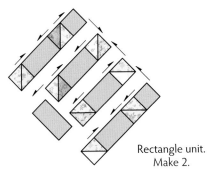

Rectangle unit.
Make 2.

Side unit 2: six half-square-triangle units; two charm triangles; one square, 4½" x 4½"; five rectangles, 4½" x 8½"

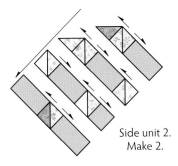

Side unit 2.
Make 2.

Square unit: six half-square-triangle units; five rectangles, 4½" x 8½"

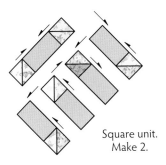

Square unit.
Make 2.

Center unit: nine half-square-triangle units; two rectangles, 2½" x 12½"; two rectangles, 2½" x 16½"

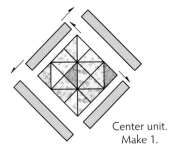

Center unit.
Make 1.

3 Follow the quilt assembly diagram below to sew the side units, square units, rectangle units, and center unit in diagonal rows. Sew the diagonal rows together. Add the corner units last. Press in the direction indicated by the arrows.

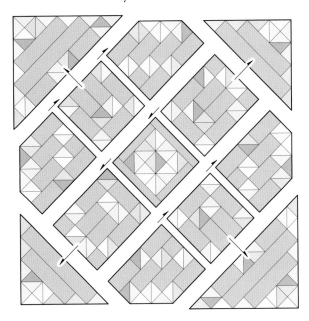

4 Trim the sides and square up the corners of the quilt, carefully handling the bias edges.

Keep the Edges in Check

Carefully stay stitch the outer edges of the quilt top to stabilize them before layering and basting. Stitch a scant ¼" from the raw edge on all sides, and the stitching will be hidden in the binding.

Finishing the Quilt

For help with any of the finishing steps, go to ShopMartingale.com/HowtoQuilt for free downloadable information.

1 Layer, baste, and quilt your quilt, or take it to your favorite long-arm quilter for finishing.

2 Using the peach 2½"-wide strips, make and attach binding.

Nash, Small

*This pint-sized version of the larger "Nash" quilt on page 12
not only calls for fewer blocks, but you also start with smaller
pieces to end up with this charming little quilt.*

"Nash, Small," designed and made by Carrie Nelson; machine quilted by Louise Haley

FINISHED QUILT: 30" x 30" • FINISHED BLOCK: 7½" x 7½"

Materials

Yardage is based on 42"-wide fabric, except where noted.

9 assorted light 5" squares for blocks

50 assorted medium or dark 5" squares for blocks and outer border

⅓ yard of light fabric for inner border

⅜ yard of fabric for binding

1⅛ yards of fabric for backing

35" x 35" piece of batting

Cutting

From *each* of the light squares, cut:

1 square, 5" x 5"; cut into quarters diagonally to yield 4 triangles (36 total)

From *each* of 26 medium or dark squares, cut:

1 border strip, 2½" x 5" (26 total)

1 strip, 2" x 5" (26 total)

From *each* of 18 medium or dark squares, cut:

1 strip, 2" x 5" (18 total)

1 strip, 2⅜" x 5"; crosscut each strip into 2 squares, 2⅜" x 2⅜" (36 total)

From *each* of 5 medium or dark squares, cut:

2 strips, 2" x 5" (10 total)

From the remaining medium or dark square, cut:

2 strips, 2" x 5"; crosscut into 4 squares, 2" x 2"

From the light fabric for inner border, cut:

4 strips, 2" x 23"

From the binding fabric, cut:

130" of 2"-wide bias binding

Piecing the Blocks

For each block, you'll need the following pieces:

- **Four-patch unit:** four different 2⅜" squares
- **Inner triangles:** four matching light quarter-square triangles
- **Outer triangles:** four different strip-pieced triangles

Use a scant ¼"-wide seam allowance throughout. After sewing each seam, press the seam allowances in the direction indicated by the arrows (or press them open).

1 Lay out four 2⅜" squares in a four-patch arrangement. Sew the squares together in pairs, and then sew the pairs together to make a four-patch unit. Make nine four-patch units, each measuring 4¼" square.

Make 9.

2 Sew matching light quarter-square triangles to the sides of the four-patch units from step 1. Make nine units and trim them to 5⅞" square, making sure to leave a ¼" seam allowance beyond the outermost points of the four-patch units.

Make 9.

3 Sew three 2" x 5" strips together along their long edges to make 18 strip-pieced squares. The strip-pieced squares should measure 5" square.

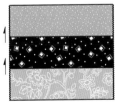

Make 18.

4 Cut each strip-pieced square in half diagonally to make two half-square triangles. Cut a total of 36 triangles, taking care to have all the squares aligned in the same direction as shown. The direction of the strips in the triangles does matter!

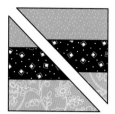

Cut 36 triangles.

5 Fold each triangle in half and finger-crease to mark the center of the long side. Stitch triangles to opposite sides of the unit from step 2, matching the center crease to the crossed seams. Sew triangles to the remaining sides of the unit to complete the block. Repeat to make a total of nine blocks.

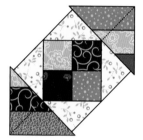 

Make 9.

6 Using a square ruler, trim each block to measure 8" square. To properly align the ruler, the 4" lines on the ruler should be aligned with the outermost points of the light triangles. Make sure that both points are lined up before trimming; that way the points will match when the blocks are sewn together. There will likely be a ⅜" seam allowance between the outer edge of the block and the outermost points of the light triangles. Carrie chose to trim less off the block to keep the strips a uniform size. You're welcome to trim a lot or a little. The most important thing is that the blocks are all trimmed to the same size and that you have at least ¼" seam allowance.

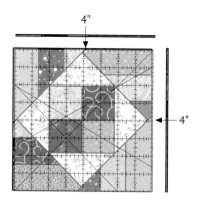

Assembling the Quilt Top

1 Lay out the blocks in three rows of three blocks each as shown in the quilt assembly diagram on page 121.

2 Sew the blocks together into rows, pressing the seam allowances in opposite directions from row to row (or press them open). Then sew the rows together and press. The quilt top should measure 23" x 23".

3 For the inner border, sew two light 23"-long strips to opposite sides of the quilt center. Join 2" squares to the ends of the two remaining light strips. Press the seam allowances toward the border strips. Sew these borders to the top and bottom of the quilt top and press the seam allowances toward the inner border.

4 For the outer border, sort the 2½" x 5" border strips into the following groups:

- **Side borders:** two groups of six strips each
- **Top and bottom borders:** two groups of seven strips each

Join each group of rectangles end to end to make four long strips. Press the seam allowances in one direction (or press them open). For the side borders, trim the two shorter strips to measure 2½" x 26". For the top and bottom borders, trim the two longer strips to measure 2½" x 30".

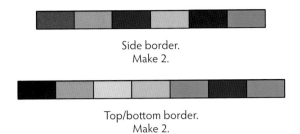

Side border.
Make 2.

Top/bottom border.
Make 2.

5 Sew the border strips to the sides and then the top and bottom of the quilt top, keeping the pinked edges on the outside. Press the seam allowances toward the outer border.

Finishing the Quilt

For help with any of the finishing steps, go to ShopMartingale.com/HowtoQuilt for free downloadable information.

1 Layer, baste, and quilt your quilt, or take it to your favorite long-arm quilter for finishing.

2 Using the 2"-wide binding strips, make and attach binding.

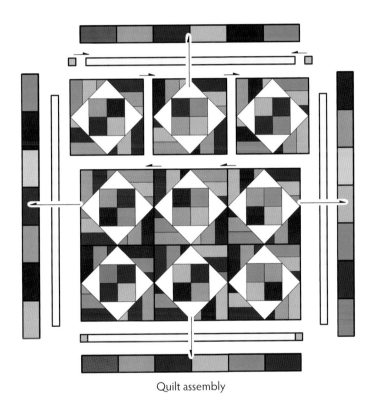

Quilt assembly

Simply Charming

Don't be shy about mixing your boldest, brightest charm squares, because anything goes in this quilt! With its decidedly scrappy appearance and prairie-point edging, it is indeed simply charming!

"Simply Charming," designed and made by Jodi Crowell

FINISHED QUILT: 78" x 78" (EXCLUDING PRAIRIE POINTS) • FINISHED BLOCK: 9" x 9"

Materials

Yardage is based on 42"-wide fabric, except where noted.

456 assorted light print 5" squares for blocks and prairie points

424 assorted medium and/or dark print 5" squares for blocks and prairie points

7½ yards of fabric for backing (3 widths pieced horizontally)

84" x 84" piece of batting

Cutting

All measurements include a ¼"-wide seam allowance.

From the assorted light 5" squares, cut:

100 squares, 3⅞" x 3⅞"; cut in half diagonally to yield 200 triangles

356 squares, 3½" x 3½"

From the assorted medium and/or dark 5" squares, cut:

100 squares, 3⅞" x 3⅞"; cut in half diagonally to yield 200 triangles

324 squares, 3½" x 3½"

Piecing the Blocks

1 Join each light triangle to a medium or dark triangle along the long edges to make 200 half-square-triangle units as shown. Press the seam allowance toward the darker triangle. Each unit should measure 3½" square.

Make 200.

2 Arrange half-square-triangle units and 3½" squares in rows as shown. Sew the squares and units into rows; press the seam allowances in alternate directions from row to row. Sew the rows

together to complete the block; press. Make the number of blocks indicated for each combination of pieces.

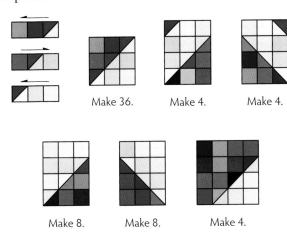

Make 36.   Make 4.   Make 4.

Make 8.   Make 8.   Make 4.

Assembling the Quilt Top

1 Refer to the quilt assembly diagram below to arrange the blocks into eight horizontal rows of eight blocks each.

2 Sew the blocks in each row together; press the seam allowances in alternate directions from row to row. Sew the rows together; press the seam allowances in one direction.

Quilt assembly

Finishing the Quilt

For help with any of the finishing steps, go to ShopMartingale.com/HowtoQuilt for free downloadable information. Layer, baste, and quilt your quilt, or take it to your favorite long-arm quilter for finishing; make sure no quilting stitches lie within ½" of the quilt edges to allow for the placement of the prairie points.

Adding the Prairie Points

1 To make prairie points, fold each remaining 3½" light square and medium and/or dark square in half horizontally, wrong sides together; press. Then fold the two ends in toward the center on the diagonal as shown; press. Make 100 light prairie points and 104 medium and/or dark prairie points.

Fold.   Fold.

2 Starting at one end of a quilt side, pin the cut edge of each medium and/or dark prairie point to the cut edge of the quilt top, aligning each prairie point with a square as shown and placing the folded side against the right side of the quilt top. Pin the backing out of the way. Sewing through the quilt top and batting only, stitch the prairie points to all four edges of the quilt, using a ¼"-wide seam allowance.

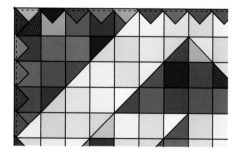

3 Center each of the light prairie points between two of the medium and/or dark prairie points as shown. Align the cut edges and pin in place. Sew the prairie points to all four edges of the quilt, using a scant ¼"-wide seam allowance.

4 Trim the batting close to the stitching. Fold the prairie points out, turning the seam allowance in toward the batting, and lightly press on the right side. Trim the backing fabric so that it extends ⅜" beyond the edge of the quilt top. Then turn the seam allowance of the backing under, covering the seam allowance and the lines of stitches. Finish the back of the quilt using a blind stitch. Add quilting stitches along the edge of the quilt if necessary.

Jamie's Quilt

This quilt features a fabulous masculine color scheme. The optical illusion adds a unique "spin" that looks difficult, but isn't. This is the perfect project for honing your skill at making half-square-triangle units.

"Jamie's Quilt," pieced by Claudia Plett; designed and machine quilted by Le Ann Weaver

FINISHED QUILT: 68½" x 82½" • FINISHED BLOCK: 12" x 12"

Materials

Yardage is based on 42"-wide fabric, except where noted. Fat quarters are 18" x 21".

130 assorted cream print 5" squares for blocks

65 assorted blue print 5" squares for blocks and sashing cornerstones

54 assorted brown print 5" squares for blocks

6 fat quarters of assorted blue prints for blocks and outer border

4 fat quarters of assorted brown prints for blocks and sashing

1⅓ yards of brown print for inner border, corner squares, and binding

5 yards of fabric for backing

73" x 87" piece of batting

Cutting

Refer to the cutting diagrams above right for cutting the brown and blue fat quarters.

From the 4 brown print fat quarters, cut a total of:

31 rectangles, 2½" x 12½"

16 squares, 5" x 5" (add to the 54 brown charm squares for blocks)

From the 6 blue print fat quarters, cut a total of:

18 rectangles, 5½" x 15½"

18 squares, 5" x 5" (add to the 65 blue charm squares for blocks)

From *each* of 50 cream print 5" squares, cut:

4 squares, 2½" x 2½" (200 total)

From *each* of 40 cream print 5" squares, cut:

2 rectangles, 2" x 3½" (80 total)

From *the remaining* 40 cream print 5" squares, cut:

2 rectangles, 2" x 5" (80 total)

From *each* of 50 brown print 5" squares, cut:

4 squares, 2½" x 2½" (200 total)

From *each* of 20 brown print 5" squares, cut:

4 squares, 2" x 2" (80 total)

From *each* of 40 blue print 5" squares, cut:

4 squares, 2½" x 2½" (160 total)

From *each* of 40 blue print 5" squares, cut:

2 rectangles, 2" x 5" (80 total)

From *each* of the 3 remaining blue print 5" squares, cut:

4 squares, 2½" x 2½" (12 total)

From the brown print yardage, cut:

7 strips, 2½" x 42"

4 squares, 5½" x 5½"

8 strips, 2¼" x 42"

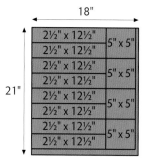
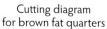

Cutting diagram
for brown fat quarters

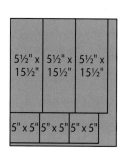

Cutting diagram
for blue fat quarters

Piecing the Blocks

1 Draw a diagonal line from corner to corner on the wrong side of each cream 2½" square and on 80 of the blue 2½" squares. Pair cream and brown, cream and blue, and blue and brown squares right sides together. Sew ¼" on both sides of the marked lines and then cut the squares apart to make half-square-triangles units as shown. Press the seam allowances toward the darker prints. Trim the units to measure 2" x 2".

Make 240.   Make 160.   Make 160.

Trim and Treat

When you have a lot of half-square-triangle units to trim, invite friends or your stitching group to get together and have a trimming tea party! Have plenty of rotary cutters and mats available—along with cookies, of course!

2 Using the brown 2" squares, cream 2" x 3½" rectangles, cream 2" x 5" rectangles, blue 2" x 5" rectangles, and the half-square-triangle units from step 1, make quarter-block units as shown. Make sure to rotate the half-square-triangle units into the correct position before sewing. Press the seam allowances as indicated. The units should measure 6½" x 6½".

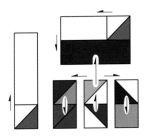 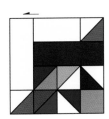

Make 80.

3 Combine four units from step 2 as shown to complete a block. Make 20 blocks. Blocks should measure 12½" x 12½".

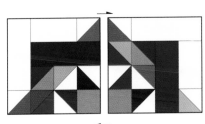

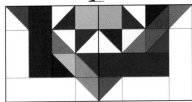

Make 20.

Assembling the Quilt Top

1 Join four blocks and three of the brown 2½" x 12½" strips into a row. Press the seam allowances toward the strips. Make five rows.

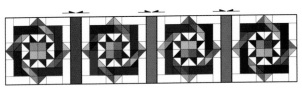

Make 5.

2 Using the remaining 16 brown 2½" x 12½" strips and the 12 blue 2½" cornerstones, make four sashing rows as shown. Press the seam allowances toward the strips.

Make 4.

3 Matching the seam intersections, sew the block rows and sashing rows together to form the quilt center, referring to the quilt assembly diagram on page 128. Press the seam allowances toward the sashing rows.

Adding the Borders

1 For the inner border, stitch the brown 2½" strips together end to end. Measure the length of the quilt top and cut two strips the length of the quilt from this long strip. Add the strips to the sides of the quilt, pressing the seam allowances toward the borders. Measure the width of the quilt and cut two strips to this length for the top and bottom of the quilt. Add the strips to the quilt and press.

2 Sew the 18 blue rectangles together end to end for the outer borders. Press the seam allowances open. Measure your quilt through the center both ways and cut two side borders and a top and a bottom border to the correct measurements.

3 Stitch the side borders to the sides of your quilt top and press the seam allowances toward the outer border.

4 Add the brown 5½" squares to the ends of the top and bottom borders. Stitch the top and bottom borders to your quilt top. Press toward the outer border.

Finishing the Quilt

For help with any of the finishing steps, go to ShopMartingale.com/HowtoQuilt for free downloadable information.

1 Layer, baste, and quilt your quilt, or take it to your favorite long-arm quilter for finishing.

2 Using the brown 2¼"-wide strips, make and attach binding.

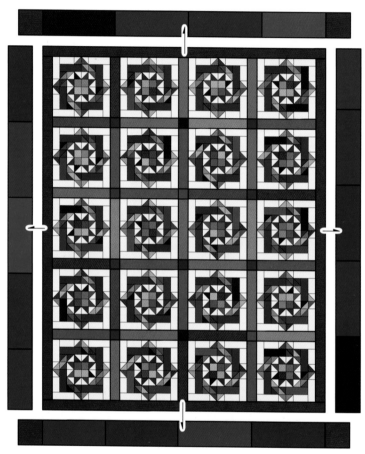

Quilt assembly

3

Fat Eighths
9" x 21" RECTANGLES

Everything's Coming Up Rainbows

Krista created the original version of this quilt as a mini wall hanging for a Flickr swap. She set rainbow colors against a light-gray background, which really made them pop. Even in this larger bed-sized quilt, this pattern is a great way to use small pieces of your favorite prints.

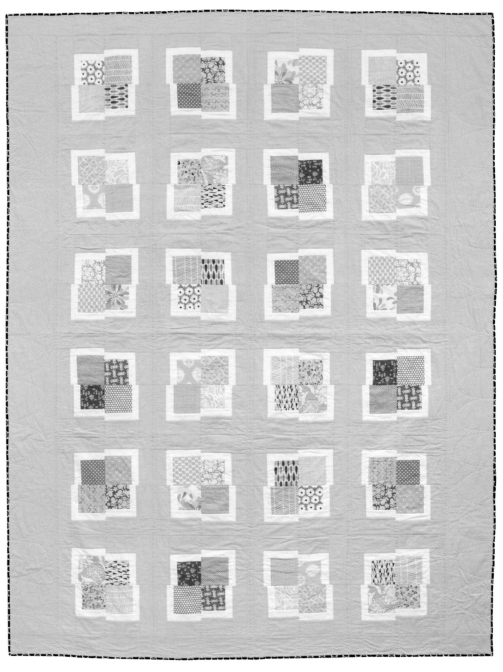

"Everything's Coming Up Rainbows," designed and made by Krista Fleckenstein

FINISHED QUILT: 70" x 90" • FINISHED BLOCK: 14" x 14"

Materials

Yardage is based on 42"-wide fabric, except where noted. Fat eighths are 9" x 21".

4⅞ yards of light-gray solid for blocks and border
1¼ yards of white solid for blocks
1 fat eighth *each* of 4 assorted red prints for blocks
1 fat eighth *each* of 4 assorted orange prints
   for blocks
1 fat eighth *each* of 4 assorted yellow prints
   for blocks
1 fat eighth *each* of 4 assorted green prints for blocks
1 fat eighth *each* of 4 assorted blue prints for blocks
1 fat eighth *each* of 4 assorted purple prints
   for blocks
¾ yard of dark print for binding
5½ yards of fabric for backing
76" x 96" piece of batting

Cutting

Divide the assorted prints into two sets; each set will have two each of the red, orange, yellow, green, blue, and purple prints. Label the sets A and B.

From *each* of the set A prints, cut:
1 square, 9" x 9" (12 total)
From *each* of the set B prints, cut:
1 square, 8" x 8" (12 total)
From the white solid, cut:
24 rectangles, 1½" x 9"
24 rectangles, 1½" x 11"
24 rectangles, 1½" x 8"
24 rectangles, 1½" x 10"
From the *lengthwise* grain of the light-gray solid, cut:
4 strips, 7½" x 42½"
From the remainder of the light-gray solid, cut:
24 rectangles, 2½" x 11"
24 rectangles, 2½" x 15"
24 rectangles, 3" x 10"
24 rectangles, 3" x 15"
4 strips, 3½" x 35½"
From the dark print, cut:
8 strips, 2½" x 42"

Piecing the Blocks

The blocks are made in two sets, A and B, using the designated group of fabrics for each set.

Set A

1 Sew white 1½" x 9" rectangles to opposite sides of an assorted 9" square. Press the seam allowances toward the rectangles.

2 Sew white 1½" x 11" rectangles to the two remaining sides of the square. Press the seam allowances toward the rectangles.

3 Sew light-gray 2½" x 11" rectangles to opposite sides of the square from step 2. Sew light-gray 2½" x 15" rectangles to the two remaining sides of the square to complete the block. Press the seam allowances toward the newly added rectangles. The

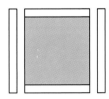

block should measure 15" x 15". Repeat the process to make 12 blocks total.

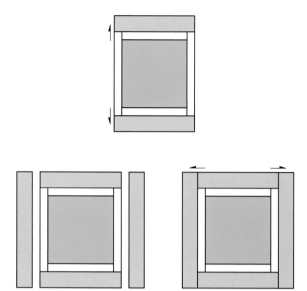

Make 12.

Set B

1 Sew white 1½" x 8" rectangles to opposite sides of an assorted 8" square. Press the seam allowances toward the rectangles.

2 Sew white 1½" x 10" rectangles to the two remaining sides of the square. Press the seam allowances toward the rectangles.

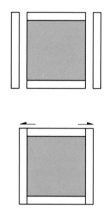

3 Sew light-gray 3" x 10" rectangles to opposite sides of the square from step 2. Sew light-gray 3" x 15" rectangles to the two remaining sides of the square to complete the block. Press the seam allowances toward the newly added rectangles. The block should measure 15" x 15". Repeat the process to make 12 blocks total.

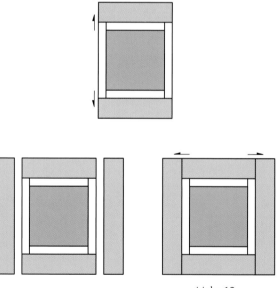

Make 12.

Final Block Assembly

1 Cut each of the set A blocks in half horizontally and vertically as shown to make four quarter blocks. The blocks should measure 7½" x 7½". Make 48 quarter blocks, keeping like fabrics together.

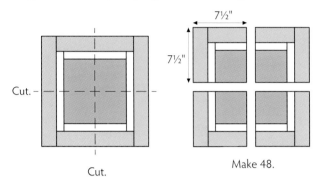

Cut.

Cut.

7½"

7½"

Make 48.

2 Repeat step 1, using the set B blocks to make 48 quarter blocks, keeping like fabrics together.

3 Lay out two different A quarter blocks and two different B quarter blocks from the same color family as shown. Sew the quarter blocks together in pairs and press the seam allowances to one side. Join the pairs; press. The block should measure 14½" x 14½".

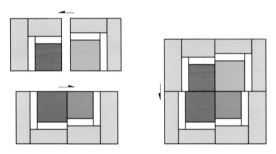

4 Repeat step 3 with the remaining quarter blocks to make 24 blocks total. You should have four blocks each from the red, orange, yellow, green, blue, and purple prints.

Assembling the Quilt Top

1 Referring to the quilt assembly diagram for color placement, arrange the blocks in six rows of four blocks each. Sew the blocks together in rows. Press the seam allowances in opposite directions from row to row.

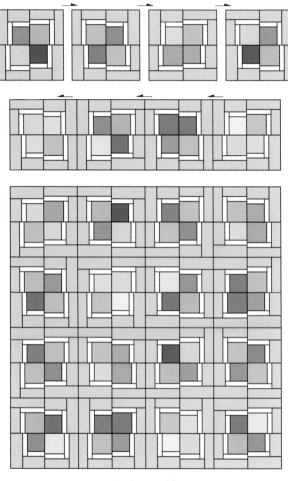

Quilt assembly

2 Join the rows. Press the seam allowances in one direction. The quilt top should measure 56½" x 84½".

3 Join the light-gray 7½" x 42½" strips in pairs to make two 84½"-long strips. Sew these strips to opposite sides of the quilt top as shown on page 134. Press the seam allowances toward the border.

4 Join the light-gray 3½" x 35½" strips in pairs to make two 70½"-long strips. Sew these strips to the top and bottom of the quilt top. Press the seam allowances toward the border.

Finishing the Quilt

For help with any of the finishing steps, go to ShopMartingale.com/HowtoQuilt for free downloadable information.

1 Layer, baste, and quilt your quilt, or take it to your favorite long-arm quilter for finishing.

2 Using the dark-print 2½"-wide strips, make and attach binding.

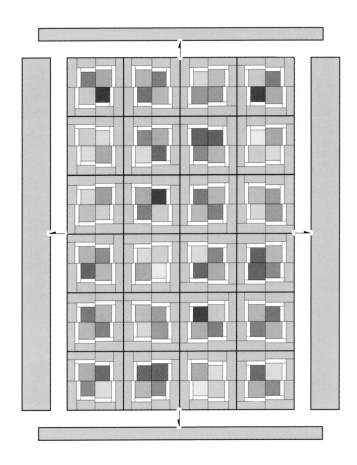

Vertigo

You'll fall head over heels for this dizzyingly bright, playful quilt. Audrie used two different values of a single color in each vertical strip, creating a mesmerizing optical effect that adds to the fun!

"Vertigo," designed and made by Audrie Bidwell

FINISHED QUILT: APPROXIMATELY 40" x 41"

Materials

Yardage is based on 42"-wide fabric, except where noted. Fat eighths are 9" x 21". This quilt is made using 5 color groups, each containing 6 different shades of a single color. It calls for fat eighths, but scraps at least 7" x 13" will also work.

1 fat eighth *each* of 6 assorted purple solids
1 fat eighth *each* of 6 assorted teal solids
1 fat eighth *each* of 6 assorted green solids
1 fat eighth *each* of 6 assorted yellow solids
1 fat eighth *each* of 6 assorted gray solids
⅜ yard of gray print for binding
2⅜ yards of fabric for backing
47" x 48" piece of batting

Cutting

All measurements include a ¼"-wide seam allowance.

From *each* of the fat eighths, cut:
1 rectangle, 7" x 13"; crosscut into 4 strips, various widths x 13" (120 total)*

From the gray print, cut:
5 strips, 2¼" x 42"

*Be sure to cut each strip a slightly different width; it's OK if the cuts are slightly skewed, but don't make them too wonky or you may encounter problems when trying to assemble the quilt top. The four strips should have a combined width of 7".

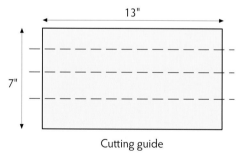

Cutting guide

Fabric Facts

Quilt fabrics used are Robert Kaufman Kona Cotton Solids (Black, Pepper, Coal, Gold, Yarrow, Curry, Corn Yellow, Canary, Maize, Teal Blue, Caribbean, Lagoon, Robin Egg, Aqua, Moss, Olive, Hibiscus, Mulberry, Magenta, Violet, Pansy, and Thistle) and Moda Bella Solids (Steel, Silver, Feather, Turquoise, Terrain Cactus, Curry, Light Lime, and Chartreuse).

Making the Strip Sets

1 Stack the strips from each of the 30 fabrics separately. Within each color group, arrange the strips from light to dark and label the stacks from A (lightest) to F (darkest).

2 Pair the strips within each color grouping as follows: A and D, B and E, C and F. Sew the strips together in pairs, randomizing the strip widths. Join matching pairs to create one strip set for each color/value pairing. Press the seam allowances to one side. Make 3 strip sets from each color group for a total of 15.

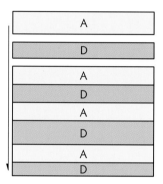

Make 3 strip sets of each color group;
15 total.

3 Square up the strip sets by trimming all edges with a rotary cutter and ruler. Cut each strip set into four sections of equal width, which can range from 2½" to 3" depending on the finished width of your strip sets. For example, if the strip set is 12" wide, cut each section 3" wide.

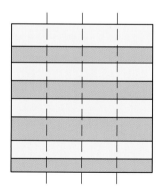

Cut 4 equal-width sections.

Assembling the Quilt Top

1 Sew four matching pieced segments end to end. Press the seam allowances in one direction. Repeat for each set of matching strips to make 15 two-color columns. Trim the columns to the same length.

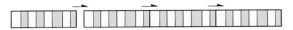

2 Arrange the strips on your design wall. In the quilt shown, Audrie arranged her strips from light to dark, working through the color sequence gray, yellow, teal, green, and purple three times. To achieve the quilt's optical effect, the tops of the columns must alternate between dark and light values. Rotate columns as necessary to achieve correct value placement.

3 Sew the columns together and press the seam allowances open to avoid bulk.

Finishing the Quilt

For help with any of the finishing steps, go to ShopMartingale.com/HowtoQuilt for free downloadable information.

1 Layer, baste, and quilt your quilt, or take it to your favorite long-arm quilter for finishing.

2 Using the gray 2¼"-wide strips, make and attach binding.

Quilt assembly

Woodland Sunset

Rebecca loves scrap quilts, but generally limited her scraps to one style of fabric per project. That was until she saw a quilt that mixed batiks and Civil War reproduction prints. It was love at first sight! With this quilt she showcases a unique blend of contemporary and traditional fabrics using a traditional block in a contemporary setting. If you're new to making scrappy quilts or hesitant, this is the perfect pattern to give scraps a try.

"Woodland Sunset," designed and made by Rebecca Silbaugh

FINISHED QUILT: 48½" x 58½" • FINISHED BLOCK: 7" x 7" • FINISHED BORDER BLOCK: 3" x 3"

Materials

Yardage is based on 42"-wide fabric, except where noted. Fat eighths are 9" x 21".

16 fat eighths of assorted dark fabrics for blocks
13 fat eighths of assorted light fabrics for blocks
¾ yard of dark print for setting triangles
½ yard of dark stripe for outer border
⅓ yard of medium-value fabric for inner border
½ yard of dark fabric for binding
3 yards of fabric for backing
54" x 64" piece of batting

Cutting

Keep the pieces separated by size as you cut them to make the blocks easier to assemble later.

From *each* of the 13 light fat eighths, cut:
1 square, 7½" x 7½"; crosscut into 5 strips,
    1½" x 7½". Crosscut each strip into:
    1 rectangle, 1½" x 4" (65 total; 1 is extra)
    1 rectangle, 1½" x 3½" (65 total; 1 is extra)
5 squares, 3" x 3" (65 total; 1 is extra)

From the remainder of the light fat eighths, cut a *total* of:
32 squares, 2½" x 2½"
36 squares, 2" x 2"
18 squares, 1½" x 1½"

From *each* of the 16 dark fat eighths, cut:
1 strip, 3" x 20"; crosscut into 4 squares, 3" x 3"
    (64 total)
2 strips, 1½" x 20"; crosscut into:
    2 rectangles, 1½" x 4½" (32 total)
    4 rectangles, 1½" x 3½" (64 total)
    4 rectangles, 1½" x 2½" (64 total)
    4 squares, 1½" x 1½" (64 total)

From the remainder of the dark fat eighths, cut a *total* of:
36 squares, 2" x 2"
18 squares, 2½" x 2½"

From the dark print yardage, cut:
4 squares, 11¼" x 11¼"; cut into quarters diagonally
    to yield 16 side setting triangles (2 are extra)
2 squares, 6" x 6"; cut in half diagonally to yield
    4 corner setting triangles

From the medium-value fabric, cut:
5 strips, 1½" x 42"
From the dark stripe, cut:
4 strips, 3½" x 42"
From the dark binding fabric, cut:
6 strips, 2¼" x 42"

Making the Center Blocks

1 Mark a diagonal line from corner to corner on the wrong side of each light 3" square. Randomly pair each marked light square right sides together with a dark 3" square. Sew ¼" from each side of the drawn line. Cut along the drawn line, and press the seam allowances toward the dark fabric. Make 128 half-square-triangle units. Square up each unit to measure 2½" x 2½".

Make 128.

2 Randomly select two dark 1½" squares and sew them together. Make 32 units. Press the seam allowances in one direction.

Make 32.

3 Randomly select dark 1½" x 2½" rectangles and sew them to the bottom of each unit from step 2 as shown. Press the seam allowances toward the rectangles. Sew the remaining dark 1½" x 2½" rectangles to the left side of each of these units. Press the seam allowances toward the newly added rectangles.

Make 32.

4 Repeat step 3 with the dark 1½" x 3½" rectangles.

Make 32.

5 Sew a dark 1½" x 4½" rectangle to the bottom of each unit from step 4 to complete the log-cabin units. Press the seam allowances toward the newly added rectangles. Make 32 units, each measuring 4½" x 4½".

Make 32.

6 Randomly select two half-square-triangle units from step 1 and sew them together as shown. Press the seam allowances in the direction indicated. Make 32 units.

Make 32.

7 Randomly select two half-square-triangle units and a light 2½" square and sew them together as shown. Press the seam allowances toward the light square. Make 32 units.

Make 32.

8 Sew the units from step 6 to the top of each log-cabin unit from step 5. Press the seam allowances toward the log-cabin units. Sew the units from step 7 to the right side of each of these units. Press the seam allowances toward the log-cabin units.

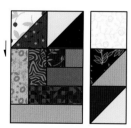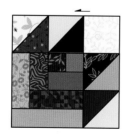

Make 32.

9 Randomly select two light 1½" x 3½" rectangles and sew them together as shown to make a pieced left-side strip. Make 32 left-side strips. In the same manner, select and sew two light 1½" x 4" rectangles together to make a pieced bottom strip. Make 32 bottom strips.

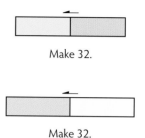

Make 32.

Make 32.

10 Sew a pieced left-side strip to the left side of each unit from step 8, positioning them so the seam allowances are pointing toward the top of the blocks. Press the seam allowances toward the pieced strips. Add a pieced bottom strip to the bottom of each of these units, positioning them so the seam allowances are pointing toward the left side of the blocks. Press the seam allowances toward the bottom strips. Make 32 blocks, each measuring 7½" x 7½".

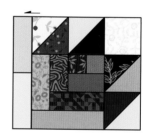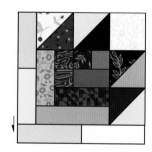

Make 32.

Making the Border Blocks

1 Mark a diagonal line from corner to corner on the wrong side of each light 2" square. Pair each marked light square right sides together with a dark 2" square. Sew ¼" from each side of the drawn line. Cut along the drawn line, and press the seam allowances toward the dark fabric. Make 72 half-square-triangle units. Square up each unit to measure 1½" x 1½".

Make 72.

2 Randomly select two half-square-triangle units from step 1 and sew them together as shown. Press the seam allowances in the direction indicated. Make 18 units.

Make 18.

3 Randomly select two half-square-triangle units and a light 1½" square and sew them together as shown. Press the seam allowances toward the light square. Make 18 units.

Make 18.

4 Sew the units from step 2 to the top of each dark 2½" square. Press the seam allowances toward the squares. Sew the units from step 3 to the right side of each of these units. Press the seam allowances toward the squares. Make 18 blocks, each measuring 3½" x 3½".

Make 18.

Choosing Border and Setting Fabrics

No matter which fabrics you use within a quilt, nothing dictates the feel of the quilt like the borders and large setting pieces. If you use 100 different fabrics within a quilt but choose a blue border, the quilt will almost always read blue as a whole.

Sometimes the best option for large pieces, if you want the quilt to still read as scrappy, is to use neutrals. However there are exceptions to every rule, so audition border fabrics to get the result you're looking for.

Assembling the Quilt Top

1 Refer to the quilt assembly diagram on page 142 to lay out the center blocks in diagonal rows as shown. Pay close attention to the orientation of the blocks. Sew the blocks in each row together. Press the seam allowances in alternating directions from row to row.

2 Onto the end of each sewn row, stitch a dark side setting triangle. Make sure you are sewing the short side of the triangle to the blocks, and that the bottom edges of the blocks and triangles are aligned. Press the seam allowances in the same direction as the others in the row.

3 Join the rows. Press the seam allowances away from the center.

4 Find and pin-mark the midpoint of each corner block's raw edge and the midpoint of each dark corner setting triangle's long edge. Matching midpoints, sew a corner setting triangle to each corner of the quilt top. Press the seam allowances toward the triangles.

5 Trim the quilt edges ¼" from the block points.

6 Sew the medium-value 1½"-wide strips end to end to make one long strip. Measure the length of the quilt top through the middle and near each edge; determine the average of these three measurements. From the pieced strip, cut two inner-border strips to the average length. Sew these strips to the sides of the quilt top, matching the ends and easing in any excess. Press the seam allowances toward the border strips.

7 Measure the width of the quilt top through the middle and near each edge; determine the average of these measurements. From the remainder of the pieced medium-value strip, cut two strips to the length of the average width. Sew these strips to the top and bottom of the quilt top. Press the seam allowances toward the border strips.

8 To make the pieced outer borders, sew four border blocks to one end of a dark striped 3½"-wide strip as shown on page 142. Make two. Press the seam allowances toward the striped strip. Measure the quilt-top length as described in step 6,

and trim each border strip to the average length, cutting the excess from the striped end of each strip.

Side border.
Make 2.

9 Sew five border blocks to one end of each of the remaining two dark striped strips as shown. Make two. Press the seam allowances toward the striped strip. Measure the width of the quilt top as described in step 7, and trim each border strip to the length of the average width, cutting the excess from the striped end of each strip.

Top/bottom border.
Make 2.

10 Referring to the quilt assembly diagram, sew the side outer-border strips to the quilt top and then attach the top and bottom outer borders. Press the seam allowances toward the inner border.

Finishing the Quilt

For help with any of the finishing steps, go to ShopMartingale.com/HowtoQuilt for free downloadable information.

1 Layer, baste, and quilt your quilt, or take it to your favorite long-arm quilter for finishing.

2 Using the dark 2¼"-wide strips, make and attach binding.

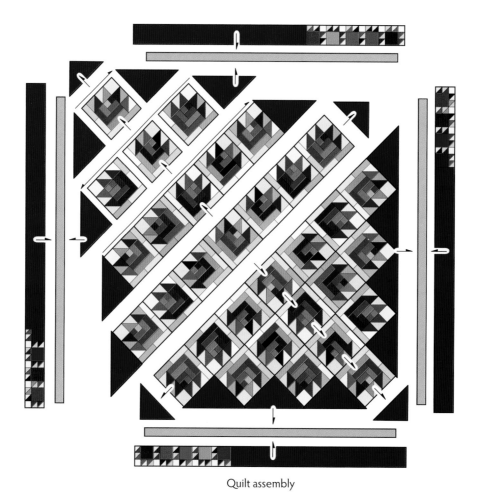

Quilt assembly

4

Fat Quarters
18" x 21" RECTANGLES

Vintage Cherries

Pull your favorite fat quarters from your stash to make this fabulous quilt. Created with the holidays in mind, it will be a winner throughout the winter season—and well beyond.

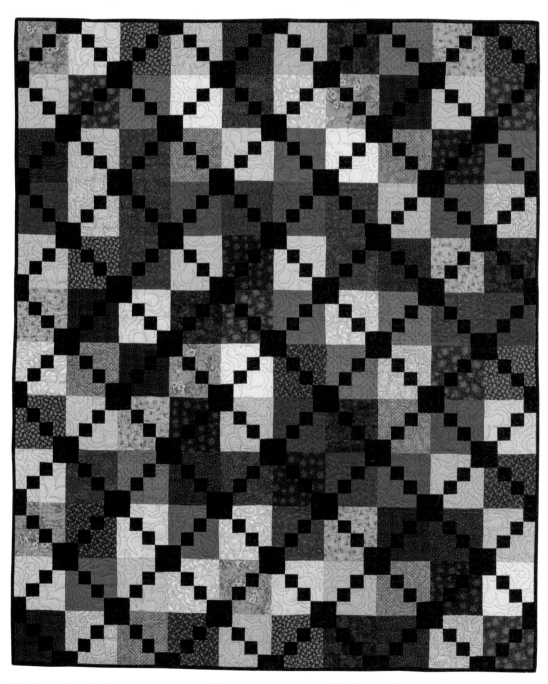

"Vintage Cherries," designed and made by Jeanne Large and Shelley Wicks; machine quilted by Laila Nelson

FINISHED QUILT: 60½" x 72½" • FINISHED BLOCK: 6" x 6"

Materials

Yardage is based on 42"-wide fabric, except where noted. Fat quarters are 18" x 21".

24 fat quarters in various prints of pink, red, burgundy, brown, and beige for blocks
1⅝ yards of black tone on tone for blocks
⅝ yard of black fabric for binding
4 yards of fabric for backing
70" x 82" piece of batting

Cutting

Cut all strips across the width of fabric.

From the black tone on tone, cut:

24 strips, 2" x 42"; crosscut each strip into 2 strips, 2" x 21" (48 total)

From *each* of the 24 fat quarters, cut:

2 strips, 2" x 21" (48 total)
2 strips, 3½" x 21" (48 total); crosscut each strip into 5 squares, 3½" x 3½" (240 total)

From the black binding fabric, cut:

7 strips, 2½" x 42"

Piecing the Blocks

1 Sew a print 2" x 21" strip to a black 2" x 21" strip to make a strip set. Press the seam allowances toward the black fabric. Make a total of 48 strip sets. Crosscut each strip set into 10 segments, 2" wide (480 total).

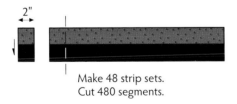

Make 48 strip sets.
Cut 480 segments.

2 Sew two matching segments together as shown to make a four-patch unit. Make 240 units.

Make 240.

3 Sew a matching 3½" square to one side of each four-patch unit. Press the seam allowances toward the 3½" square. Sew two of these sections together to make one block. Press the seam allowances to one side. Make 120 blocks.

Make 120.

Pressing Pointer

If you have a bulky corner or lots of points coming together, try pressing the seam allowances open rather than to one side. A little bit of spray starch also helps when dealing with stubborn seams.

Assembling the Quilt Top

1 Arrange the blocks into 12 rows of 10 blocks each, rotating the blocks to form the chain as shown in the quilt assembly diagram below.

2 Sew the blocks together into rows, and then sew the rows together. Press.

Finishing the Quilt

For help with any of the finishing steps, go to ShopMartingale.com/HowtoQuilt for free downloadable information.

1 Layer, baste, and quilt your quilt, or take it to your favorite long-arm quilter for finishing.

2 Using the black 2½"-wide strips, make and attach binding.

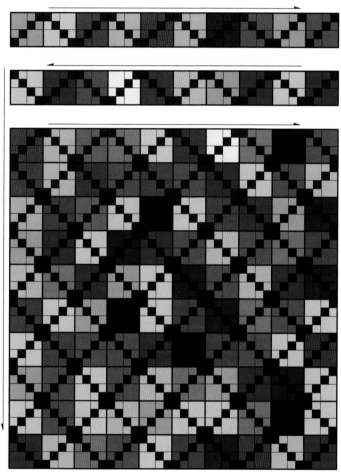

Quilt assembly

Ray of Light

The light-value batik fabrics really glow in this quilt. The juxtaposition of the lights and darks establishes the pattern and creates a sense of movement. The design may look difficult, but Sally Schneider's easy method for making shaded four-patch units speeds up the assembly process. And, you don't need to cut any triangles, which is a bonus to many quiltmakers.

"Ray of Light," designed and pieced by Regina Girard;
machine quilted by Karen Burns of Compulsive Quilting

FINISHED QUILT: 50½" x 60½" • FINISHED BLOCK: 10" x 10"

Materials

Yardage is based on 42"-wide fabric, except where noted. Fat quarters are 18" x 21".

5 dark fat quarters (1 each of blue, purple, black, red, and orange) for blocks*

5 light fat quarters (1 each of yellow, pink, light blue, light orange, and gray) for blocks*

1⅞ yards of dark batik for border and binding

3½ yards of fabric or flannel for backing

57" x 67" piece of batting

6" x 6" square of template plastic

If you don't have at least 21" of usable fabric across each fat quarter, you'll need two of each color.

Cutting

Separate your fat quarters into pairs of one light and one dark fabric and keep them together as you cut the pieces. Refer to the cutting diagram below.

From each fat quarter, cut:

1 strip, 5½" x 21"; crosscut into 3 rectangles, 5½" x 6½"

2 strips, 3" x 21"; crosscut each strip into 3 rectangles, 3" x 4" (6 total), and 3 squares, 3" x 3" (6 total)

1 strip, 5½" x 21"; crosscut into 1 rectangle, 5½" x 6½". Trim the remaining strip to 3" wide, and cut:

    2 rectangles, 3" x 4"

    2 squares, 3" x 3"

From the *lengthwise* grain of the dark batik, cut:

4 strips, 5½" x 50½"

5 strips, 2½" x 54"

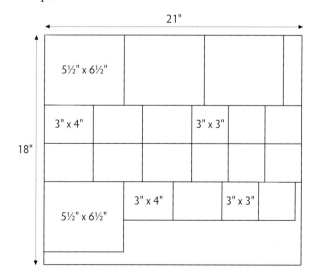

Making the Block Units

You'll make two different pieced units, A and B, with the lights and darks reversed between them.

Unit A   Unit B

Unit A

1 Working with the pieces you cut from each pair of light and dark fat quarters, gather the light 3" squares, the dark 3" x 4" rectangles, and the light 5½" x 6½" rectangles.

2 Sew a light 3" square to the end of each dark 3" x 4" rectangle. Press the seam allowances toward the rectangles.

3 Sew two matching rectangle units together as shown, carefully matching the outside edges.

4 Clip through the seam allowances in the middle of the unit. (Don't worry if you clip through the stitching; you'll cut the units diagonally through the middle in step 7.) Open the unit and press the seam allowances toward the dark rectangles, changing the pressing direction at the clip.

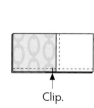 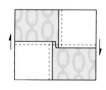

Clip.

5 Cut the template plastic into a 5½" square; cut the square in half diagonally to make a template for marking sewing lines on the units.

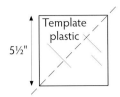

6 Align the corner and left edge of the template with the corner and left edge of the sewn rectangle as shown. Draw a diagonal line, making sure the line goes from the corner of the sewn rectangle and passes a few threads beyond the corner of the square at the block center. You may need to switch marking pencils for your light and dark fabrics. Flip the block and mark the stitching line on the opposite side as well.

7 With right sides together, pin a light 5½" x 6½" rectangle to the pieced unit. Sew on each diagonal marked line, starting on the side of the rectangle, not the point. (Your machine may eat the fabric if you start on the point.) Cut between the sewing lines with your rotary cutter to make two units.

 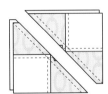

8 Open the units and press the seam allowances toward the pieced triangles. Repeat to make a total of eight A units from each fabric pair. Make a total of 40 A units.

Unit A.
Make 40.

Unit B

1 Working with the same color combination as your first group of A units, gather the dark 3" squares, the light 3" x 4" rectangles, and the dark 5½" x 6½" rectangles.

2 Sew a dark 3" square to the end of each light 3" x 4" rectangle. Press the seam allowances toward the squares.

3 Sew the rectangle units together as shown, carefully matching the outside edges.

4 Clip through the seam allowances in the middle of the unit. Open the unit and press the seam allowances toward the dark squares, changing the pressing direction at the clip.

 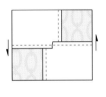

Clip.

5 Repeat the marking, sewing, and cutting process as for the A units, combining the pieced unit with a dark 5½" x 6½" rectangle. Make eight B units from each fabric pair, for a total of 40 B units.

Unit B.
Make 40.

Assembling the Blocks

Arrange the A and B units on your design wall as shown, distributing the color and pattern evenly before sewing the units into blocks. (If you prefer a more random color placement, sew the units into blocks first, and then arrange the blocks.) To make each block, sew the top A and B units together. Press the seam allowances toward the B unit. Repeat with the bottom units. Join the rows. Press the seam allowances up or down, alternating the direction from block to block. Repeat to make 20 blocks.

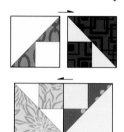 

Assembling the Quilt Top

1 Sew the blocks together into rows. Press the seam allowances in opposite directions from row to row. Join the rows. Press the seam allowances in the same direction. The quilt top should measure 40½" x 50½".

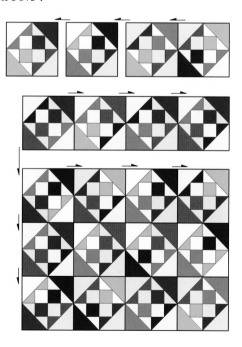

2 Sew the 5½" x 50½" border strips to the sides of the quilt top. Press the seam allowances toward the border strips.

3 Repeat with the remaining border strips at the top and bottom of the quilt top.

Finishing the Quilt

For help with any of the finishing steps, go to ShopMartingale.com/HowtoQuilt for free downloadable information.

1 Layer, baste, and quilt your quilt, or take it to your favorite long-arm quilter for finishing.

2 Using the dark-batik 2½"-wide strips, make and attach binding.

Three Steps Forward

Whether you're building your quilting skills or you're a seasoned quilter, you'll find "Three Steps Forward" an uplifting pattern. The easy-to-make Jacob's Ladder block, constructed with squares and half-square-triangle units, will elevate your confidence in no time.

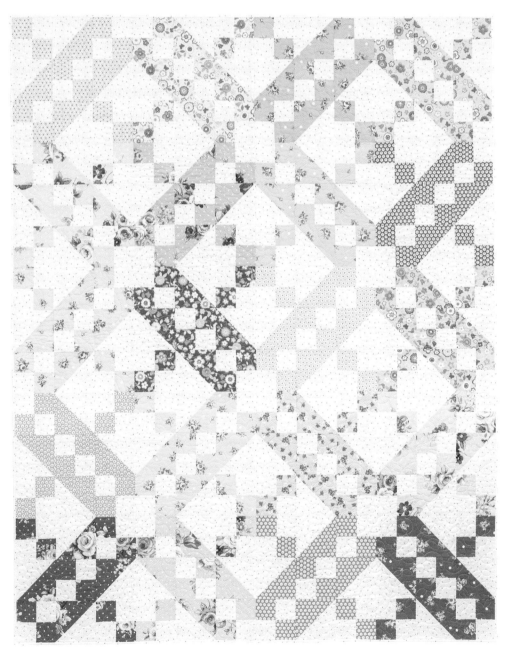

"Three Steps Forward," designed and pieced by Victoria L. Eapen; machine quilted by Al Kuthe

FINISHED QUILT: 72½" x 90½" • **FINISHED BLOCK:** 18" x 18"

Materials

Yardage is based on 42"-wide fabric, except where noted. Fat quarters are 18" x 21".

1 fat quarter *each* of 20 assorted florals for blocks
4⅜ yards of white print for blocks and binding
6 yards of fabric for backing
78" x 96" piece of batting

Cutting

From *each* of the 20 assorted florals, cut:

2 strips, 3½" x 21"; crosscut into 10 squares,
   3½" x 3½" (200 total)
1 strip, 7" x 21"; crosscut into 2 squares, 7" x 7"
   (40 total)

From the white print, cut:

19 strips, 3½" x 42"; crosscut into 200 squares,
   3½" x 3½"
8 strips, 7" x 42"; crosscut into 40 squares, 7" x 7"
9 strips, 2¼" x 42"

Piecing the Blocks

1 Sew each floral 3½" square to a white-print
3½" square to make a two-patch unit. Press the
seam allowances toward the floral squares. Sew two
matching two-patch units together as shown to
make a four-patch unit. The unit should measure
6½" x 6½". Repeat to make 20 sets of five matching
units (100 total).

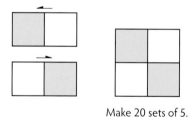

Make 20 sets of 5.

2 Draw a diagonal line from corner to corner on
the wrong side of each white-print 7" square.
Layer each white square with a floral 7" square, right
sides together. Sew ¼" from each side of the marked
lines to make two half-square-triangle units from

each pair (20 sets of four matching units). Press the
seam allowances toward the floral triangles. Trim
each unit to 6½" x 6½".

Make 20 sets of 4.

3 Using pieces from the same floral fabric, arrange
five four-patch units and four half-square-
triangle units into three horizontal rows as shown.
Sew the units in each row together. Press the seam
allowances in alternating directions from row to row.
Sew the rows together. Press the seam allowances in
one direction. Repeat to make a total of 20 blocks.

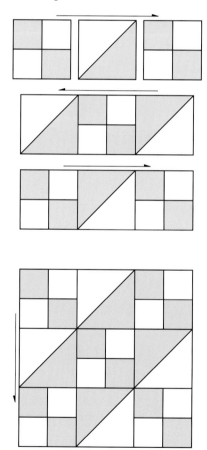

Make 20.

Assembling the Quilt Top

Arrange the blocks into five horizontal rows of four blocks each. Rotate every other block 90° so that the four-patch units form a diagonal line across the quilt as shown. Sew the blocks in each row together. Press the seam allowances in alternating directions from row to row. Sew the rows together. Press the seam allowances in one direction.

Finishing the Quilt

For help with any of the finishing steps, go to ShopMartingale.com/HowtoQuilt for free downloadable information.

1 Layer, baste, and quilt your quilt, or take it to your favorite long-arm quilter for finishing.

2 Using the white-print 2¼"-wide strips, make and attach binding.

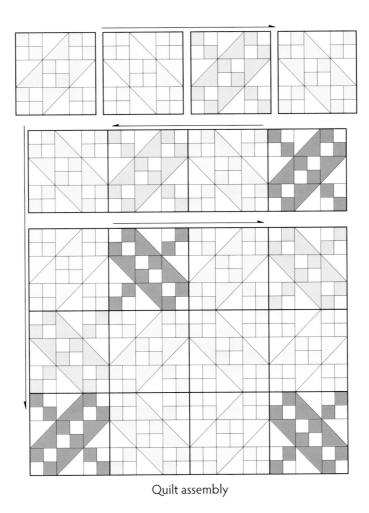

Quilt assembly

Blue Skies Ahead

Guarantee blue patchwork skies year-round with a simple but sweet quilt featuring dreamy clouds and happy birds. Fusible fleece, adhered to the wrong side of the cloud fabric, keeps the blue background fabrics from showing through the white clouds. The fusible fleece also gives the appliqués structure so the clouds hold up to the machine quilting, and avoids the stiffness that fusible web can create. The appliqués are machine stitched, making the blocks quick and easy to put together.

"Blue Skies Ahead," designed, pieced, and appliquéd by Adrienne Smitke; machine quilted by Dawna Callahan

FINISHED QUILT: 60½" x 68½" • FINISHED BLOCK: 8" x 8"

Materials

Yardage is based on 42"-wide fabric, except where noted. Fat quarters are 18" x 21".

14 fat quarters of assorted blue prints for blocks
7 fat quarters of assorted white-on-white fabrics
    for clouds
1 fat quarter of red fabric for birds
1⅛ yards of blue fabric for border and binding
4⅛ yards of fabric for backing*
1½ yards of 45"-wide fusible fleece for clouds
66" x 74" piece of batting
¼ yard of 20"-wide fusible web for birds
Felt-tipped erasable fabric pen
8½" x 11" piece of clear template plastic
Curved quilter's safety pins (optional)

Consider a soft flannel for the backing to make this quilt extra cozy.

Cutting

From *each* of the blue fat quarters, cut:
4 squares, 8½" x 8½" (56 total)
From the blue fabric for border and binding, cut:
7 strips, 2½" x 42"
7 strips, 2¼" x 42"

Appliquéing the Blocks

1 Using the appliqué patterns on page 157, trace and cut out one cloud and one bird from the template plastic. The cloud pattern has already been reversed for fusible appliqué.

2 On the fleece side of your fusible fleece, use the cloud template and a felt-tipped erasable fabric pen to trace 39 clouds. Cut out the clouds, leaving at least ½" beyond the drawn lines. Following the manufacturer's instructions, fuse six clouds each to the wrong side of six white-on-white fat quarters and three clouds to the wrong side of the seventh fat quarter. Cut out the clouds on the lines.

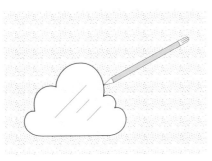

3 Use a curved quilter's safety pin to secure a cloud to the center of a blue square, positioning the cloud as shown. Using straight pins, pin the edges generously to secure. Machine appliqué the cloud to the block using a blanket stitch or zigzag stitch. Repeat with the remaining white clouds for a total of 39 cloud blocks.

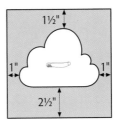 

Make 39.

4 Use the bird template to trace one regular and one reversed bird onto the paper side of the fusible web. Cut out the birds, leaving at least ½" beyond the drawn lines. To keep the shapes supple, cut out the center of the birds, leaving a ¼" margin all the way around.

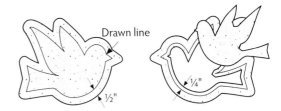

5 Following the manufacturer's instructions, fuse the birds to the wrong side of the red fat quarter. Cut out the shapes on the drawn lines and fuse each bird to a blue square. Machine stitch around each bird to secure.

Make 1 and 1 reversed.

Assembling the Quilt Top

1 Lay out the blocks as shown below or arrange them in any order you like. This is a great opportunity to personalize your quilt and make it your own!

2 Sew the blocks into horizontal rows. Press the seam allowances in opposite directions from row to row. Join the rows. Press the seam allowances in one direction.

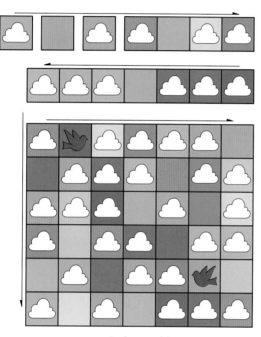

Quilt assembly

3 Sew the seven blue 2½" x 42" strips end to end to make one long strip. Press the seam allowances open. Cut two strips, 64½" long, and sew to the sides of the quilt top. Press the seam allowances toward the borders.

4 Cut two strips, 60½" long, and sew to the top and bottom of the quilt top. Press the seam allowances toward the borders.

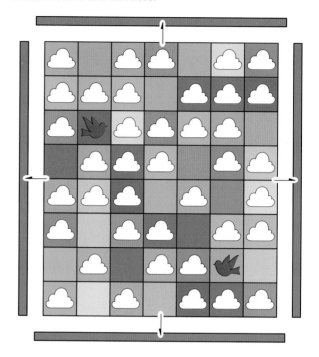

Finishing the Quilt

For help with any of the finishing steps, go to ShopMartingale.com/HowtoQuilt for free downloadable information.

1 Layer, baste, and quilt your quilt, or take it to your favorite long-arm quilter for finishing.

2 Using the blue 2¼"-wide strips, make and attach binding.

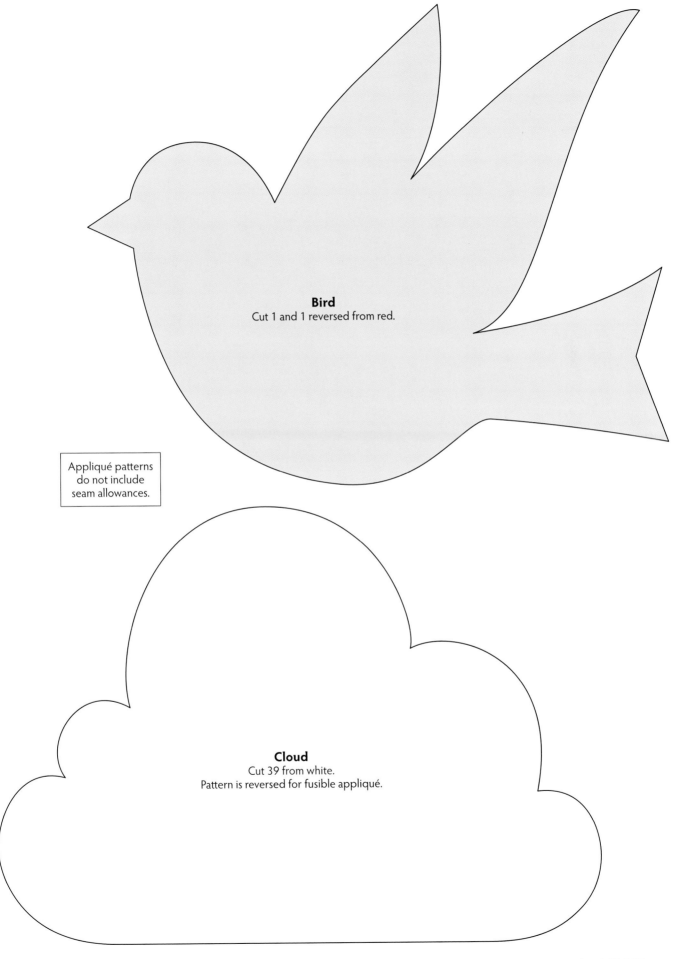

Bird
Cut 1 and 1 reversed from red.

Appliqué patterns
do not include
seam allowances.

Cloud
Cut 39 from white.
Pattern is reversed for fusible appliqué.

Retrolicious!

Black and white pathways run through this quilt, making the happy colors pop. The cutting and piecing are super easy; it's the color placement that's a bit tricky. Since each of the alternate blocks is different, instructions are given row by row, building the inner border in right along with the piecing.

"Retrolicious!," designed and pieced by Cornelia Gauger;
machine quilted by Cindy Glancy of Dancing Thread Long-Arm Quilting

FINISHED QUILT: 60½" x 80½" • FINISHED BLOCK: 10" x 10"

Materials

Yardage is based on 42"-wide fabric, except where noted. Fat quarters are 18" x 21".

2 fat quarters *each* of the following colors* (12 total): green, orange, red, blue, yellow, and pink for blocks

2 fat quarters of different black prints for blocks

2 fat quarters of different white prints for blocks

1⅛ yards of black-and-white print for blocks and borders

⅝ yard of black solid for binding

4⅞ yards of fabric for backing

67" x 87" piece of batting

For each color, choose fat quarters that contrast in value—a light red and a medium red, for example.

Cutting

From *each* of the 12 colored fat quarters, cut:

2 strips, 5½" x 18"; crosscut each strip into 3 squares, 5½" x 5½" (72 total)

2 strips, 3" x 18"; crosscut each strip into 6 squares, 3" x 3" (144 total)

2 strips, 1" x 12½" (24 total). From *2* of the fat quarters, cut 1 additional strip to make 26 total strips.

From *each* of the black and the white fat quarters, cut:

7 strips, 3" x 18"; crosscut into 42 squares, 3" x 3" (168 total; 1 square from each fat quarter will be left over)

From the black-and-white print, cut:

12 strips, 3" x 42"; cut *5* of the strips into:
   10 rectangles, 3" x 10½"
   10 rectangles, 3" x 5½"
   4 squares, 3" x 3"

From the black solid, cut:

8 strips, 2½" x 42"

Piecing the Large Four Patch Blocks

Pair contrasting 5½" squares of each color—light green and medium green, for example—and sew together. Make two. Press the seam allowances toward the darker fabric. Join the units to make one large four-patch unit. Repeat to make three four-patch units in each color for a total of 18.

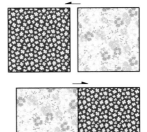 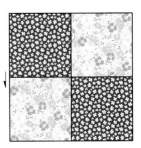

Make 3 in each color.

Assembling the Alternate Blocks

It's easier to place the colors correctly if you assemble the alternate blocks row by row. You may also find it easier to join each row to the previous one as you go so that they don't get out of sequence.

1 Pair 3" squares of each color and sew together. Make 12 in each color for a total of 72 units.

Make 12 in each color.

2 Sew white and black 3" squares together as shown. Repeat to make a total of 17 units in those fabrics. Repeat with the remaining black and white squares for another 17 units. Sew two different units together to make 17 small four-patch units.

Make 17 of each.

Four-patch unit. Make 17.

Assembling the Quilt Top

1 For row 1 (also the top inner border), join a black-and-white square, a black square, a green pair, a white square, a black-and-white 10½" rectangle, a black square, a yellow pair, a white square, a black-and-white 10½" rectangle, a black square, a red pair, a white square, and a black-and-white square.

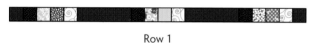

Row 1

2 For row 2, make two inner-border units as follows: For the left inner border, sew a black square and a white square to opposite ends of a green pair. For the right inner border, sew a white square and a black square to opposite ends of a red pair.

Make 1.   Make 1.

3 Make an alternate block for row 2, using two white squares, two black squares, a green pair, a pink pair, a yellow pair, a black-and-white four-patch unit, and a 5½" black-and-white rectangle.

Repeat, using one yellow pair, one green pair, and one red pair.

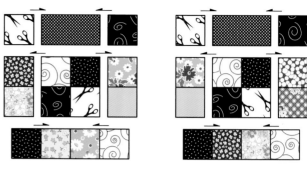

Make 1.   Make 1.

4 Assemble row 2 using the units made in steps 2 and 3, a large green four-patch unit, a large yellow four-patch unit, and a large red four-patch unit. Sew row 2 to row 1. Press the seam allowances toward row 1.

Row 1

Row 2

5 For row 3, make three alternate blocks as shown, paying careful attention to the placement of the pieces in each block.

Make 1.   Make 1.

Make 1.

6 Assemble row 3 using a black-and-white 10½"
rectangle at both ends, the alternate blocks from
step 5, a large pink four-patch unit, and a large green
four-patch unit. Sew this row to the first two rows.
Press the seam allowances (and all subsequent horizontal seam allowances) toward the previous row.

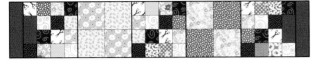

Row 3

7 Assemble and attach rows 4–8 in the same manner, making the alternate blocks as you go.

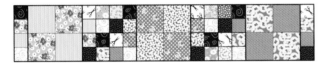

Row 4

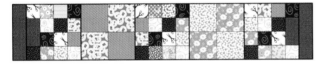

Row 5

Row 6

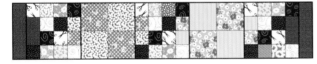

Row 7

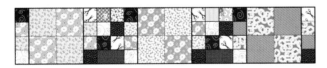

Row 8

8 For row 9 (the bottom inner border), assemble
the pieces as shown and sew to row 8.

Row 9

Adding the Outer Border

1 Sew three black-and-white 3" x 42" strips
together and press the seam allowances open. Cut
two strips, 55½" long, and sew to the top and bottom
of the quilt top. Press the seam allowances toward
the outer border.

2 Sew the remaining four black-and-white 3" x 42"
strips together and press the seam allowances
open. Cut two strips, 80½" long, and sew to the sides
of the quilt top. Press the seam allowances toward
the outer border.

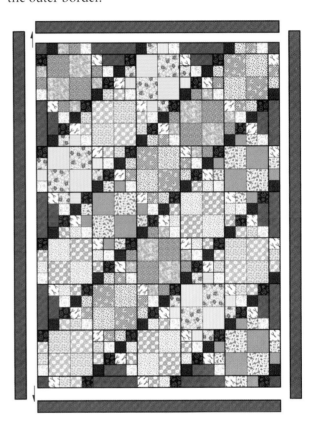

3 To create the faux piping just inside the binding, sew seven colored 1" x 12½" strips together,
end to end. Press the seams allowances open, and
then press the strip in half lengthwise, wrong sides
together. Make two strips.

Make 2.

4 Using washable fabric glue or a long stitch, baste a piping strip to each side of the quilt top, aligning the raw edges of the piping with the edges of the quilt top. Trim the piping strips even with the quilt top at both ends.

5 Repeat at the top and bottom of the quilt, using six 1" x 12½" strips for each.

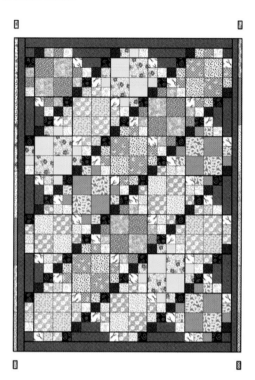

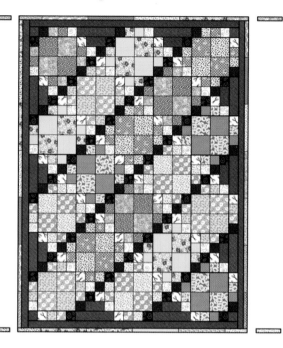

Finishing the Quilt

For help with any of the finishing steps, go to ShopMartingale.com/HowtoQuilt for free downloadable information.

1 Layer, baste, and quilt your quilt, or take it to your favorite long-arm quilter for finishing.

2 Using the black 2½"-wide strips, make and attach binding.

Jigsaw

This project makes great use of fat quarters or scraps. And it's one puzzle that is easy to solve! Simply cut your pieces and assemble the columns for a quick quilt, one that's sure to be loved.

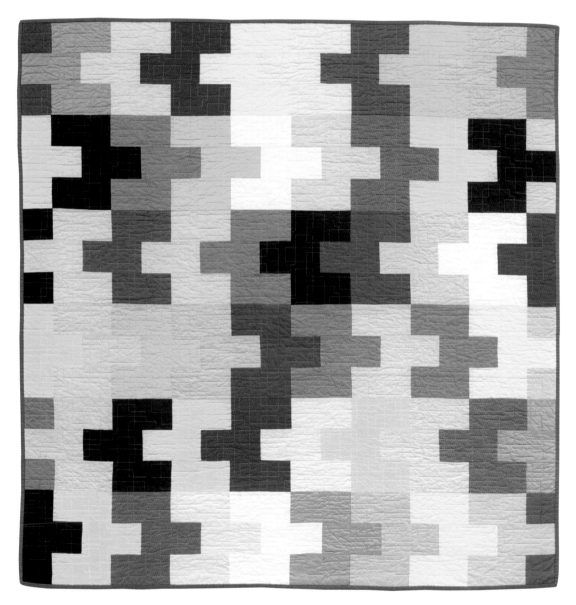

"Jigsaw," designed and pieced by Amy Ellis; quilted by Natalia Bonner

FINISHED QUILT: 54½" x 54½"

Materials

Yardage is based on 42"-wide fabric, except where noted. Fat quarters are 18" x 21".

¼ yard or 1 fat quarter *each* of 20 assorted solids*
½ yard of blue solid for binding
3½ yards of fabric for backing
60" x 60" piece of batting

Amy used Robert Kaufman Kona Cotton in the following colors: Snow, Bubble Gum, Midnight, Ruby, Cheddar, Amber, Lemon, Corn Yellow, Green Tea, Grass Green, Ice Frappe, Lagoon, Bluebell, Regatta, Lilac, Bright Peri, Ash, Tan, Earth, and Espresso.

Cutting

From *each of 12* solids, cut:
2 strips, 3½" x 42" (or 4 strips, 3½" x 21");
   crosscut into:
   7 rectangles, 3½" x 6½" (84 total)
   2 squares, 3½" x 3½" (24 total)
From *each* of the remaining 8 solids, cut:
2 strips, 3½" x 42"; crosscut into 9 rectangles,
   3½" x 6½" (72 total)
From the blue solid, cut:
6 strips, 2½" x 42"

Don't Be Mixed Up!

When cutting solids, Amy likes to open strips before crosscutting the squares and rectangles. This way she always know which side is up. To lay out this quilt, group like-colored pieces in threes and pin them together as a unit. The squares will pair with one rectangle. This will help you decide on color placement and assemble the quilt efficiently.

Assembling the Quilt Top

This quilt is assembled in rows, and there are no blocks to piece.

1 To find a pleasing arrangement of color, lay out the solid rectangles and squares in six rows on a design wall. Each row will have three strips and consist of 10 colors, with a square/rectangle group at both ends of each row. Once you have found a nice arrangement, stack the rows and move to the sewing machine.

2 To keep your colors in order and avoid confusion, chain piece across each strip. Press the seam allowances as shown. You will have six rectangles left over.

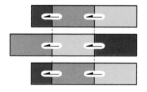 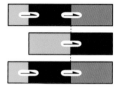

Rows 1, 3, and 5   Rows 2, 4, and 6

3 After pressing, clip the threads between two chain-pieced strips in a row, then line up the top and bottom edges to stagger the pieces. Use a few pins to ensure even distribution, and sew the two strips together. In the same way, sew the strip to the other side of the row and press the seam allowances to one side. Repeat to make six rows total.

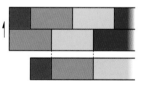

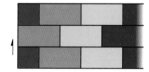

Make 6 rows.

4 Nesting the seams, join the rows to complete the quilt top. Press seam allowances in one direction.

Quilt assembly

Finishing the Quilt

For help with any of the finishing steps, go to ShopMartingale.com/HowtoQuilt for free down-loadable information.

1 Layer, baste, and quilt your quilt, or take it to your favorite long-arm quilter for finishing.

2 Using the blue 2½"-wide strips, make and attach binding.

Make It a Twin

To make a twin-size quilt measuring 72" x 96", use the following materials and cutting information.

MATERIALS

½ yard *each* of 20 assorted solids

¾ yard of blue solid for binding

6½ yards of fabric for backing

78" x 102" piece of batting

CUTTING

Refer to "Don't Be Mixed Up!" on page 164.

From *each of 16* fabrics, cut:

4 strips, 3½" x 42"; cut into:

    19 rectangles, 3½" x 6½" (304 total; 8 are extra)

    2 squares, 3½" x 3½" (36 total)

From *each of 4* fabrics, cut:

3 strips, 3½" x 42"; cut into 18 rectangles, 3½" x 6½" (72 total)

From the blue solid, cut:

9 strips, 2½" x 42"

ASSEMBLING THE QUILT TOP

On a design wall or other flat surface, lay out the solid rectangles and squares in eight rows as shown in the assembly diagram below. Each row will have three strips and consist of 17 colors, with a square/rectangle group at both ends of each row. Once you have a pleasing arrangement, assemble the quilt as described on page 164.

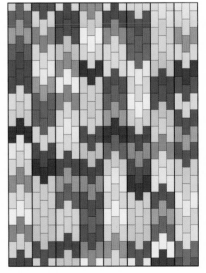

Quilt assembly

Lost and Found

The simple Carrie Nation block sparkles in this super-quick quilt. Thanks to the values reversing in alternate blocks, the diagonal chain seems to appear and disappear—to be lost and found. The blocks are made in pairs, and each fat quarter makes two blocks. For a less-scrappy look, purchase multiples of your favorite fat quarters. Mary used two of the green fabrics twice.

"Lost and Found," designed and pieced by Mary Green; machine quilted by Krista Moser
FINISHED QUILT: 48½" x 72½" • FINISHED BLOCK: 12" x 12"

Materials

Yardage is based on 42"-wide fabric, except where noted. Fat quarters are 18" x 21".

12 fat quarters of coordinating light and medium prints for blocks
2⅝ yards of dark-purple print for blocks
⅝ yard of pink print for binding
3 yards of fabric for backing (crosswise seam)
54" x 78" piece of batting

Cutting

From the dark-purple print, cut:

17 strips, 3½" x 42"; from 5 of the strips, cut a total of 48 squares, 3½" x 3½"
12 strips, 2" x 42"

From *each* fat quarter, cut:

3 strips, 3½" x 21"; from 1 of the strips, cut 4 squares, 3½" x 3½" (48 total)
2 strips, 2" x 21" (24 total)

From the pink print, cut:

7 strips, 2½" x 42"

Piecing the Blocks

Make one pair of blocks (A and B) at a time using the dark-purple fabric and one of the fat-quarter fabrics.

1 Cut a dark-purple 3½" x 42" strip in half and sew the halves to 3½" strips of fat-quarter fabric. Press the seam allowances on one strip set toward the dark-purple fabric and the seam allowances on the other set toward the fat-quarter fabric.

2 Cut four 3½" units from each strip set for a total of eight units. Keep the units separated into two piles based on the direction of the seam allowances.

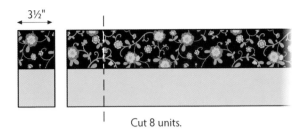

Cut 8 units.

3 Cut a dark-purple 2" x 42" strip in half and sew the halves to 2" strips of fat-quarter fabric. Press the seam allowances on both strip sets toward the dark purple. Cut eight 2" units from each strip set for a total of 16 units.

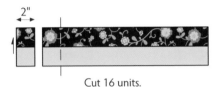

Cut 16 units.

4 Sew the 2" units together in pairs to make four-patch units. Make eight four-patch units.

Make 8.

5 To make block A, sew four dark-purple 3½" squares, the step 2 units with the seams pressed toward the dark-purple fabric, and four of the four-patch units together in rows as shown, making sure to orient the four-patch units correctly. Press the seam allowances toward the dark-purple fabric. Join the rows. Press the seam allowances in one direction.

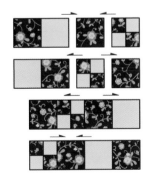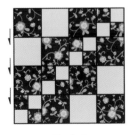

Block A

6 To make block B, sew four fat-quarter 3½" squares, the step 2 units with the seams pressed toward the fat-quarter fabric, and four of the four-patch units together in rows as shown. Again, make sure the four-patch units are oriented correctly. Press the seam allowances toward the fat-quarter fabric. Join the rows. Press the seam allowances in one direction.

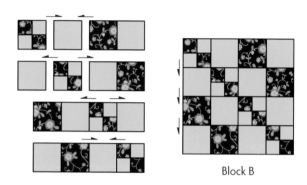

Block B

7 Repeat steps 1–6 to make a total of 24 blocks—one A and one B from each fat quarter.

Assembling the Quilt Top

Arrange the blocks in six horizontal rows of four blocks each. Sew the blocks together in rows. Press the seam allowances in opposite directions from row to row. You may need to re-press some of the block

seams to get them to nest nicely. Join the rows. Press the seam allowances in one direction.

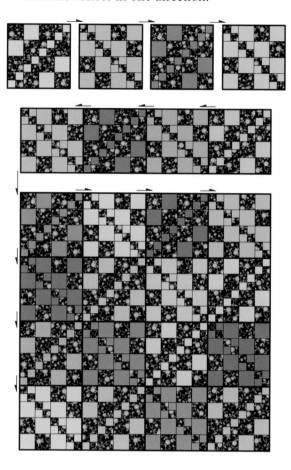

Finishing the Quilt

For help with any of the finishing steps, go to ShopMartingale.com/HowtoQuilt for free downloadable information.

1 Layer, baste, and quilt your quilt, or take it to your favorite long-arm quilter for finishing.

2 Using the pink 2½"-wide strips, make and attach binding.

Grandmother's Thimble

Regina's inspiration for this quilt came from the antique thimbles that her grandmother used when stitching or darning. The quilt combines two all-time favorite quilt blocks, Snowball and Nine Patch, with a Tumbler/Thimble block. Using Japanese Daiwabo taupe fabrics gives this quilt an old feel.

"Grandmother's Thimble," designed and pieced by Regina Girard; machine quilted by Karen Burns of Compulsive Quilting

FINISHED QUILT: 77" x 86" • FINISHED BLOCKS: Snowball and Nine Patch: 4½" x 4½", Small Thimble: 3" tall, Large Thimble: 4¼" tall

Materials

Yardage is based on 42"-wide fabric, except where noted. Fat quarters are 18" x 21".

10 assorted fat quarters for large and small Thimble blocks

5 light fat quarters for Snowball blocks

4 light fat quarters for Nine Patch blocks

4 dark fat quarters for Nine Patch blocks

3 dark fat quarters for Snowball blocks

2⅝ yards of dark-brown fabric for outer border and binding

5¼ yards of fabric for backing

83" x 92" piece of batting

8½" x 11" piece of template plastic

Cutting

To avoid confusion, group the light and dark fat quarters used for each of the 3 different blocks before cutting.

Snowball Blocks

From *each* light fat quarter, cut:

3 strips, 5" x 21"; crosscut each strip into 4 squares, 5" x 5" (60 total)

From *each* dark fat quarter, cut:

8 strips, 2" x 21"; crosscut each strip into 10 squares, 2" x 2" (240 total)

Nine Patch Blocks

From *each* light fat quarter, cut:

7 strips, 2" x 21" (28 total)

From *each* dark fat quarter, cut:

8 strips, 2" x 21" (32 total)

Thimble Blocks

Use the template plastic to make large and small Thimble templates from the patterns on page 174. You'll need a total of 80 large Thimbles and 144 small Thimbles.

From each of the assorted fat quarters, cut:

1 strip, 4¾" x 21"; crosscut into 5 large Thimbles (50 total)

1 strip, 4¾" x 21"; crosscut into 3 large Thimbles (30 total)

2 strips, 3½" x 21"; crosscut into 12 small Thimbles (120 total)

From the remainder of each fat quarter, cut:

2 small Thimbles (20 total)

From the leftover fabric scraps, cut:

4 total additional small Thimbles*

*You may be able to cut only partial Thimbles if your fabric is less than 22" wide. Use these partial Thimbles on the ends of the strips for constructing the center; it will be trimmed square later.

Outer Border

From the *lengthwise* grain of the dark-brown fabric, cut:

2 strips, 7½" x 72"

2 strips, 7½" x 77"

4 strips, 2½" x 90"

Making the Nine Patch Blocks

Pair your fabrics for the Nine Patch blocks, one light and one dark, to make four sets of fabrics.

1 Sew a light 2" x 21" strip between two dark 2" x 21" strips to make strip set A. Press the seam allowances toward the dark strips. Repeat to make three of strip set A. Crosscut each strip set into 2" units for a total of 30 units.

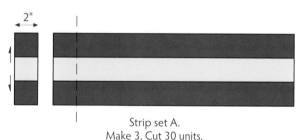

Strip set A.
Make 3. Cut 30 units.

2 Sew a dark 2" x 21" strip between two light 2" x 21" strips to make strip set B. Press the seam allowances toward the dark strip. Repeat to make two of strip set B. Crosscut each strip set into 2" units for a total of 15 units.

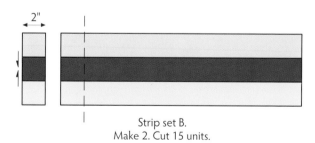

Strip set B.
Make 2. Cut 15 units.

3 Lay out two A units with one B unit as shown to form a Nine Patch block. Join the rows, being careful to nest the seam intersections. Press the seam allowances toward the A units. Repeat to make 15

Nine Patch blocks for each set of fabrics for a total of 60 Nine Patch blocks.

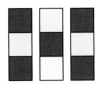

Make 60.

Piecing the Snowball Blocks

Use the 2" and 5" squares to make the Snowball blocks. Mark a diagonal line from corner to corner on the wrong side of each 2" square. Position a square on each corner of a 5" square and sew on the marked lines. Cut off the excess fabric at each corner, leaving a ¼" seam allowance. Press the resulting triangle corners open. For an alternative method, see the tip below. Make 60 total 5" Snowball blocks.

Make 60.

Fast Snowballs

If you don't want to take time to mark the diagonal lines on the 2" squares, mark your sewing machine using removable tape instead. When sewing your 2" squares onto the 5" background square, start at the corner. Use the marked line to keep your sewing line straight by keeping the lower point of the small square on the line.

Assembling the Quilt Center

It may look difficult to sew these Thimble blocks together, but it's easy once you get the hang of it.

1 Align two small Thimbles side by side, one with the narrow end at the top and one with the wide end at the top.

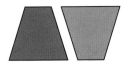

2 Flip the right Thimble over onto the left Thimble, keeping the right edges aligned. The measurement from the point of the bottom Thimble to the overlapping edge of the top Thimble should be ¼" as shown.

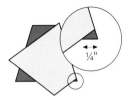

3 Sew using a ¼" seam allowance.

 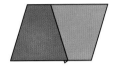

4 In the same manner, join a total of 12 Thimbles in a horizontal row, alternating their placement so they nest. Repeat to make 12 horizontal rows.

Make 12.

5 Arrange the rows, flipping every other row so the wide bottom of one Thimble touches the wide top of the Thimble in the next row. Press the seam allowances in opposite directions from row to row. Sew the rows together, being careful to butt the seam intersections. Press the seam allowances upward.

6 Using a rotary cutter and long ruler, trim the section to 27½" wide.

27½"

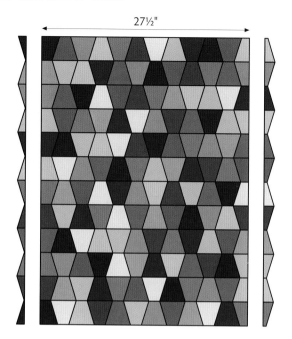

Making the Nine Patch and Snowball Sections

1 Sew one Nine Patch block between two Snowball blocks. Press the seam allowances toward the Nine Patch block. Repeat to make a total of eight rows.

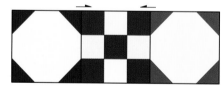

Make 8.

2 Sew one Snowball block between two Nine Patch blocks. Press the seam allowances toward the Nine Patch blocks. Repeat to make a total of eight rows.

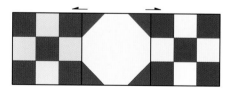

Make 8.

3 Alternate four of the Snowball rows with four of the Nine Patch rows. Sew the rows into a vertical section. Press the seam allowances toward the

bottom of the column. Make another section and press the seam allowances upward.

Make 2.

4 Attach the sections to the Thimble center as shown, with a Snowball row at the top of the left section and a Nine Patch row at the top of the right section. Press the seam allowances toward the Thimbles.

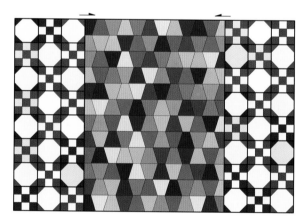

5 Arrange six Snowball blocks and six Nine Patch blocks into a horizontal row, alternating the blocks and placing a Nine Patch on the left end and a Snowball block on the right end. Sew the blocks together in a row. Press the seam allowances toward the Nine Patch blocks. Repeat to make a total of six rows.

Make 6.

6 Sew three rows together as shown to make the top section. Press the seam allowances downward. Sew the remaining three rows together to make the bottom section.

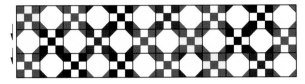

Make 2.

7 Attach the sections to the top and bottom edges of the quilt top, flipping the second section to align the Snowball/Nine Patch pattern running up and down. Press the seam allowances toward the center section.

Making the Large Thimble Border

1 Arrange 20 of the large Thimbles in a horizontal row. Sew the Thimbles together. Press the seam allowances in one direction. Repeat to make a total of four border rows.

Make 4.

2 Trim the ends of two borders to measure 63½". Sew a border to each side of the quilt top. Press the seam allowances toward the border.

3 Trim the ends of each remaining border to measure 63". Sew to the top and bottom of the quilt top. Press the seam allowances toward the border.

Adding the Outer Border

Sew the 7½" x 72" border strips to the sides of the quilt top. Press the seam allowances toward the outer border. Sew the dark-brown 7½" x 77" strips to the top and bottom. Press the seam allowances toward the outer border.

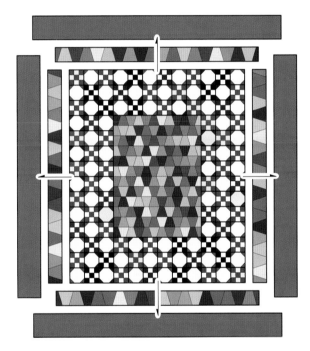

Finishing the Quilt

For help with any of the finishing steps, go to ShopMartingale.com/HowtoQuilt for free downloadable information.

1 Layer, baste, and quilt your quilt, or take it to your favorite long-arm quilter for finishing.

2 Using the dark-brown 2½"-wide strips, make and attach binding.

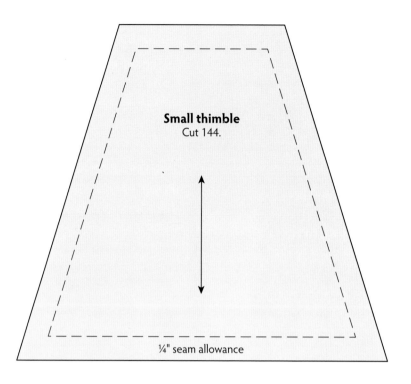

Small thimble
Cut 144.

¼" seam allowance

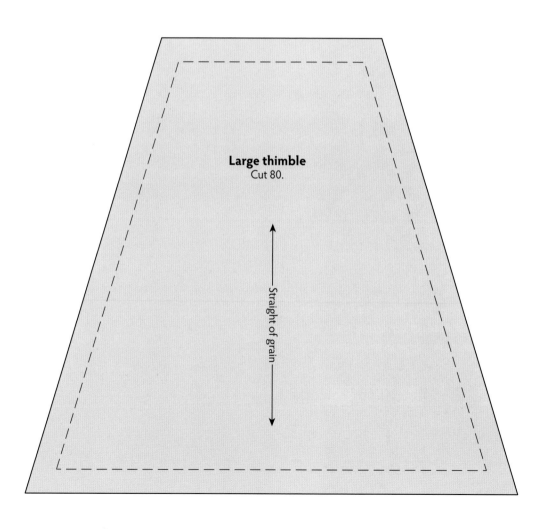

Large thimble
Cut 80.

Straight of grain

Flower Power

Turn a stack of your favorite fat quarters into this whimsical quilt. You can use the leftovers on the back for a coordinated look and no waste. The appliqué work is minimal and uses easy shapes. Fused raw-edge appliqué is also quick—the sewing machine does all the work! Add a couple of yo-yos and buttons for flower centers for an extra bit of pop.

"Flower Power," designed and made by Terry Martin; machine quilted by Adrienne Reynolds

FINISHED QUILT: 68" x 72½" • FINISHED BLOCK: 4½" x 4½"

Materials

Yardage is based on 42"-wide fabric, except where noted. Fat quarters are 18" x 21".

13 assorted fat quarters for patchwork quilt center

2⅛ yards of black floral for border and binding

1 fat quarter *each* of 3 coordinating prints for flower, stem, and leaf appliqués

Scraps of yellow fabric for flower centers

4¼ yards of fabric for backing

74" x 79" piece of batting

1⅞ yards of 18"-wide lightweight paper-backed fusible web

45 mm and 60 mm yo-yo makers (optional)

9 yellow ½"-diameter buttons

Cutting

All measurements include ¼"-wide seam allowances.

From *each* of the 13 fat quarters for the quilt center, cut:
3 strips, 5" x 21" (39 total)

From the black floral, cut:
7 strips, 7½" x 42"
8 strips, 2¼" x 42"

Assembling the Quilt Top

1 Randomly select three different 5" strips and sew them together along the long edges to make a strip set. Press the seam allowances in one direction. Repeat to make a total of 13 strip sets. Crosscut each strip set into four segments, 5" wide (52 total).

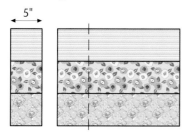

Make 13 strip sets.
Cut 4 segments from each (52 total).

2 Randomly select four segments and sew them together end to end to make a row, making sure all the seam allowances are pressed in the same direction. Repeat to make a total of 13 rows.

Make 13.

3 Join the rows, rotating the rows as needed so the seam allowances are pressed in opposite directions from row to row.

4 Using the patterns on pages 177 and 178, trace five large flower petal shapes, 10 small flower petal shapes, and 35 stem/leaf shapes onto the paper side of the fusible web. Roughly cut around each shape. Follow the manufacturer's instructions to fuse the five large flower petal shapes and 15 of the stem/leaf shapes to the wrong side of one of the coordinating fat quarters. Cut out the shapes on the marked lines. Cut the stem/leaf shapes in half lengthwise along the center cutting line. Fuse the 10 small flower petal shapes to a different coordinating fat quarter and fuse the 20 remaining stem/leaf shapes to the remaining coordinating fat quarter. Cut out the shapes on the marked lines. Remove the paper backing from all of the pieces.

5 Referring to the photo on page 175 and the quilt assembly diagram below, arrange the shapes on the quilt top as shown or create your own unique arrangement. When you're satisfied with the results, fuse the shapes in place.

6 Using a narrow zigzag stitch, hem stitch, or decorative machine stitch, stitch around the outer edges of each fused shape. This is recommended if the quilt will be laundered frequently and not simply hung as a wall hanging.

7 Measure the quilt top to measure and trim the black floral 7½"-wide strips to fit. Sew the borders to the quilt and press the seam allowances toward the border strips.

Quilt assembly

Finishing the Quilt

For help with any of the finishing steps, go to ShopMartingale.com/HowtoQuilt for free downloadable information.

1 Layer, baste, and quilt your quilt, or take it to your favorite long-arm quilter for finishing.

2 Using the black floral 2¼"-wide strips, make and attach binding.

3 Follow the manufacturer's instructions included with the yo-yo maker to make one large and two small yo-yos from the fabric scraps. With the open side down, sew the large yo-yo to the center of the large flower and the small yo-yos to the center of the two small flowers. Sew three yellow buttons to the center of each yo-yo.

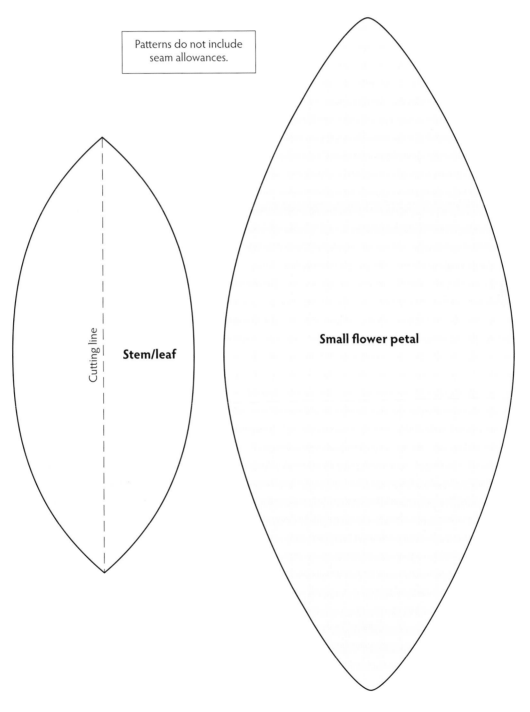

Patterns do not include seam allowances.

Cutting line

Stem/leaf

Small flower petal

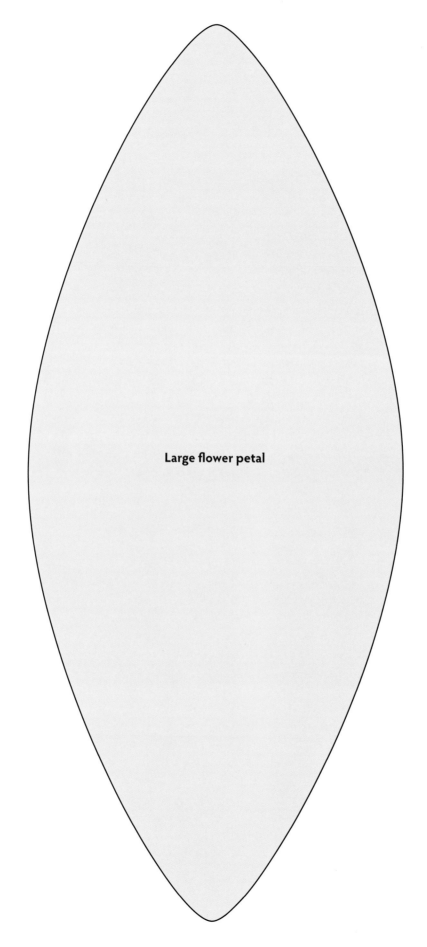

Large flower petal

Pieces of Eight

Just like pirates in the movies, Vickie too would like to have nine pieces of eight. (A "piece of eight," or peso de ocho, is a Spanish silver dollar.) But instead of pirating, she settled for a quilt design with nine blocks that form interlocking eights. This block is a jewel made with just squares and half-square-triangle units.

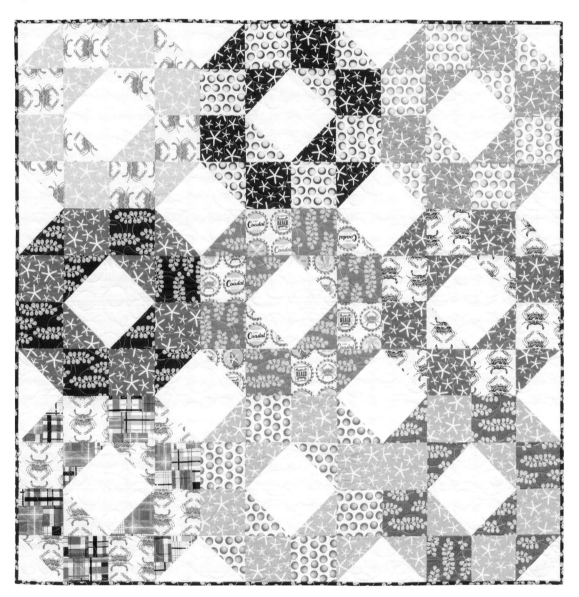

"Pieces of Eight," designed and pieced by Victoria L. Eapen; machine quilted by Al Kuthe

FINISHED QUILT: 54½" x 54½" • **FINISHED BLOCK: 18" x 18"**

Materials

Yardage is based on 42"-wide fabric, except where noted.

¼ yard or fat quarter *each* of 18 assorted prints for blocks

1⅛ yards of light solid for blocks

½ yard of blue print for binding

3⅓ yards of fabric for backing

60" x 60" piece of batting

Cutting

From the light solid, cut:

6 strips, 5½" x 42"; crosscut into 36 squares, 5½" x 5½"

From *each* of the 18 assorted prints, cut:

4 squares, 5" x 5" (72 total)

2 squares, 5½" x 5½" (36 total)

From the blue print, cut:

6 strips, 2¼" x 42"

Piecing the Blocks

1 Draw a line diagonally from corner to corner on the wrong side of each light 5½" square. Layer each light square right sides together with a print 5½" square. Sew ¼" from both sides of the marked lines and cut apart on the marked lines to make two half-square-triangle units from each pair (18 sets of four matching units total). Press the seam allowances toward the print triangles. Trim each unit to 5" x 5".

Make 18 sets of 4.

2 Select two different sets of four matching units from step 1 along with their matching 5" squares. Arrange the pieces into four horizontal rows as shown. Sew the pieces in each row together. Press the seam allowances in alternate directions from row to row. Sew the rows together. Press the seam allowances

in one direction. The completed block should measure 18½" x 18½". Repeat to make a total of nine blocks.

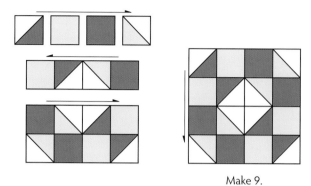

Make 9.

Assembling the Quilt Top

Arrange the rows into three horizontal rows of three blocks each, rotating the blocks so that the seam allowances nest together. Sew the blocks in each row together. Press the seam allowances in alternating directions from row to row. Sew the rows together. Press the seam allowances in one direction.

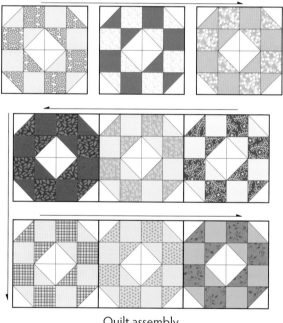

Quilt assembly

Finishing the Quilt

For help with any of the finishing steps, go to ShopMartingale.com/HowtoQuilt for free downloadable information.

1 Layer, baste, and quilt your quilt, or take it to your favorite long-arm quilter for finishing.

2 Using the blue-print 2¼"-wide strips, make and attach binding.

Charmed, I'm Sure

This quilt features seven dark-value prints for the star points. After selecting those fabrics, choose seven fat quarters each of medium-value prints and of medium- to dark-value prints to coordinate with the hand-dyed fabrics. Once you've done that, all that's left are the light and black pieces—the easy ones!

"Charmed, I'm Sure," designed and pieced by Susan Dissmore; machine quilted by Eileen Peacher

FINISHED QUILT: 66" x 78" • FINISHED BLOCK: 12" x 12"

Materials

Yardage is based on 42"-wide fabric, except where noted. Fat quarters are 18" x 21".

9 fat quarters of assorted light prints for blocks and outer border*

7 fat quarters of assorted black prints for outer border*

1 fat quarter *each* of dark prints in green, blue, red, brown, purple, gold, and gray for blocks and outer border (7 total)

1 fat quarter *each* of medium-dark to dark prints in green, blue, red, brown, purple, gold, and gray for blocks and outer border (7 total)

1 fat quarter *each* of medium-value prints in green, blue, red, brown, purple, gold, and gray for blocks and outer border (7 total)

¾ yard of black print for binding

5 yards of fabric for backing

74" x 86" piece of batting

More than one fat quarter of the same print was included in the assortment.

Cutting

All measurements include ¼" seam allowances.

From *each* of the dark and medium green, blue, red, brown, and purple prints, cut:

3 strips, 3⅞" x 21". Cut the strips into 12 squares, 3⅞" x 3⅞"; cut the squares in half diagonally to yield 24 triangles (240 total).

1 strip, 4¼" x 21". Cut the strip into 4 squares, 4¼" x 4¼"; cut the squares into quarters diagonally to yield 16 triangles (160 total).

From *each* of the medium-dark/dark green, blue, red, brown, purple, and gray prints, cut:

2 strips, 3⅞" x 21". Cut the strips into 9 squares, 3⅞" x 3⅞"; cut the squares in half diagonally to yield 18 triangles (108 total; 1 extra of green, blue, brown, and gray).

1 strip, 4¼" x 21". Cut the strip into 4 squares, 4¼" x 4¼"; cut the squares into quarters diagonally to yield 16 triangles (96 total).

From the dark gray print, cut:

3 strips, 3⅞" x 21". Cut the strips into 12 squares, 3⅞" x 3⅞"; cut the squares in half diagonally to yield 24 triangles.

From the medium-gray print, cut:

3 strips, 3⅞" x 21". Cut the strips into 12 squares, 3⅞" x 3⅞"; cut the squares in half diagonally to yield 24 triangles.

1 strip, 4¼" x 21". Cut the strip into 4 squares, 4¼" x 4¼"; cut the squares into quarters diagonally to yield 16 triangles.

From *each* of the dark, medium-dark/dark, and medium gold prints, cut:

2 strips, 3⅞" x 21". Cut the strips into 8 squares, 3⅞" x 3⅞"; cut the squares in half diagonally to yield 16 triangles (48 total).

1 strip, 4¼" x 21". Cut the strip into 4 squares, 4¼" x 4¼"; cut the squares into quarters diagonally to yield 16 triangles (48 total).

From *each* of 6 assorted light prints, cut:

3 squares, 7¼" x 7¼"; cut the squares into quarters diagonally to yield 12 triangles for blocks (72 total).

6 squares, 3⅞" x 3⅞"; cut the squares in half diagonally to yield 12 triangles (72 total).

From *1* of the remaining light prints, cut:

1 strip, 7¼" x 21". Cut the strip into 2 squares, 7¼" x 7¼"; cut the squares into quarters diagonally to yield 8 triangles for blocks.

1 strip, 3⅞" x 21". Cut the strip into 4 squares, 3⅞" x 3⅞"; cut the squares in half diagonally to yield 8 triangles.

From *each* of the 2 remaining light prints, cut:

2 strips, 7¼" x 21". Cut the strips into 3 squares, 7¼" x 7¼"; cut the squares diagonally into quarters to yield 12 triangles for border (24 total; 3 extra per print).

From *each* of 4 black prints, cut:

1 square, 7¼" x 7¼"; cut the square into quarters diagonally to yield 4 triangles (16 total)

4 rectangles, 3½" x 12½" (16 total)

From *1* black print, cut:

2 strips, 3⅞" x 21". Cut the strips into 10 squares, 3⅞" x 3⅞"; cut the squares in half diagonally to yield 20 triangles.

1 square, 7¼" x 7¼"; cut the square into quarters diagonally to yield 4 triangles (2 extra)

2 rectangles, 3½" x 12½"

From *1* black print, cut:

3 strips, 3⅞" x 21". Cut the strips into 14 squares, 3⅞" x 3⅞"; cut the squares in half diagonally to yield 28 triangles.

From *1* black print, cut:

4 strips, 3½" x 21". Cut the strips into:

    4 rectangles, 3½" x 6½"

    4 rectangles, 3½" x 9½"

From the black print for binding, cut:

8 strips, 2½" x 42"

Making the Star Blocks

1 Using the dark triangles cut from 3⅞" squares, sew two matching triangles to each short side of the light triangles (designated for blocks) cut from 7¼" squares as shown. Make the amount indicated for each color. Press the seam allowances toward the dark triangles and trim the dog-ears.

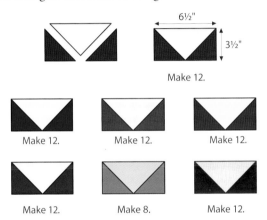

Make 12.

Make 12. Make 12. Make 12.

Make 12. Make 8. Make 12.

2 Using the triangles cut from 3⅞" squares, sew a medium triangle to a light triangle along their longest edges to make a half-square-triangle unit. Make the amount indicated for each color. Press the seam allowances toward the medium triangles and trim the dog-ears.

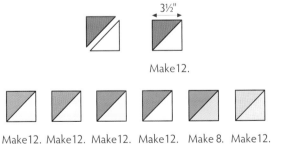

Make 12.

Make 12. Make 12. Make 12. Make 12. Make 8. Make 12.

Fabric Placement

When constructing the units in steps 1 and 2, match the same light print with the same dark- and medium-value prints for consistency.

3 Repeat step 2 using the medium and medium-dark triangles. Press the seam allowances toward the medium-dark triangles and trim the dog-ears.

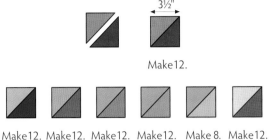

Make 12.

Make 12. Make 12. Make 12. Make 12. Make 8. Make 12.

4 Sew the units from step 3 together as shown to make pinwheel units. Press the seam allowances as indicated. Press the final seam allowance open.

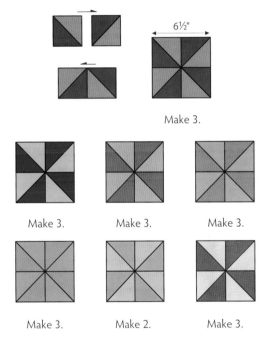

Make 3.

Make 3. Make 3. Make 3.

Make 3. Make 2. Make 3.

5 Sew the units from steps 1, 2, and 4 together in rows as shown to make the Star blocks. Press the seam allowances as indicated. Make a total of 20 blocks in the color combinations shown.

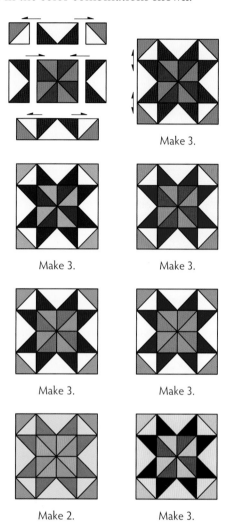

Make 3.

Make 3.   Make 3.

Make 3.   Make 3.

Make 2.   Make 3.

Making the Border Blocks

1 Using the triangles cut from medium and medium-dark green, blue, red, brown, purple, and gold 4¼" squares, sew the triangles together as shown to make larger triangles. Make eight of

each color combination. Press the seam allowances toward the darker fabric and trim the dog-ears.

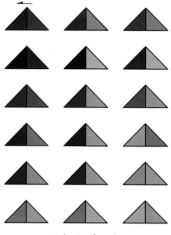

Make 8 of each.

2 Referring to the color combinations for the border blocks shown on page 185, arrange the triangle units from step 1, the triangles cut from black and light 7¼" squares, and the triangles cut from black and medium-dark 3⅞" squares into two rows as shown. Sew the pieces in each row together. Press the seam allowances as indicated. Sew the rows together. Press the seam allowances open and trim the dog-ears. Add a black 3½" x 12½" rectangle to the top of each unit. Press the seam allowances toward the rectangles. Make one of each color combination.

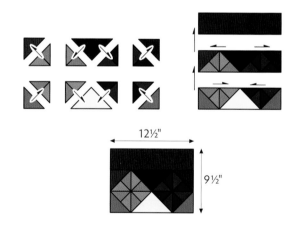

12½"

9½"

Border blocks.
Make 1 of each.

3 As described in step 1, sew the medium and medium-dark gray triangles cut from 4¼" squares together to make larger triangles.

Make 16.

4 Sew the gray triangles from step 3 to the remaining black and medium-dark gray, blue, green, and brown triangles cut from 3⅞" squares as shown. Don't press the seam allowances at this time.

3½"

Make 12

Make 1 of each.

5 Arrange and sew the units from step 4 together as shown. Press the seam allowances as indicated. Press the final seam allowance open.

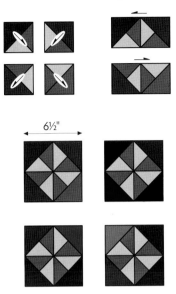

6½"

Make 1 of each.

6 Sew a black 3½" x 6½" rectangle to one side of each unit from step 5 as shown. Press the seam allowances toward the rectangles. Sew a black 3½" x 9½" rectangle to the top of each unit to complete the border corner blocks. Press the seam allowances toward the rectangles.

9½"

Border corner blocks.
Make 1 of each.

Assembling the Quilt Top

Referring to the quilt assembly diagram, arrange and sew the Star blocks, the border blocks, and the border corner blocks into rows as shown. Press the seam allowances open. Sew the rows together to form the quilt top. Press the seam allowances open.

Finishing the Quilt

For help with any of the finishing steps, go to ShopMartingale.com/HowtoQuilt for free downloadable information.

1 Layer, baste, and quilt your quilt, or take it to your favorite long-arm quilter for finishing.

2 Using the black 2½"-wide strips, make and attach binding.

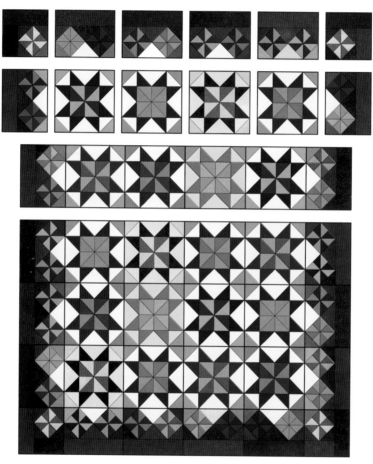

Quilt assembly

S-C-H-Double-Oh-L

Spells school! Remember this fun jump-rope jingle from your grade-school days?
The dark-blue chain running through this quilt reminds us of twirling jump ropes.
Remember Double Dutch and "Don't Forget the Red Hot Peppers"? We used feedsack
reproduction prints to make this nostalgic quilt. Dick and Jane would just love it!

"S-C-H-Double-Oh-L," designed and pieced by Barbara Groves and Mary Jacobson

FINISHED QUILT: 80" x 80" • FINISHED BLOCK: 8" x 8"

Materials

Yardage is based on 42"-wide fabric, except where noted. Fat quarters are 18" x 21".

24 coordinating fat quarters for blocks
2 yards of dark-blue print for blocks and inner border
1⅝ yards of green print for outer border
⅔ yard of orange print for binding
7½ yards of fabric for backing
88" x 88" piece of batting

Cutting

From *each* fat quarter, cut:
1 strip, 5" x 21" (24 total); crosscut the strips into a
   total of 64 squares, 5" x 5"
2 strips, 4½" x 21" (48 total); crosscut the strips into a
   total of 144 squares, 4½" x 4½"*

From the dark-blue print, cut:
8 strips, 5" x 42"; crosscut into 64 squares, 5" x 5"
7 strips, 2½" x 42"

From the green print, cut:
8 strips, 6¼" x 42"

From the orange print, cut:
9 strips, 2¼" x 40"

Keep like prints together in pairs.

Piecing the Blocks

1 Layer one coordinating print 5" square and one
dark-blue 5" square right sides together. Using a
¼" seam allowance, stitch along two opposite sides
of the squares as shown.

2 Cut down the center of the squares as shown and
press the seam allowances open. Make a total of
128 two-patch units.

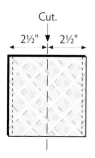 

Make 128.

3 With right sides together, layer the two-patch
units, aligning the seams and reversing the color
placement as shown. Using a ¼" seam allowance,
stitch along two opposite sides, making sure to stitch
across the previous seam lines.

4 Cut down the center of the sewn units as shown
and press the seam allowances open. Make 128
Four Patch blocks.

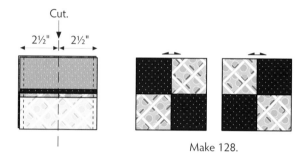

Make 128.

5 For each Double Four Patch block, choose two
matching Four Patch blocks and two matching 4½" squares; the print should be different from
the ones used in the Four Patch blocks. You will
have extra 4½" squares, so choose your favorites.
Arrange and sew the blocks as shown. The blocks
should measure 8½" x 8½". Make 64 Double Four
Patch blocks.

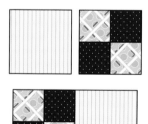 

Make 64.

Assembling the Quilt Top

1 Arrange the blocks into eight rows of eight blocks each, rotating the blocks as shown. Sew the blocks into rows.

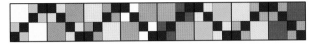

Make 4.

Make 4.

2 Sew the rows together. The quilt should now measure 64½" x 64½".

3 Piece the seven dark-blue 2½" x 42" strips together end to end for the inner border.

4 Measure the quilt from top to bottom through the middle to determine the length of the side borders. From the pieced strip, cut the side borders to the needed length and attach them to the sides of the quilt.

5 Measure the quilt from side to side through the middle, including the side borders, to determine the length of the top and bottom borders. From the pieced strip, cut the top and bottom borders to the needed length and attach them to the quilt. The quilt should now measure 68½" x 68½".

6 Piece the eight green 6¼" x 42" strips together end to end for the outer border. Repeat the measuring and cutting process as you did for the inner border and add the outer border to the quilt. The quilt should now measure 80" x 80".

Finishing the Quilt

For help with any of the finishing steps, go to ShopMartingale.com/HowtoQuilt for free downloadable information.

1 Layer, baste, and quilt your quilt, or take it to your favorite long-arm quilter for finishing.

2 Using the orange-print 2¼"-wide strips, make and attach binding.

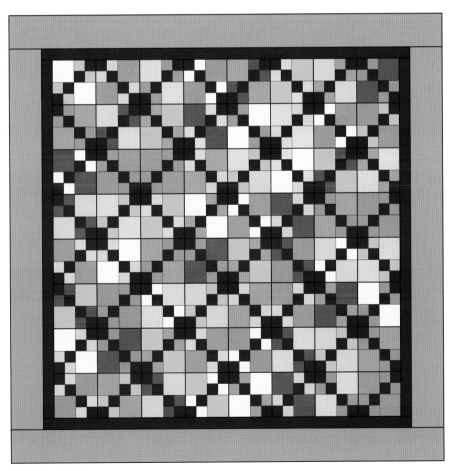

Shakespeare in Leaves

The Pacific Northwest is blessed with wonderful autumn weather, and crisp winds blow away the usual gray clouds to reveal beautiful blue skies. Mary was inspired by the numerous shades the leaves turn in the fall—and captured some of their beauty in this Maple Leaf quilt. You can almost see the blue pinwheels on this quilt spinning in the wind!

"Shakespeare in Leaves," designed and pieced by Mary J. Burns; machine quilted by Karen Burns of Compulsive Quilting

FINISHED QUILT: 68½" x 78½" • FINISHED BLOCK: 12" x 18"

Materials

Yardage is based on 42"-wide fabric, except where noted. Fat quarters are 18" x 21".

1 fat quarter *each* of 2 different light-blue prints for Pinwheel blocks

1 fat quarter *each* of 2 different dark-blue prints for Pinwheel blocks

2 fat quarters of red prints for Maple Leaf blocks

1 fat quarter each of yellow, orange, lime-green, and black prints for Maple Leaf blocks (for a scrappier look, use 12 different prints for leaves)

3 yards of dark-gray print for sashing strips and binding

1½ yards of sky-blue print for block backgrounds

4¾ yards of fabric for backing

74" x 84" piece of batting

½"-wide bias bar

Cutting

From *each* of the light-blue and dark-blue fat quarters, cut:

5 strips, 3¼" x 21"; crosscut into 20 rectangles, 3¼" x 4½" (80 total)

From *each* of the red, yellow, orange, lime-green, and black fat quarters, cut:

1 strip, 9¼" x 18"; crosscut into:
    1 rectangle, 9¼" x 13¼"
    2 rectangles, 1½" x 9¼"

2 strips, 5¼" x 18"; crosscut into 4 rectangles, 5¼" x 7½"

From the sky-blue print, cut:

2 strips, 4½" x 42"; crosscut into 12 rectangles, 4½" x 6½"

From the remaining sky-blue print, cut on the *lengthwise* grain:

2 strips, 9¼" wide; crosscut into 6 rectangles, 9¼" x 13¼"

3 strips, 7½" wide; crosscut into 24 rectangles, 5¼" x 7½"

From the dark-gray print, cut:

6 strips, 6½" x 42"; crosscut into 16 rectangles, 6½" x 12½"

2 strips, 18½" x 42"; crosscut into 15 rectangles, 4½" x 18½"

8 strips, 2½" x 42"

Cutting Triangles from Rectangles

Unlike squares cut in half diagonally, triangles cut from rectangles are not identical regardless of the direction you cut. Carefully follow the instructions for cutting all rectangles to ensure that your blocks turn out as planned.

Making the Pinwheel Blocks

1 Make four stacks of light-blue 3¼" x 4½" rectangles, with 10 rectangles in each stack. Working with only four pieces at a time, cut the rectangles in the first two stacks in half diagonally in one direction. Label these as A triangles. Cut the rectangles in the remaining two stacks in half diagonally in the opposite direction and label these as A reversed triangles (AR). You'll have 40 of each.

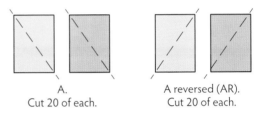

A.
Cut 20 of each.

A reversed (AR).
Cut 20 of each.

2 Stack and cut the dark-blue 3¼" x 4½" rectangles in the same way to yield 40 dark-blue B triangles and 40 dark-blue B reversed triangles (BR).

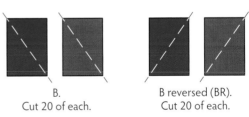

B.
Cut 20 of each.

B reversed (BR).
Cut 20 of each.

To Pin or Not to Pin?

That is the question. If you sew carefully with a scant ¼" seam allowance, you shouldn't need to pin these units because they'll be trimmed to size. However, be careful not to stretch the bias edges as you sew the triangles; a walking foot is very helpful.

3 Sew a light-blue A triangle and a dark-blue B triangle together, matching the end points along the longest edges of the triangles as shown. Sew the triangles together using a scant ¼" seam allowance. Chain piece the remaining A and B triangles together for efficiency. Press the seam allowances toward the dark-blue fabric. Make a total of 40 pieced rectangle units.

Make 20 of each.

4 In the same manner, sew a light-blue AR triangle and a dark-blue BR triangle together. Press the seam allowances toward the dark-blue fabric. Make a total of 40 pieced rectangle units.

Make 20 of each.

5 To trim the pinwheel units, position the ruler with the 2½" mark on the seam at one corner and the 3½" mark on the seam at the opposite corner. Trim ⅛" to ¼" off the two edges. Then rotate the unit (or your ruler) and line up the clean-cut edges with the 2½" and 3½" ruler marks and trim the remaining two sides. Each trimmed rectangle should measure 2½" x 3½".

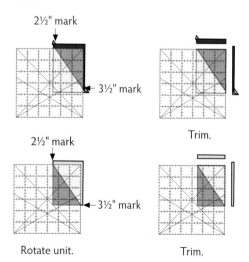

6 Arrange each Pinwheel block using two A/B units and two AR/BR units; 10 blocks will "spin" to the right and 10 blocks will "spin" to the left. Sew the units together in rows. Press the seam allowances open to reduce the bulk. Join the rows. Mary used one pin when joining the rows, sticking the pin all the way through both pieces at the center intersection of the points. Press the seam allowances open. Make 10 of each Pinwheel block.

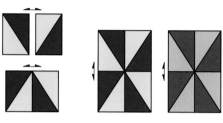

Make 10 of each.

Making the Maple Leaf Blocks

1 For both the colored leaf fabrics and the sky-blue fabric, cut the 5¼" x 7½" rectangles in half diagonally, from top right to bottom left, right side up, as shown. Cut the 9¼" x 13¼" rectangles in half diagonally in the opposite direction, from top left to bottom right, right side facing up.

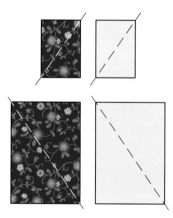

2 Sew each small leaf-print triangle and a small sky-blue triangle together, matching the end points along the longest edges of the triangles. Chain piece the units using a scant ¼" seam allowance. Press the seam allowances toward the sky fabric. Make four rectangle units from each fat quarter for a total of 48 small leaf/sky rectangles.

Make 48.

3 As you did with the Pinwheel blocks, trim the rectangle units, this time aligning the 4½" and 6½" marks with the diagonal seam. The trimmed units should measure 4½" x 6½".

4 Use the 1½" x 9¼" rectangles to make the leaf stems. Fold each rectangle in half lengthwise, *wrong* sides together, and stitch ¼" from the long raw edges. Insert the bias bar into the resulting fabric tube, and rotate the tube so that the seam allowance is centered along one flat side of the bias bar. Press flat. The finished stems will measure approximately ½" wide.

The Bridge Is the Thing

Because these long, skinny triangle tips have a tendency to get tangled in with your bobbin thread when sewing, use a bridge—a square scrap of fabric with which you always start and end your chain sewing. Sewing on the scrap fabric first creates enough thread tension to feed the triangle tips safely without having the feed dogs eat them. Ending a chain with a bridge sets you up for the next chain.

5 Pin or glue baste one end of the stem perpendicular to the diagonal edge of a large sky triangle, centering the stem along the edge. Pin or glue baste the free end of the stem to the sky triangle 1¼" from the corner. Machine appliqué the stem to the block in a gentle curve using a narrow zigzag stitch and matching thread. Stitch the inside of the curve first, and then sew the outside edge.

6 Sew a large leaf triangle and a large sky triangle together, matching the end points along the diagonal edges of the triangles and sandwiching the stem between the layers. Carefully press the seam allowances toward the leaf fabric. Make two units from each fat quarter for a total of 12 large leaf/sky rectangles.

1¼"

7 Trim the units, this time aligning the 8½" and 12½" marks with the diagonal seam. The trimmed units should measure 8½" x 12½".

8½"

12½"

Make 12.

8 To assemble each Maple Leaf block, sew two small leaf/sky rectangle units to one 4½" x 6½" sky rectangle as shown. Press the seam allowances toward the sky rectangle.

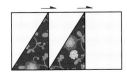

9 Sew two small leaf/sky rectangle units end to end as shown. Press the seam allowances downward.

10 Sew the unit from the previous step to the right edge of the large leaf rectangle. Press the seam allowances toward the large rectangle. Add the unit made in step 8 to the top. Press the seam allowances toward the large rectangle. The block should measure 12½" x 18½". Make 12 Maple Leaf blocks.

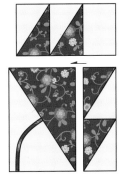 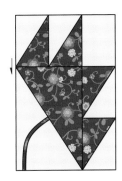

Make 12.

Assembling the Quilt Top

1 Referring to the quilt assembly diagram below, arrange the Maple Leaf blocks and dark-gray 4½" x 18½" sashing strips in three horizontal rows of four blocks each. Sew a sashing strip between the blocks and to the left and right ends of each row. Press the seam allowances toward the sashing strips. The rows should measure 68½" long.

2 Sew the Pinwheel blocks and the dark-gray 6½" x 12½" sashing strips into four horizontal rows, alternating the direction the pinwheels spin from row to row. (Sew with the Pinwheel blocks on top to intersect the points precisely and avoid catching the seam allowances.) Press the seam allowances toward the sashing strips. The rows should measure 68½" long.

3 Join the rows, paying attention to the direction the pinwheels spin and matching the block intersections. Press the seam allowances in one direction.

Finishing the Quilt

For help with any of the finishing steps, go to ShopMartingale.com/HowtoQuilt for free downloadable information.

1 Layer, baste, and quilt your quilt, or take it to your favorite long-arm quilter for finishing.

2 Using the dark-gray 2½"-wide strips, make and attach binding.

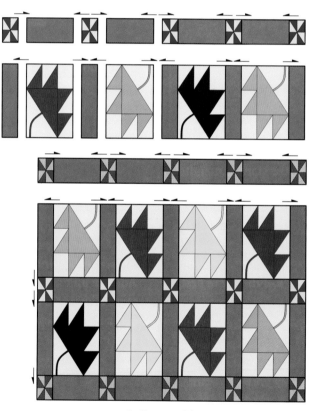

Quilt assembly

Quick Bricks

Fat quarters are so irresistible.
Grab a bundle of your favorites and go!

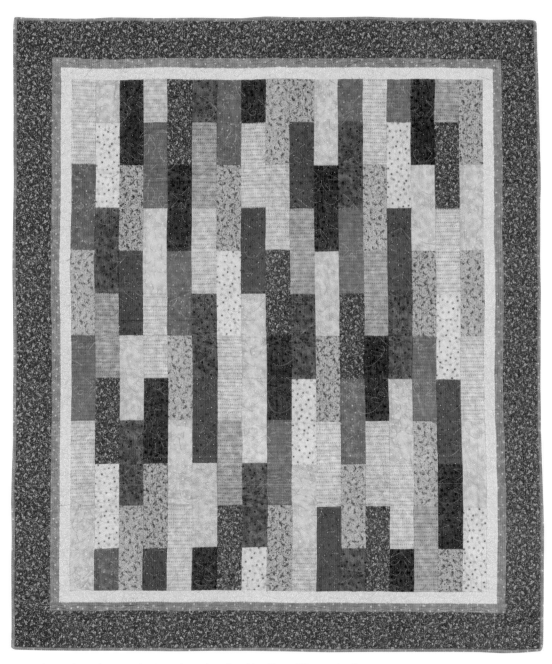

"Quick Bricks," designed, pieced, and quilted by Sara Diepersloot
FINISHED QUILT: 59" x 69"

Materials

Yardage is based on 42"-wide fabric, except where noted. Fat quarters are 18" x 21".

14 fat quarters of orange, red, blue, and green prints
  for bricks
1 yard of red print for outer border
⅜ yard of orange print for inner border
⅓ yard of green print for middle border
⅝ yard of fabric for binding
3¾ yards of fabric for backing
65" x 75" piece of batting

Cutting

Be sure to cut across the 21" length of each fat quarter.

From *each* of the 14 fat quarters, cut:
4 strips, 3¼" x 21"; crosscut into 8 rectangles,
  3¼" x 10" (112 total; 2 are extra)
From the orange print, cut:
6 strips, 1¾" x 42"
From the green print, cut:
6 strips, 1½" x 42"
From the red print, cut:
7 strips, 4" x 42"
From the binding fabric, cut:
7 strips, 2¼" x 42"

Assembling the Quilt Top

This quilt top isn't pieced using traditional blocks, but rather in rows of vertical blocks. To help in the layout of your quilt top, use a design wall, or the floor or a large table if you don't have a design wall. Lay out all the rectangles before sewing so that you can play with the fabric placement until the layout and color arrangement are pleasing to you. Try to space the colors and different fabrics evenly throughout the quilt.

You'll make two different vertical rows, one with six rectangles and one with seven. They will alternate in the quilt layout. Note that you will have two extra rectangles.

1 To make row 1, sew together six rectangles end to end. Make nine rows; press all the seam allowances in the same direction.

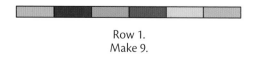

Row 1.
Make 9.

2 To make row 2, sew together seven rectangles end to end. Make eight rows; press all the seam allowances in the same direction.

Row 2.
Make 8.

3 Trim the first and last rectangle in each row 2, measuring 5" from the seam line as shown. Now each row 2 should be the same length as row 1.

4 Alternating rows 1 and 2, sew the rows together to complete the quilt top.

5 Attach the inner, middle, and outer borders, one at a time, by measuring the quilt top after each addition and piecing and trimming the border strips to fit your quilt top.

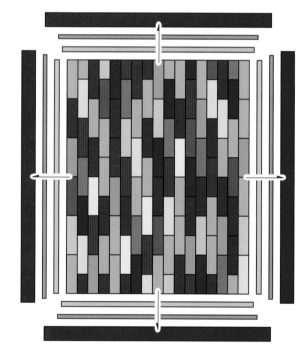

Finishing the Quilt

For help with any of the finishing steps, go to ShopMartingale.com/HowtoQuilt for free downloadable information.

1 Layer, baste, and quilt your quilt, or take it to your favorite long-arm quilter for finishing.

2 Using the 2¼"-wide binding strips, make and attach binding.

Don's Goose

This quilt is a favorite in Jeanne's family. The warm colors and flying geese will always evoke memories of the wonderful man after whom the quilt is named, Jeanne's dad, Don. His life was full of friends, family, and love.

"Don's Goose," designed and pieced by Jeanne Large and Shelley Wicks; machine quilted by Wendy Findlay

FINISHED QUILT: 56" x 72" • FINISHED BLOCK: 8" x 8"

Materials

Yardage is based on 42"-wide fabric, except where noted. Fat quarters measure 18" x 21".

12 fat quarters of assorted beige fabrics for blocks
9 fat quarters of assorted brown and gold fabrics for blocks
6 fat quarters of assorted red fabrics for blocks
1½ yards of dark-brown fabric for border and binding
3⅝ yards of fabric for backing
64" x 80" piece of batting

Cutting

All strips are cut across the width of the fabric unless otherwise specified. Use a variety of the fat quarters for each cut you make to ensure a scrappy look in your finished quilt.

From the 12 assorted beige fabrics, cut a *total* of:
48 strips, 2¾" x 21"; crosscut each strip into 6 squares, 2¾" x 2¾" (288 total)
6 strips, 4" x 21"; crosscut each strip into 4 squares, 4" x 4". Cut each square in half diagonally to yield 2 triangles (48 total).

From the 15 assorted red, brown, and gold fabrics, cut a total of:
24 strips, 5" x 21"; crosscut each strip into 6 rectangles, 2¾" x 5" (144 total)
16 strips, 5⅝" x 21"; crosscut each strip into 3 squares, 5⅝" x 5⅝" (48 total). Cut each square in half diagonally to yield 2 triangles (96 total).
6 strips, 4" x 21"; crosscut each strip into 4 squares, 4" x 4". Cut each square in half diagonally to yield 2 triangles (48 total).

From the dark-brown fabric for border and binding, cut:
7 strips, 4½" x 42"
7 strips, 2½" x 42"

Piecing the Blocks

1 Using a pencil and ruler, lightly draw a diagonal line on the wrong side of each beige 2¾" square.

2 Layer one of the marked squares over one end of a 2¾" x 5" rectangle as shown. Sew from corner to corner directly on the drawn line. Fold the top corner back and align it with the corner of the rectangle beneath it; press. Trim away the excess layers of fabric beneath the top triangle, leaving a ¼" seam allowance. Repeat to make a total of 144 units.

In the same manner, layer a beige square on the opposite end of the rectangle as shown and stitch, press, and trim to make a flying-geese unit. The quilt shown has mostly matching beige fabrics on each side of a flying-geese center, but a couple of flying-geese use mismatched beige prints. Make 144.

Make 144.

3 Join three flying-geese units along their long sides as shown. Press the seam allowances to one side. Repeat for a total of 48 units.

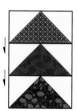

Make 48.

4 Sew a 5⅝" triangle to each long side of each unit from step 3. The end points of the triangles will be slightly longer than the flying-geese units. Evenly distribute the excess triangle fabric at each end of the flying-geese units as shown. Press the seam allowances toward the triangles just added.

5 Sew a red, brown, or gold 4" triangle to the top of each unit from step 4 and a beige 4" triangle to the bottom of each unit, adjusting the end points as you did in step 4. Press the seam allowances toward the triangles just added. Trim each block to measure 8½" x 8½".

Make 48.

Assembling the Quilt Top

1 Arrange the blocks into eight rows of six blocks each, rotating the blocks to form the design as shown in the quilt assembly diagram at right.

Pressed to Perfection

When multiple points come together at a corner, it's sometime beneficial to press the seam allowances open. This quilt is an example of this situation. All the seam allowances at the joining of the blocks and the rows have been pressed open. This will prevent large lumps from forming at the corners.

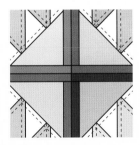

2 Sew the blocks together into rows, and then sew the rows together; press.

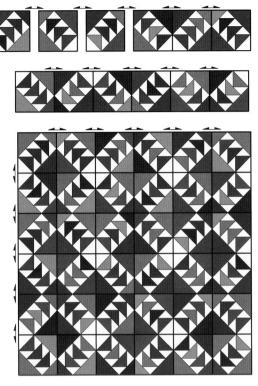

Quilt assembly

3 Sew the dark-brown 4½" x 42" strips together end to end to make one long continuous strip. From this strip, cut two strips, 56½" long, and two strips, 64½" long.

4 Sew the 64½"-long strips to the sides of the quilt; press. Sew the 56½"-long strips to the top and bottom of the quilt; press.

Finishing the Quilt

For help with any of the finishing steps, go to ShopMartingale.com/HowtoQuilt for free downloadable information.

1 Layer, baste, and quilt your quilt, or take it to your favorite long-arm quilter for finishing.

2 Using the dark-brown 2½"-wide strips, make and attach binding.

5

Jelly Rolls
2½" x 42" STRIPS

Slushie

With three different fabrics in each block, the Trip around the World block allows you to play with endless fabric combinations. In this version, the blended pieced blocks are dotted with a punch of fruity lime-and-cream setting blocks.

"Slushie," designed and pieced by Cassie Barden;
machine quilted by Karen Burns of Compulsive Quilting

FINISHED QUILT: 73" x 73" • FINISHED BLOCK: 10" x 10"

Materials

Yardage is based on 42"-wide fabric, except where noted.

20 strips, 2½" x 42", of assorted prints

8 strips, 2½" x 42", of assorted solids (or prints that read as solids)

1½ yards of cream print for setting blocks

1½ yards of pink-and-teal print for outer border

⅝ yard of bright-pink print for inner border

½ yard of teal print for setting triangles

⅜ yard of lime print for center setting blocks

⅔ yard of fabric for binding

4½ yards of fabric for backing

79" x 79" piece of batting

Sorting the Precut Fabrics

Each block uses four 2½"-wide strips. Cassie made two identical blocks from each set of four strips. First choose eight Jelly Roll strips for the block corners and centers; these will be fabric A. For these corner patches, Cassie chose a fabric that reads as a solid to add consistency and structure to the block.

Cutting

From *each of the 8* strips for fabric A, cut:

1 strip, 2½" x 21", and 2 squares, 2½" x 2½"

From the cream print, cut:

16 strips, 3" x 42"; crosscut the strips into:

    18 rectangles, 3" x 5½"

    18 rectangles, 3" x 10½"

    12 rectangles, 3" x 5⅞"

    12 rectangles, 3" x 10⅞"

    2 rectangles, 3" x 6¼"

    2 rectangles, 3" x 11¼"

From the lime print, cut:

9 squares, 5½" x 5½"

From the teal print, cut:

6 squares, 5⅞" x 5⅞"

1 square, 6¼" x 6¼"

From the bright-pink print, cut:

6 strips, 2½" x 42"

From the pink-and-teal print, cut:

7 strips, 6½" x 42"

From the binding fabric, cut:

8 strips, 2½" x 42"

Making the Trip around the World Blocks

You can mix and match your strips as desired. Sew two blocks at a time and press the seam allowances open or to the side as you go.

1. Choose a set of four strips, including one 2½" x 21" strip and two squares of fabric A. As you select the other three strips, cut them in half by simply snipping along the center fold line. For two blocks, you'll need one half strip and two squares of fabric A, one whole strip cut in half for fabric B, one whole strip cut in half for fabric C, and one half strip for fabric D. Mark each strip with its designation of A, B, C, or D. As you sew the strips to each other, it's important not to get them mixed up.

A	B	C	B	A
B	C	D	C	B
C	D	A	D	C
B	C	D	C	B
A	B	C	B	A

Fabric placement guide

2. Make three strip sets as shown. Sew strip A to a strip B, sew a strip B to a strip C, and sew a strip C to strip D. Crosscut each strip set into eight segments, 2½" wide.

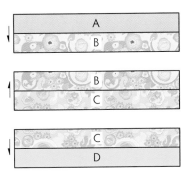

3 Using four of each of the segments and one 2½" square A, sew together into rows as shown. Join the rows. Press the seam allowances to one side. Repeat to make a second block.

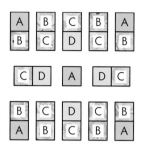

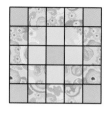

Make 2.

4 Repeat steps 1–3 using the remaining 2½" strips to make a total of 16 blocks.

Making the Alternate Blocks

1 Sew cream 3" x 5½" rectangles to opposite sides of a lime square; press the seam allowances open.

2 Sew a cream 3" x 10½" rectangle to each remaining side; press the seam allowances open. Repeat to make a total of nine setting blocks.

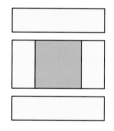

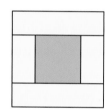

Setting block.
Make 9.

Making the Setting Triangles

1 Sew cream 3" x 5⅞" rectangles to opposite sides of a teal 5⅞" square; press the seam allowances open. Sew a 3" x 10⅞" rectangle to each remaining side; press the seam allowances open.

2 Draw a diagonal line from corner to corner through the center of your block. Stay stitch a scant ¼" from either side of the line. The long edges of the triangles will be cut along the bias and could easily stretch, distorting the edges of your quilt, but stay stitching before you cut the triangles will prevent this. Cut the block in half along the marked line.

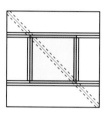
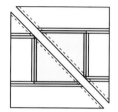

3 Repeat steps 1 and 2 with the remaining teal squares to make 12 side setting triangles total.

4 For the corner setting triangles, sew cream 3" x 6¼" rectangles to opposite sides of the teal 6¼" square; press the seam allowances open.

5 Sew a 3" x 11¼" rectangle to each remaining side; press the seam allowances open.

6 Draw diagonal lines from corner to corner through the center of your block. Stay stitch a scant ¼" outside the drawn lines as you did before. Cut the block into quarters diagonally to make four corner setting triangles.

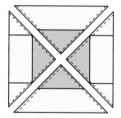

Assembling the Quilt Top

1 Sew the blocks and setting triangles together in diagonal rows as shown, and then sew the rows together. Press the seam allowances open.

2 Measure the length of the quilt through the center. Sew the bright-pink inner-border strips together end to end to make one long length. Cut two strips for the sides and sew them to the quilt. Press all seam allowances away from the center. Measure the width of the quilt through the center, cut two bright-pink strips, and add them to the top and bottom. Press.

3 Measure the quilt top; piece the pink-and-teal outer-border strips together, cut, and sew them to the quilt in the same manner as the inner border.

Finishing the Quilt

For help with any of the finishing steps, go to ShopMartingale.com/HowtoQuilt for free downloadable information.

1 Layer, baste, and quilt your quilt, or take it to your favorite long-arm quilter for finishing.

2 Using the 2½"-wide binding strips, make and attach binding.

Six Degrees South

The spinning stars in this quilt appear to be sending off jagged heat waves. It's super easy to piece, with nary a triangle to cut. To re-create it, use lots of light batiks for block backgrounds and hot colors for the stars.

"Six Degrees South," designed and pieced by Kim Brackett; quilted by Nancy Troyer

FINISHED QUILT: 49½" x 61½" • FINISHED BLOCK: 6" x 6"

Materials

Yardage is based on 42"-wide fabric, except where noted.

24 strips, 2½" x 42", of assorted light batiks for blocks

12 strips, 2½" x 42", of assorted dark batiks for blocks

1⅛ yards of multicolored batik for outer border

¾ yard of pink batik for inner border and binding

3½ yards of fabric for backing

54" x 66" piece of batting

Cutting

From *each* of the 24 assorted light-batik strips, cut:

4 rectangles, 2½" x 6½" (96 total)

2 rectangles, 2½" x 4½" (48 total)

From *each* of the 12 assorted dark-batik strips, cut:

4 rectangles, 2½" x 4½" (48 total)

8 squares, 2½" x 2½" (96 total)

From the pink batik, cut:

5 border strips, 1½" x 42"

6 binding strips, 2½" x 42"

From the multicolored batik, cut:

6 border strips, 6" x 42"

Cutting from Scraps

If you prefer to use scraps, follow the instructions below. See "Cutting" above for instructions on cutting the borders and binding.

From the assorted dark prints, cut:

48 rectangles, 2½" x 4½"

96 squares, 2½" x 2½"

From the assorted light prints, cut:

96 rectangles, 2½" x 6½"

48 rectangles, 2½" x 4½"

Piecing the Blocks

1 Layer a dark 2½" square right sides together on one end of a light 2½" x 6½" rectangle. Stitch diagonally from corner to corner of the square as shown. Trim the excess corner fabric, leaving a ¼" seam allowance. Press. Make 96.

Make 96.

2 Layer a dark 2½" x 4½" rectangle perpendicularly with a light 2½" x 4½" rectangle as shown, with right sides together and corner edges aligned. Stitch from corner to corner where the pieces intersect. Trim the excess fabric from the corner, leaving a ¼" seam allowance. Press the seam allowances toward the dark fabric. Make 48.

Make 48.

3 Sew two units from step 1 and one unit from step 2 together as shown. Press. Make a total of 48 blocks.

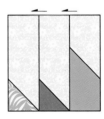

Make 48.

Assembling the Quilt Top

1 Arrange the blocks in eight horizontal rows of six blocks each, rotating the blocks as shown. Sew the blocks together in rows, pressing the seam allowances as shown. Join the rows. Press the seam allowances in the same direction.

2 Join the pink 1½"-wide strips end to end. Measure the length of the quilt top and from the long strip, cut two inner-border strips to this length. Sew the strips to the sides of the quilt. Measure the width of the quilt top and cut two inner-border strips to this length. Sew the strips to the top and bottom of the quilt. Press all seam allowances toward the borders.

3 In the same manner, use the multicolored 6"-wide strips to make and attach outer borders.

Finishing the Quilt

For help with any of the finishing steps, go to ShopMartingale.com/HowtoQuilt for free downloadable information.

1 Layer, baste, and quilt your quilt, or take it to your favorite long-arm quilter for finishing.

2 Using the pink 2½"-wide strips, make and attach binding.

Apple of My Eye

This quilt started out to be a Nine Patch, but when Sue realized she was short on fabric, she turned a potential problem into a new quilt block that is reminiscent of an apple core. With this darling design, one Jelly Roll plus a background fabric is enough to make a twin-size quilt.

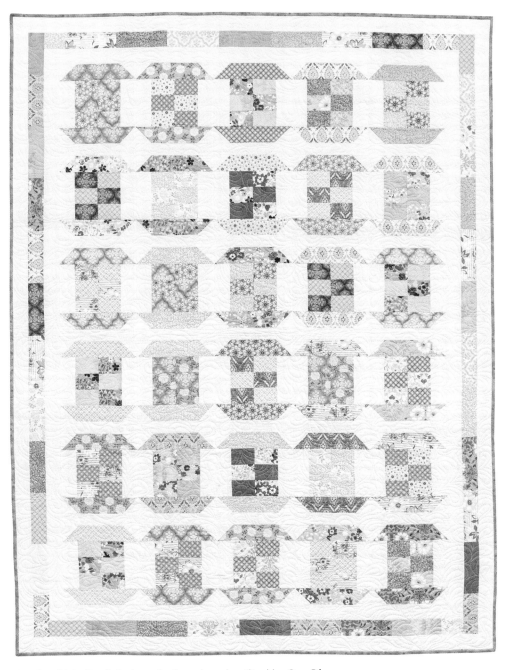

"Apple of My Eye," designed, pieced, and quilted by Sue Pfau

FINISHED QUILT: 62½" x 80" • FINISHED BLOCK: 10" x 10"

Materials

Yardage is based on 42"-wide fabric, except where noted.

40 assorted print strips, 2½" x 42", for blocks and pieced border*

3 yards of white fabric for blocks, sashing, and borders

⅔ yard of fabric for binding

5 yards of fabric for backing

69" x 86" piece of batting

Measure your strips before cutting to make sure they're at least 42" long after removing selvages.

Pick the Perfect Jelly Roll

This pattern requires most of the strips in a Jelly Roll bundle. You can use some light strips in the middle of your block, but you should pick a Jelly Roll that has mostly darks, mediums, or "busy" light strips for contrast with the background fabric.

Cutting

From the 2½"-wide strips, cut:

30 matching pairs of strips, 2½" x 10½" (60 total)

From the remaining strips and scraps, cut:

30 matching sets of 3 rectangles, 2½" x 7" (90 total)

42 rectangles, 2½" x 7"

From the white fabric, cut:

18 strips, 2½" x 42"; crosscut into:

    60 rectangles, 2½" x 6½"

    120 squares, 2½" x 2½"

15 strips, 2½" x 42"

7 strips, 2" x 42"

From the binding fabric, cut:

8 strips, 2½" x 42"

Piecing the Blocks

1 Choose two complementary sets of three matching 2½" x 7" rectangles. Sew them together to make two units as shown. Press the seam allowances toward the darker fabric. Cut the units into two 3½"-wide segments. Repeat for all 30 matching sets of 2½" x 7" rectangles. Keep the matching segments together.

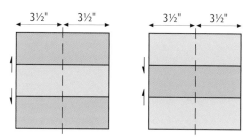

2 Sew the matching segments together as shown to make a total of 30 units.

Make 30.

3 Sew white 2½" x 6½" rectangles to opposite sides of the unit from step 2. Press the seam allowances toward the block unit.

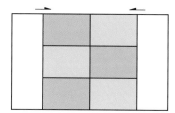

4 Draw a diagonal line from corner to corner on the wrong side of each white 2½" square. Place a marked square on each end of a 2½" x 10½" strip as shown, right sides together. Sew on the diagonal line.

Trim away the excess fabric in the corner, making sure the triangles are sewn on correctly before you trim them. Press the seam allowances toward the darker fabric.

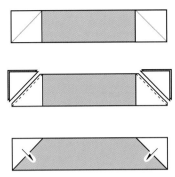

5 Sew matching strips from step 4 to the top and bottom of the block unit from step 3. Make sure the white triangles are on the outer corners. Press the seam allowances toward the strips. The block should measure 10½" square; trim if necessary. Make 30 blocks.

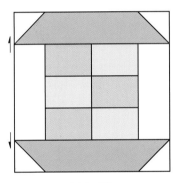

Make 30.

Block Magic!

Here's a cute—and easy—alternative to the Apple Core blocks. If you reverse the 2½" x 10½" strips when sewing them to the block, you'll have blocks that look like spools of variegated thread!

Assembling the Quilt Top

1 Arrange the blocks in six horizontal rows of five blocks each. Sew the blocks together into rows.

2 Join the white 2"-wide sashing strips end to end to make one long sashing strip. Make sure you use the strips that are 2" wide. Measure the lengths of the horizontal rows of blocks, determine the

average measurement, and cut five sashing strips to this length.

3 Place the 2"-wide sashing strips between each horizontal row and sew all of the rows together. Press the seam allowances toward the blocks.

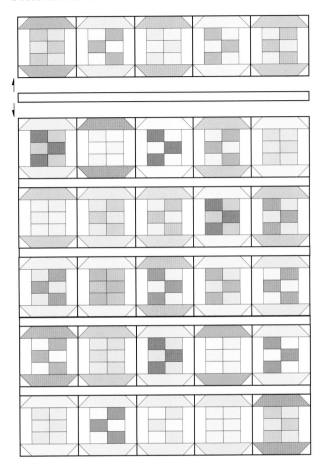

Adding the Borders

1 Join seven white 2½"-wide border strips end to end. Measure the width of the quilt through the center and trim two border strips to this length. Sew the strips to the top and bottom of the quilt. Press the seam allowances toward the quilt center.

2 Measuring the length of the quilt through the center, cut two border strips to this length and sew to the sides of the quilt. Press the seam allowances toward the quilt center.

3 Join nine 2½" x 7" rectangles end to end for the pieced border. Make two for the top and bottom of the quilt. Measure the width of the quilt through the center and trim the pieced strips equally from both ends to fit the width of the quilt. (For example, if you need to trim off 2", trim off 1" from each end.)

Sew to the top and bottom of the quilt. Press the seam allowances toward the pieced border.

Make 2.

4 Join twelve 2½" x 7" rectangles end to end. Make two for the side borders. Measure the length of the quilt through the center, including the borders just added. Trim the pieced strips equally from both ends to fit the length of the quilt. Sew to the sides of the quilt. Press the seam allowances toward the pieced border.

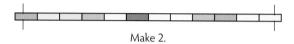

Make 2.

5 Join eight white 2½"-wide border strips end to end. Measure the width of the quilt through the

center and trim two border strips to this length. Sew the strips to the top and bottom of the quilt. Press the seam allowances toward the pieced border.

6 Measuring the length of the quilt through the center, cut two border strips to this length and sew to the sides of the quilt. Press the seam allowances toward the pieced border.

Finishing the Quilt

For help with any of the finishing steps, go to ShopMartingale.com/HowtoQuilt for free downloadable information.

1 Layer, baste, and quilt your quilt, or take it to your favorite long-arm quilter for finishing.

2 Using the 2½"-wide binding strips, make and attach binding.

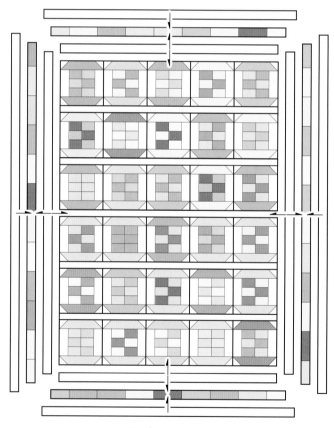

Quilt assembly

Garden Lattice

This complex-looking block with an interwoven component is actually quite easy to make. It uses one partial seam, which eliminates the need for set-in seams. And this project is perfect for using precut 2½" strips and 5" squares. You can make a very graphic quilt by using bolder prints, but pieced with floral prints in soft tones, the quilt calls to mind flowers climbing a garden trellis.

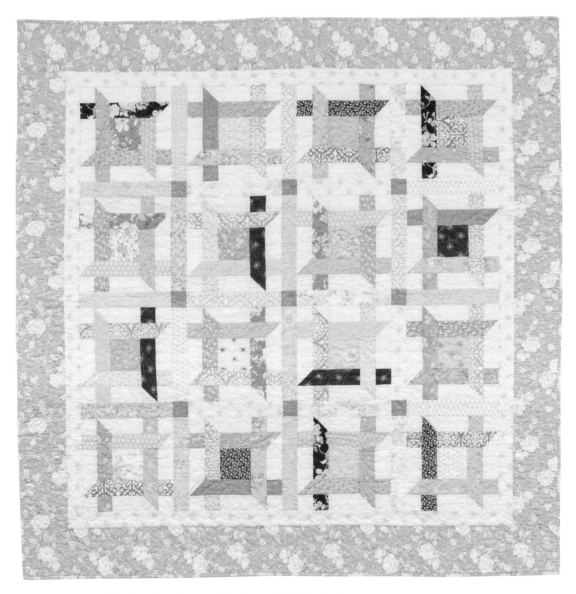

"Garden Lattice," designed and pieced by Karen Costello Soltys; machine quilted by Karen Burns of Compulsive Quilting

FINISHED QUILT: 70½" x 70½" • FINISHED BLOCK: 12" x 12"

Materials

Yardage is based on 42"-wide fabric, except where noted.

24 medium-value strips, 2½" x 42", for blocks
16 light- to medium-value squares, 5" x 5", for blocks
1 medium-value strip, 2½" x 42", for sashing squares
8 light strips, 2½" x 42", for sashing
2¼ yards of blue floral for outer border and binding
1⅓ yards of cream print for block backgrounds
½ yard of light print for inner border
4½ yards of fabric for backing
77" x 77" piece of batting

Sorting the Precut Fabrics

If you're using a Jelly Roll bundle, sort the strips into 24 medium strips for the blocks, one medium strip for sashing squares, and eight or more light strips for the sashing. Once you've selected the 24 medium strips for the blocks, further sort them into six batches of four strips each. Each group will be enough for three blocks; the key is to have an assortment of colors and prints in each group.

Cutting

From the cream print, cut:
16 strips, 2½" x 42"; crosscut into:
    64 rectangles, 2½" x 4½"
    128 squares, 2½" x 2½"
From *each* medium-value strip for blocks, cut:*
3 strips, 2½" x 8½"
3 squares, 2½" x 2½"
From the light- to medium-value 5" squares, cut:
16 squares, 4½" x 4½"
From the medium-value strip for sashing squares, cut:
9 squares, 2½" x 2½"
From *each* light strip, cut:
3 sashing strips, 2½" x 12½" (24 total)
From the light inner-border print, cut:
6 strips, 2½" x 42"
From the blue floral, cut on the *lengthwise* grain:
4 border strips, 6½" x length of fabric
4 binding strips, 2½" x length of fabric

*Each strip will make three blocks. You will have two extra pieces from the last group, which can be tossed in your scrap basket.

Piecing the Blocks

The instructions are written for making one block at a time. For each block, you'll need four 8½" strips and the four matching 2½" squares, one contrasting 4½" square, four cream 2½" x 4½" rectangles, and eight cream 2½" squares.

1 Place a cream square on the end of each 8½" strip, right sides together, and sew diagonally from corner to corner of the square as shown. Be sure to sew the angle in this direction for all strips so that the finished blocks will match those in the quilt shown.

2 Trim the excess corner fabric, leaving a ¼" seam allowance. Press the seam allowance toward the cream fabric to complete unit A.

Unit A.
Make 4 for each block.

3 Sew a cream 2½" x 4½" rectangle to one side of a colored 2½" square. Sew a cream 2½" square to the opposite side of the colored square to complete unit B. Press the seam allowances toward the cream fabric.

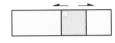

Unit B.
Make 4 for each block.

4 Lay out the pieces for one block on your sewing table. Make sure to arrange the fabrics so that the pointed ends of the colored strips appear as shown below and the units with the colored squares match up with the corresponding colored strip to complete the interwoven look.

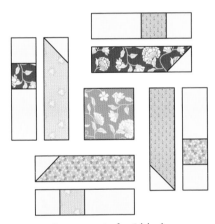

Arrange units for 1 block.

5 To assemble the block, it's easiest if you pick up one set of pieces at a time, stitch them together, and replace them in the block layout so that the colors don't become jumbled. First, sew each unit A to the unit B adjacent to it. Press the seam allowances toward the cream fabric.

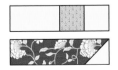 

Join unit A to unit B.

6 When all A/B units are joined, pin one of them to the 4½" center square. The A/B unit is clearly longer than the square. Simply align the end of the unit with the edge of the square as shown. Sew the unit to the square, starting at the aligned ends and stitching about 2" to 2½"; backstitch and clip the threads. Press the partial seam allowances away from the center square.

Sew partial seam.

7 Working in a counterclockwise manner, pick up the next A/B unit and stitch it to the center square unit. This time you'll be able to stitch a complete seam. Continue working your way around the block, pressing all seams away from the center square.

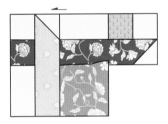

Sew complete seam.

8 After the last A/B unit has been joined, go back to the first one and complete the seam.

9 Repeat, first completing all blocks in the set of three. Then repeat all steps to make a total of 16 blocks.

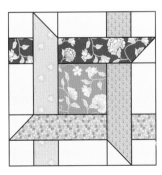

Make 16.

Easy Enlargement

The quilt shown measures 70" square, which makes a nice topper for a double or single bed, or a generous lap quilt or wall hanging. If you'd like to make a queen- or king-size bed quilt, you'll need one more Jelly Roll and charm pack. For a queen-size quilt, make 25 blocks and set them in five rows of five blocks each. For a king-size quilt, make 36 blocks set in a six-by-six arrangement. The extra Jelly Roll will also provide enough extra strips for the added sashing, but you'll need to increase the yardage for background fabric, borders, and backing.

Assembling the Quilt Top

1 Lay out the blocks in four rows of four blocks each, leaving space in between for sashing strips. Move the blocks around until you are satisfied with the color placement. Then add the scrappy light sashing strips, again moving them around until you're pleased with the balance. Add the sashing squares to the layout.

2 Sew the blocks and sashing pieces together in rows, and then sew the rows together. Press all seam allowances toward the sashing strips.

3 Cut two of the light inner-border strips in half and sew a half strip to each of the four remaining full-length strips. Measure the length of your quilt (it should be 54½"). Trim two of the inner-border strips to this length and sew them to opposite sides of the quilt. Measure the width of the quilt top (it should be 58½") and trim the remaining inner-border strips to this length. Sew them to the top and bottom of the quilt. Press all seam allowances toward the border.

4 Measure your quilt top and trim the blue-floral outer-border strips in the same manner. Sew them first to opposite sides of the quilt, followed by the top and bottom of the quilt. Press the seam allowances toward the outer border.

Finishing the Quilt

For help with any of the finishing steps, go to ShopMartingale.com/HowtoQuilt for free downloadable information.

1 Layer, baste, and quilt your quilt, or take it to your favorite long-arm quilter for finishing.

2 Using the blue-floral 2½"-wide strips, make and attach binding.

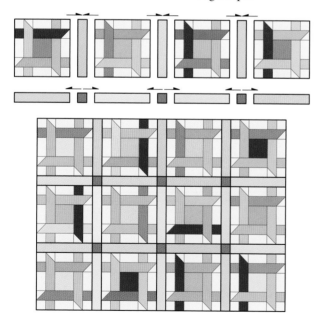

Sea Glass

For your piecing pleasure, here is a super-simple project that can be made with batiks or any style of light and dark fabrics. What fun to play around with this one! It's just as good as a walk on the beach. You could make a smaller version, with or without borders, for the perfect baby quilt.

"Sea Glass," designed and pieced by Kim Brackett; quilted by Nancy Troyer

FINISHED QUILT: 58¾" x 70" • FINISHED BLOCK: 4" x 4"

Materials

Yardage is based on 42"-wide fabric, except where noted.

22 strips, 2½" x 42", of assorted dark batiks in blue, green, and brown for blocks

18 strips, 2½" x 42", of assorted light batiks in blue, green, and tan for blocks

1⅓ yards of blue-and-green batik for outer border

½ yard of light blue-and-green batik for setting triangles

⅓ yard of brown batik for inner border

⅝ yard of blue-and-green batik for binding

4 yards of fabric for backing

63" x 74" piece of batting

Cutting

From *each of 10* dark batik strips, cut:

2 rectangles, 2½" x 4½" (20 total)

10 squares, 2½" x 2½" (100 total)

From *each of 12* dark batik strips, cut:

1 rectangle, 2½" x 4½" (12 total)

13 squares, 2½" x 2½" (156 total; 4 are extra)

From *each* of the 18 light batik strips, cut:

14 squares, 2½" x 2½" (252 total)

From the light blue-and-green batik, cut:

2 strips, 7" x 42"; crosscut into 9 squares, 7" x 7". Cut the squares into quarters diagonally to yield 36 quarter-square triangles.

From the brown batik, cut:

6 border strips, 1½" x 42"

From the blue-and-green batik, cut:

7 border strips, 6" x 42"

From the blue-and-green batik for binding, cut:

7 binding strips, 2½" x 42"

Piecing the Blocks

1 Select a pair of dark 2½" squares and a pair of light 2½" squares. Sew together one dark and one light 2½" square. Make two. Press the seam allowances toward the dark fabric. Sew the units together as shown to make a Four Patch block. Press the seam allowances in a clockwise direction. Make a total of 110 blocks.

Make 110.

2 Select a dark 2½" x 4½" rectangle, a matching 2½" square, and a light 2½" square. Sew the dark square to the light square. Press the seam allowances toward the light square. Sew the dark rectangle to the top of the unit as shown to make a Three Patch block. Press the seam allowances toward the dark rectangle. Make a total of 32 blocks.

Make 32.

Assembling the Quilt Top

1 Arrange the Four Patch blocks, Three Patch blocks, and light blue-and-green setting triangles in diagonal rows as shown. Sew the blocks together in diagonal rows, pressing the seam allowances as shown. Join the rows. Press the seam allowances in the same direction.

2 To add the borders with mitered corners, measure the length and width of your quilt top. Add 7" to each of those lengths. Sew the brown 1½"-wide strips together end to end, and cut two strips to each of your calculated lengths.

3 Sew the two side inner borders to the quilt top, matching center points. The border strips will extend beyond each end of the quilt; stop sewing ¼" from each end of the quilt top and backstitch.

Repeat to sew the top and bottom inner-border strips to the quilt top. Miter each corner, referring to ShopMartingale.com/HowtoQuilt if you need more detailed information.

4 Repeat steps 2 and 3 with the blue-and-green 6"-wide strips to add the outer border and miter the corners.

Finishing the Quilt

For help with any of the finishing steps, go to ShopMartingale.com/HowtoQuilt for free downloadable information.

1 Layer, baste, and quilt your quilt, or take it to your favorite long-arm quilter for finishing.

2 Using the blue-and-green 2½"-wide strips, make and attach binding.

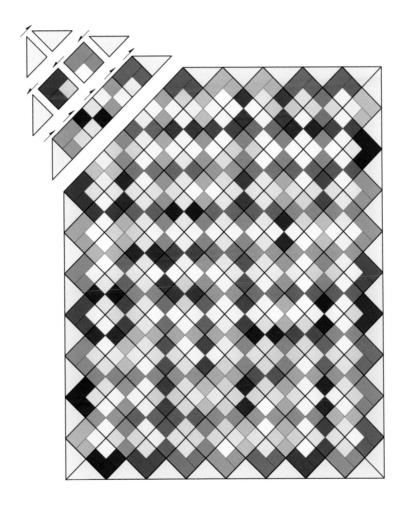

Winterberry

Mary had long been intrigued by the Leavenworth Nine Patch block. This project presented the perfect opportunity to see what she could do with it. Finding enough combinations of contrasting fabrics in a Jelly Roll can be a challenge, but the results are worth it.

"Winterberry," designed and pieced by Mary Green;
machine quilted by Karen Burns of Compulsive Quilting

FINISHED QUILT: 70" x 90" • FINISHED BLOCK: 14" x 14"

Materials

Yardage is based on 42"-wide fabric, except where noted.

17 matching pairs of strips, 2½" x 42", for color A*

10 matching pairs of strips, 2½" x 42", for color B

7 assorted strips, 2½" x 42", for color C

14 strips, 2½" x 42", of assorted prints for partial blocks

3 yards of blue print for side setting triangles, corner setting triangles, border, and binding

5½ yards of fabric for backing

77" x 97" piece of batting

*This gives you enough strips so that color A in each block will be different. If you use the remainder of these strips in the partial blocks, you won't need as many strips of assorted prints. If you want to use precut strips, you'll need 2 matching Jelly Rolls.

Sorting the Precut Fabrics

You will need three contrasting fabrics for each of the blocks and for each of the partial blocks used as setting pieces. The fabrics should have good contrast in value (dark, medium, and light) or in color. For each block, choose three colors and designate them color A, color B, and color C. Color A for the full block requires approximately 1⅓ strips, so choose these first. Choose color B next; it requires 1 strip plus about 5" of another strip. Use the leftover partial strips for color C and in the partial blocks.

Cutting

For *each* of the 17 blocks, cut:

Color A:

6 rectangles, 2½" x 6½"

2 rectangles, 2½" x 4½"

2 squares, 2½" x 2½"

Color B:

6 rectangles, 2½" x 4½"

7 squares, 2½" x 2½"

Color C:

6 squares, 2½" x 2½"

For *each* of the 14 partial blocks, cut:

Color A:

2 rectangles, 2½" x 6½"

1 square, 2½" x 2½"

Color B:

2 squares, 2½" x 2½"

Color C:

2 rectangles, 2½" x 4½"

3 squares, 2½" x 2½"

For the remainder of the quilt, cut:

Blue print:

2 strips, 12¾" x 42"; cut into 5 squares, 12¾" x 12¾". Cut into quarters diagonally to make 20 triangles.

2 squares, 12¼" x 12¼"; cut in half diagonally to make 4 triangles

8 strips, 4½" x 42"

9 strips, 2½" x 42"

Piecing the Blocks

These instructions are written for making one block at a time. Working this way will help you keep the pieces organized. Be sure to follow the diagrams for each step, taking care to orient the pieces correctly. Mary found that it was easy to get the pieces turned the wrong way.

1 Sew color B and C 2½" squares together into pairs. Press the seam allowances toward the darker squares. Set two of the pairs aside for now and sew the remaining pairs into four-patch units.

Make 2.

2 Add a color B 2½" x 4½" rectangle to each four-patch unit as shown. Press the seam allowances toward the rectangle.

Make 2.

3 Sew a color A 2½" square to a color B 2½" x 4½" rectangle; press the seam allowances toward the rectangle. Make two. Sew these units to the step 2 units as shown to complete the diagonal units.

Diagonal unit.
Make 2.

4 Sew a color B 2½" x 4½" rectangle to each remaining step 1 pair. Press the seam allowances toward the rectangle. Add a color A 2½" x 4½" rectangle to each unit as shown. Press toward the rectangle.

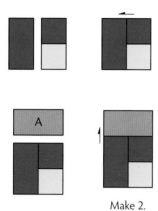

Make 2.

5 Sew a color A 2½" x 6½" rectangle to each step 4 unit. Press the seam allowances toward the rectangle to complete the corner units.

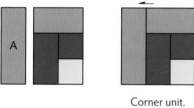

Corner unit.
Make 2.

6 Sew the diagonal units, corner units, and color A 2½" x 6½" rectangles together in rows as shown. Make sure the diagonal units are positioned correctly, with the A squares on the outside corners. Press the seam allowances toward the rectangles. Sew a color A 2½" x 6½" rectangle to each side of the remaining color B 2½" square; press the seam allowances toward the rectangles. Join the rows. Make 17 blocks.

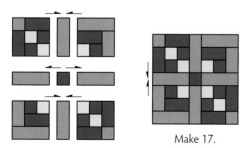

Make 17.

Piecing the Setting Triangles

Partial blocks are used to make pieced setting triangles.

1 The partial blocks consist of the diagonal unit from the main block and are used to fill in the sides and corners in the on-point layout. Refer to steps 1 through 3 of "Piecing the Blocks" on page 221 to make 14 diagonal units. (In step 1, make only the four-patch units.)

2 Add the color A 2½" x 6½" rectangles and the color C square as shown to complete the partial blocks.

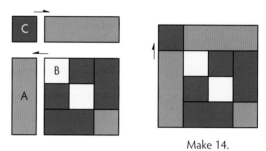

Make 14.

3 To make the side setting triangles, sew blue 12¾" quarter-square triangles to two adjacent sides of a partial block as shown. Press the seam allowances toward the triangles. Make six of these units.

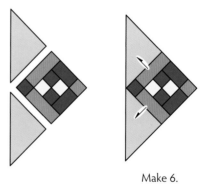

Make 6.

Setting Triangles

Some of the block corners blend into the light blue of the pieced setting triangles. Mary liked the randomness of this effect, so she left it that way. If you want all the points to stand out against the background, choose fabrics with strong contrast for the C position in the partial blocks.

4 To make the corner setting triangles, join two partial blocks, taking care to position them as shown. Add a blue 12¾" quarter-square triangle to each short side. Press the seam allowances toward the triangles. Add a blue 12¼" half-square triangle to the long side; press the seam allowances toward the triangle. Make four of these units.

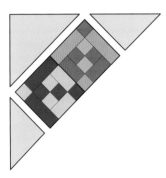

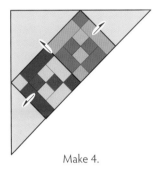

Make 4.

Assembling the Quilt Top

1 Arrange the blocks in diagonal rows, referring to the quilt assembly diagram above right for correct block orientation. The blocks are rotated from row to row so that the diagonal units and corner units match up to the same units in adjacent blocks. Position the side and corner setting triangles around the blocks. Join the blocks into rows, pressing the seam allowances in alternate directions from row to row. Add the corners last. Note that due to the way the block pieces were pressed, some adjoining seam allowances will face the same direction rather than nestle together in opposite directions. You can re-press one of the seams if you wish, or simply pin carefully to ensure accurate intersections.

2 Sew the blue 4½" x 42" strips together end to end. Measure the width of the quilt top through the center, cut two strips to this measurement, and sew them to the top and bottom edges of the quilt.

Press all seam allowances toward the borders. Measure the length of the quilt top through the center, cut two strips to this measurement, and add them to the sides of the quilt. Press.

Showcase Your Quilting

Using the same fabric for the setting triangles and the border results in lots of open area for quilting. In the quilt shown, Karen filled the space beautifully with lavish feathers. The soft, curvy lines of stitches are a nice contrast to all the straight lines in the blocks.

Finishing the Quilt

For help with any of the finishing steps, go to ShopMartingale.com/HowtoQuilt for free downloadable information.

1 Layer, baste, and quilt your quilt, or take it to your favorite long-arm quilter for finishing.

2 Using the blue 2½"-wide strips, make and attach binding.

Boxing Day

"Boxing Day" is a great pattern to use up all of your leftover strips from other projects. This design is reminiscent of pretty little presents or boxes all wrapped up for a gift exchange. Each block uses just two fabrics—the light and dark versions of the block alternate to form a pleasing overall design.

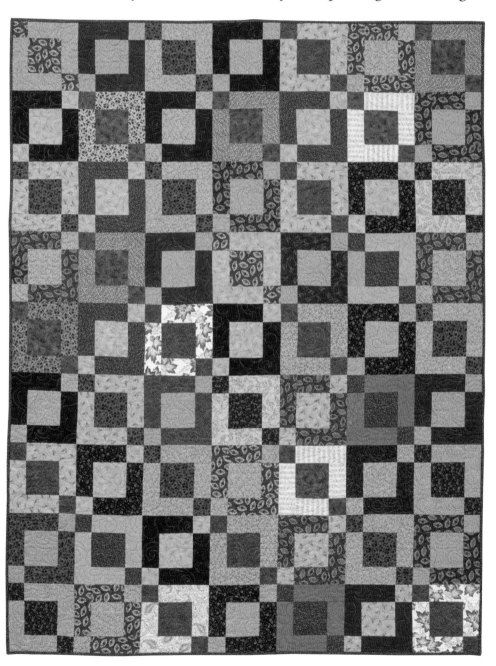

"Boxing Day," designed and pieced by Nancy J. Martin; quilted by Shelly Nolte

FINISHED QUILT: 56½" x 72½" • FINISHED BLOCK: 8" x 8"

Materials

Yardage is based on 42"-wide fabric, except where noted. Strips must be at least 22" long after squaring up the ends and removing selvages.

32 strips, 2½" x 22", of light prints for blocks

31 strips, 2½" x 22", of dark prints for blocks

1 fat quarter *each* of 4 light prints for block centers and corners

1 fat quarter *each* of 4 dark prints for block centers and corners

½ yard of dark print for binding

3⅞ yards of fabric for backing

65" x 81" piece of batting

Cutting

From *each* of the 32 light strips and 31 dark strips, cut:

2 rectangles, 2½" x 6½" (64 light and 62 dark total)

2 rectangles, 2½" x 4½" (64 light and 62 dark total)

From *each* of the light and dark fat quarters, cut:

8 squares, 4½" x 4½" (64 total)

16 squares, 2½" x 2½" (128 total)

From the dark print for binding, cut:

7 strips, 2¼" x 42"

Piecing the Blocks

You'll make two color combinations of this block: blocks with light centers and dark edges and blocks with dark centers and light edges. Pair up your fabrics, choosing one light and one dark for each block.

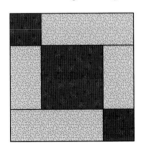 

1. Stitch a light 2½" x 4½" rectangle to each side of a dark 4½" square.

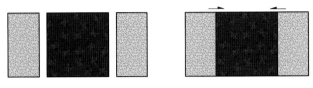

2. Stitch a dark 2½" square to a light 2½" x 6½" rectangle. Make two.

Make 2.

3. Join the units from step 2 to the top and bottom of the unit from step 1. Make sure the dark squares are in opposite diagonal corners. Make 32 blocks with dark centers and light strips on the outside edges.

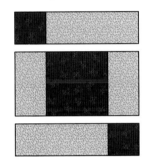 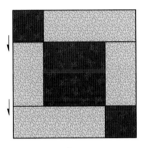

Make 32.

4. Reversing value placement, repeat to make 31 blocks with light centers and dark strips on the outside edges.

Make 31.

Assembling the Quilt Top

1 Arrange and sew the blocks into nine rows of seven blocks each, alternating the blocks with the light and dark outside edges. The four corners of the quilt should all have blocks with light outer edges. Press the seam allowances toward the blocks with dark outer edges.

2 Join the rows, matching seams. Press.

Finishing the Quilt

For help with any of the finishing steps, go to ShopMartingale.com/HowtoQuilt for free downloadable information.

1 Layer, baste, and quilt your quilt, or take it to your favorite long-arm quilter for finishing.

2 Using the dark 2¼"-wide strips, make and attach binding.

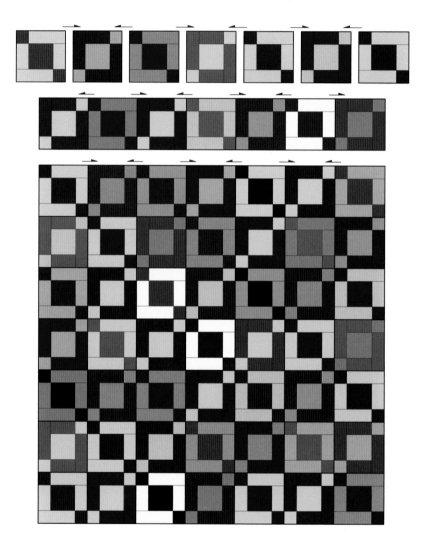

Scrap-Basket Trail

Don't be intimidated by this rather complex-looking quilt. Each block is composed of 10 easy split units, making it very simple and quick to piece. The colors and prints used in the rectangular blocks give it the look of an antique strippy quilt, but the design would be just as wonderful made in bright, contemporary prints or soft pastels.

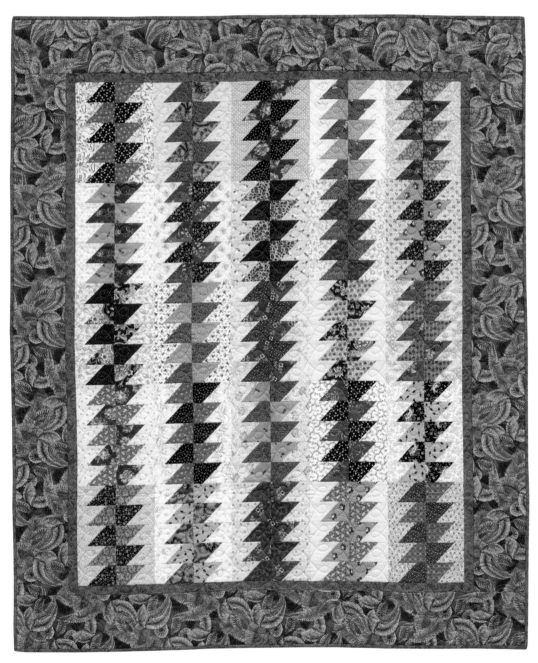

"Scrap-Basket Trail," designed and pieced by Kim Brackett; quilted by Nancy Troyer

FINISHED QUILT: 53½" x 63½" • FINISHED BLOCK: 8" x 10"

Materials

Yardage is based on 42"-wide fabric, except where noted.

25 strips, 2½" x 42", of assorted medium-dark to dark prints in red, blue, green, brown, black, and gold for blocks

25 strips, 2½" x 42", of assorted light prints for blocks

1⅛ yards of large-scale floral for outer border

⅞ yard of brown tone on tone for inner border and binding

3¾ yards of fabric for backing

58" x 68" piece of batting

Cutting

From *each* of the 25 medium-dark to dark and 25 light print strips, cut:

10 rectangles, 2½" x 3½" (250 total medium-dark to dark rectangles; 250 total light rectangles)

From the brown tone on tone, cut:

5 border strips, 1½" x 42"

7 binding strips, 2½" x 42"

From the large-scale floral, cut:

6 border strips, 6" x 42"

Cutting from Scraps

If you prefer to use scraps, follow the instructions below. See "Cutting" above for instructions on cutting the borders and binding.

From the assorted medium-dark to dark prints, cut:

50 sets of 5 rectangles, 2½" x 3½"

From the assorted light prints, cut:

25 sets of 10 rectangles, 2½" x 3½"

Piecing the Blocks

1 Select 10 matching light 2½" x 3½" rectangles and two different sets of five matching medium-dark and dark 2½" x 3½" rectangles. Make a split unit as shown by placing a light rectangle perpendicularly on the dark rectangle, right sides together and with corners aligned. Stitch from corner to corner where the pieces overlap. Trim the extra fabric from the corner, leaving a ¼" seam allowance. Press the seam allowances toward the dark fabric. Make five split units of each combination.

Make 5.

Make 5.

2 Beginning with the darker of the split units, sew five units together as shown to make the left half of the block, alternating the split units. Press the seam allowances toward the bottom of the half block. To make the right half of the block, start with the lighter of the split units at the top and alternate the colors. Press the seam allowances toward the bottom of the half block.

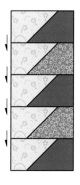 

3 Rotate the right half of the block so that the light fabric is on the outside edge and the seam allowances of the two halves oppose each other. Sew the two halves together. Press the seam allowances toward the right side of the block.

  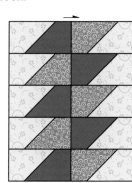

Rotate this half of the block.

4 Repeat steps 1–3 to make a total of 25 blocks.

Assembling the Quilt Top

1 Arrange the blocks in five horizontal rows of five blocks each as shown. Rotate the blocks in the second and fourth rows 180° so that the dark and medium-dark fabrics are staggered, and the center seam allowances in these rows face toward the left. Sew the blocks together in rows, pressing the seam allowances in alternating directions from row to row. Join the rows. Press the seam allowances in the same direction.

2 Measure the quilt top and piece and trim the brown 1½"-wide inner-border strips to fit. Sew the side borders on first, followed by the top and bottom borders. Repeat to add the floral 6"-wide outer-border strips. Press all seam allowances toward the just-added border.

Finishing the Quilt

For help with any of the finishing steps, go to ShopMartingale.com/HowtoQuilt for free downloadable information.

1 Layer, baste, and quilt your quilt, or take it to your favorite long-arm quilter for finishing.

2 Using the brown tone-on-tone 2½"-wide strips, make and attach binding.

Scrappy Hunter's Star

Hunter's Star is a traditional quilt-block pattern in which the stars emerge only when the blocks are set together. Typically, this pattern is made from just two or three fabrics, but using precut strips and squares lets you speed up the cutting for this striking scrappy version.

"Scrappy Hunter's Star," designed and pieced by Regina Girard;
quilted by Karen Burns of Compulsive Quilting

FINISHED QUILT: 75½" x 75½" • FINISHED BLOCK: 8½" x 8½"

Materials

Yardage is based on 42"-wide fabric, except where noted.

1 strip, 2½" x 42", and 1 matching 10" x 10" square *each* of 18 assorted light prints for blocks, pieced borders, and scrappy binding*

1 strip, 2½" x 42", and 1 matching 10" x 10" square *each* of 18 assorted dark prints for blocks, pieced borders, and scrappy binding*

2⅓ yards of green poppy print for outer border

5¼ yards of fabric for backing, or 2½ yards of 108"-wide backing fabric

82" x 82" piece of batting

Template plastic

*If you prefer to use precuts, you'll need 1 Jelly Roll for blocks and binding and 1 matching Layer Cake for blocks and pieced borders.

Choosing Fabrics

Make sure that the collection of fabrics you choose has good contrast and that most of the fabrics will read as solid in the finished quilt. You need an equal number of lights and darks for this pattern. Some medium-value fabrics can be used as either lights or darks depending on which fabrics they're paired with, but it's good to start out with primarily light and dark fabrics so that the stars will stand out.

Sorting the Precut Fabrics

1 Pair your 2½" strips with the coordinating 10" fabric squares.

2 Sort these pairs into three groups: lights, mediums, and darks.

3 Combine fabrics into pairs—one light fabric set with a dark fabric set. Mediums can be used for either light or dark depending upon the fabric that they're matched with. Each pair of fabrics will make two identical blocks.

4 If you're starting with a 40-fabric Jelly Roll and Layer Cake, choose 36 of the fabrics, leaving out four fabrics. You can accomplish this by eliminating

colors that don't fit with the rest, prints that you don't care for, or prints that are too large in scale to read as a single color. Just be sure that in the end you have an even number of lights and darks.

Cutting

To make it easier to keep the block pieces organized, cut the pieces for each block from the two fabrics and set them aside before cutting the next block. The patterns for cutting templates A and B are on page 234. Make one of each from template plastic. Refer to the cutting guide below when cutting the A and B pieces.

From each 2½" fabric strip, cut:

2 A pieces

4 B pieces

Save the leftovers from the strips for the scrappy binding.

From each 10" square, cut:

1 rectangle, 7" x 10"; trim to 7" x 7" square. Cut in half diagonally to make 2 triangles.

Save the remaining 3" x 10" and 3" x 7" strips for the pieced inner and middle borders.

From the green poppy print, cut from the *lengthwise* grain:

2 strips, 7½" x 61½"

2 strips, 7½" x 75½"

Cutting guide

Piecing the Blocks

1 Use a ruler or a point-trimming tool to trim the points off the A pieces as shown, trimming ¼" from the point. Do not trim points from the B pieces.

2 Arrange one dark A piece and two light B pieces as shown for one block.

3 Flip one of the light B pieces over on top of the dark A piece, right sides together and aligned as shown. The triangle tip should extend ¼" beyond piece A. Sew together.

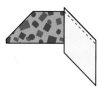

4 Attach the other light B piece to the opposite end of the unit in the same manner. Press the seam allowances toward the dark fabric.

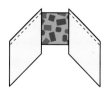
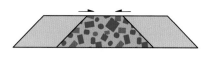

5 Repeat steps 2–4 with the light A piece and two dark B pieces for the same block. Press seam allowances toward the dark fabric.

6 Sew a triangle to the short edge of each star-point unit made in steps 2–5, matching the triangle fabric to the center fabric of the star-point units. Don't worry if your edges don't match at this stage; the triangles are cut oversized and will be trimmed later. For a dark triangle, press the seam allowances toward the triangle; for a light triangle, press the seam allowances toward the star-point units.

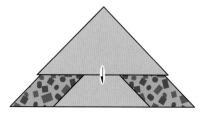
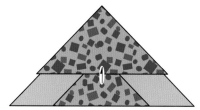

7 Sew the resulting triangle units together to create the block, being sure that the seam intersections of the A and B pieces match. Butt the seams together

and use a pin to align the points if desired. You will make two blocks from each set of light and dark fabrics for a total of 36 blocks. Press the seam allowances toward the star-point unit with the dark fabric in the center.

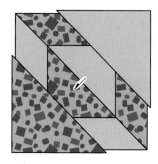

Trimming the Blocks

You'll need to trim each block to 9" x 9". Use a large square ruler with a line on the 45° diagonal and trim all four sides of the block to make sure your star points are the same length.

1 Line up the diagonal line on the ruler with the diagonal seam of the block. The inner point of opposite star points should be 2¼" from the edges of the block.

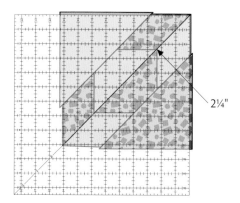

2 Trim the right and top edges of the block.

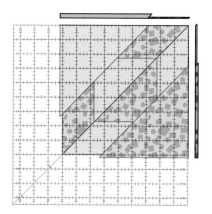

3 Rotate the block 180°, align the ruler with the block in the same way, and trim the right and top edges of the block to make it 9" square.

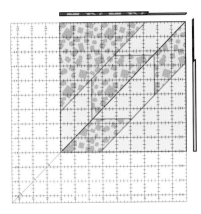

4 Repeat steps 1–3 to trim all 36 blocks.

Assembling the Quilt Top

1 Arrange the blocks in six horizontal rows of six blocks each, alternating the placement of the light and dark star points as shown to create the stars.

2 Sew the blocks into rows and press the seam allowances open. Sew the rows together; press the seam allowances open. The quilt center should measure 51½" x 51½".

3 If necessary, trim the remaining 7"- and 10"-long strips cut from the 10" squares so that they're exactly 3" wide.

4 Referring to the assembly diagram, arrange and sew three light 10" strips and four dark 7" strips together, alternating them as shown for the inner side borders. Make two and press the seam allowances toward the dark fabrics. Trim to 51½" long and sew to the sides of the quilt. Repeat for the top and bottom borders using four light 10" strips and three dark 7" strips for each. Trim to 56½" and sew to the top and bottom of the quilt. Press seam allowances toward the border.

5 For the middle side borders, piece together three light 7" strips and four dark 10" strips, alternating them as before; press the seam allowances toward the dark fabrics. Make two, trim to 56½", and sew to the sides of the quilt. Repeat for the top and bottom borders, sewing four light 7" strips and four dark 10" strips together for each border. Press and trim to 61½". Sew to the top and bottom of the quilt.

6 Attach the poppy-print 61½" outer-border strips to the sides and the 75½" strips to the top and bottom of the quilt. Press the seam allowances toward the outer border.

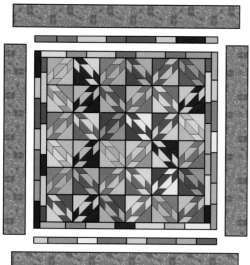

Finishing the Quilt

For help with any of the finishing steps, go to ShopMartingale.com/HowtoQuilt for free downloadable information.

1 Layer, baste, and quilt your quilt, or take it to your favorite long-arm quilter for finishing.

2 Trim the ends of 22 of the leftover 2½"-wide strips to 45°; all of the ends should be trimmed with the angles facing in the same direction. Sew the strips together to create a scrappy binding that's approximately 314" long. Use this strip to make and attach binding.

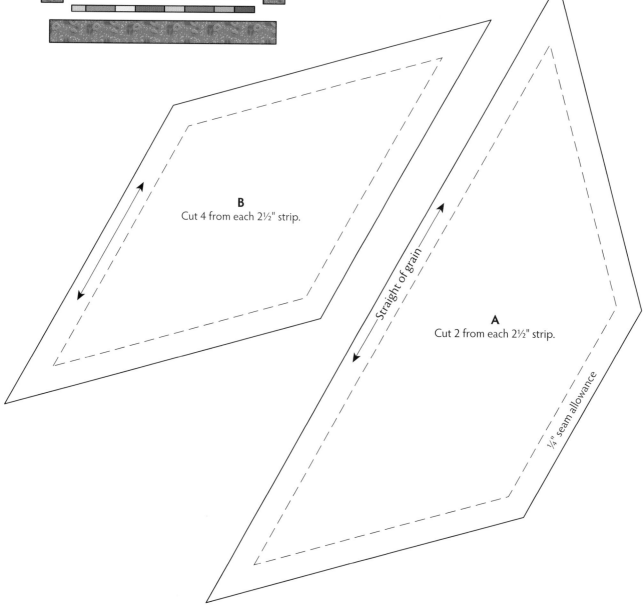

B
Cut 4 from each 2½" strip.

Straight of grain

A
Cut 2 from each 2½" strip.

¼" seam allowance

Barn Raising

Simple squares and triangles form a light and dark design area in each block. Rotating the blocks as you would do for a Log Cabin quilt creates bands of color that form this Barn Raising design. You can also set the blocks in many other ways, as you would typical Log Cabin blocks.

"Barn Raising," designed and pieced by Nancy J. Martin; quilted by Wanda Rains

FINISHED QUILT: 52" x 72" • FINISHED BLOCK: 10" x 10"

Materials

Yardage is based on 42"-wide fabric, except where noted.

30 strips, 2½" x 22", of assorted light prints for blocks

30 strips, 2½" x 22", of assorted dark prints for blocks

14 strips, 2½" x 22", of assorted dark-red prints for block accents and inner border

¼ yard *each* of 4 light fabrics for blocks

¼ yard *each* of 4 dark fabrics for blocks

1 yard of medium print for outer border

½ yard of fabric for binding

3½ yards of fabric for backing

60" x 80" piece of batting

Cutting

From *3* of the light strips, cut:
24 squares, 2½" x 2½"
From *3* of the dark strips, cut:
24 squares, 2½" x 2½"
From the dark-red accent strips, cut:
24 squares, 2½" x 2½"
11 strips, 1½" x 22"
From *each* of the 4 light fabrics, cut:
1 strip, 3" x 42"; crosscut into 12 squares, 3" x 3" (48 total)
From *each* of the 4 dark fabrics, cut:
1 strip, 3" x 42"; crosscut into 12 squares, 3" x 3" (48 total)
From the medium print, cut:
6 strips, 5¼" x 42"
From the binding fabric, cut:
7 strips, 2¼" x 42"

Piecing the Blocks

1 Using the light 2½" x 22" strips and following the illustrations below, sew three strip sets in each combination to make the units for the blocks. Cut each strip set into eight segments, 2½" wide, for a total of 24 segments from each combination.

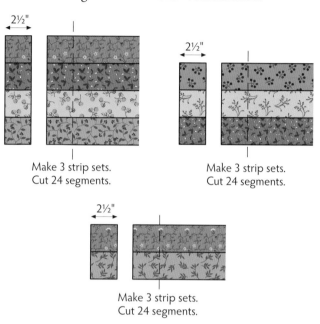

Make 3 strip sets.
Cut 24 segments.

Make 3 strip sets.
Cut 24 segments.

Make 3 strip sets.
Cut 24 segments.

2 Using the dark 2½" x 22" strips, repeat step 1. Cut each strip set into eight segments, 2½" wide, for a total of 24 segments from each combination.

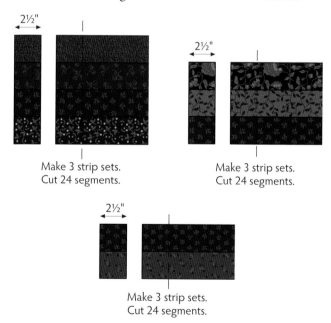

Make 3 strip sets.
Cut 24 segments.

Make 3 strip sets.
Cut 24 segments.

Make 3 strip sets.
Cut 24 segments.

3 Layer a light 3" square with a dark 3" square, right sides together. Mark a diagonal line on the wrong side of the light square from corner to corner. Stitch ¼" from each side of the marked line and then cut apart on the line. Press the resulting half-square-triangle units open. Repeat with all light and dark 3" squares to make a total of 96 units. Trim the completed units to 2½" x 2½".

2½"

Cut 96.

4 Sew the light and dark units, half-square-triangle units, and accent squares into rows. Stitch the rows together to make a block. Make 24 blocks.

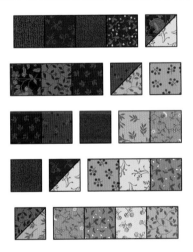

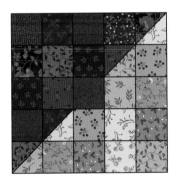

Make 24.

Assembling the Quilt Top

1 Arrange the blocks into six rows of four blocks each, rotating them as shown. Sew blocks together in rows, pressing in opposite directions from row to row. Join the rows to make the quilt top.

2 Join the dark-red 1½"-wide strips end to end. Measure your quilt top and trim the strips to fit to add the inner border.

3 Add the medium-print 5¼"-wide strips in the same manner for the outer border.

Finishing the Quilt

For help with any of the finishing steps, go to ShopMartingale.com/HowtoQuilt for free downloadable information.

1 Layer, baste, and quilt your quilt, or take it to your favorite long-arm quilter for finishing.

2 Using the 2¼"-wide binding strips, make and attach binding.

Generations

You can use the last tiny bits of your favorite fabrics in this scrappy quilt. Use high-contrast light and dark fabrics to make sure the design doesn't become lost. Or use a single background fabric for even more definition.

"Generations," designed and pieced by Kim Brackett; quilted by Nancy Troyer

FINISHED QUILT: 59½" x 75½" • FINISHED BLOCK: 6" x 6"

Materials

Yardage is based on 42"-wide fabric, except where noted.

26 strips, 2½" x 42", of assorted dark prints in red, blue, brown, green, gold, and black for blocks and sashing

28 strips, 2½" x 42", of assorted light prints in tan, beige, and cream for blocks and sashing

1⅓ yards of blue print for outer border

1 yard of brown print for inner border and binding

4¼ yards of fabric for backing

64" x 80" piece of batting

Cutting

From *each of 18* assorted dark print strips, cut:

4 rectangles, 2½" x 4½" (72 total)

8 squares, 2½" x 2½" (144 total)

From *each of 8* assorted dark print strips, cut:

3 rectangles, 2½" x 4½" (24 total)

10 squares, 2½" x 2½" (80 total; 5 are extra)

From *each of 21* assorted light print strips, cut:

3 rectangles, 2½" x 6½" (63 total)

2 rectangles, 2½" x 4½" (42 total)

4 squares, 2½" x 2½" (84 total)

From *each of 7* assorted light print strips, cut:

3 rectangles, 2½" x 6½" (21 total; 2 are extra)

1 rectangle, 2½" x 4½" (7 total; 1 is extra)

5 squares, 2½" x 2½" (35 total; 5 are extra)

From the brown print, cut:

6 border strips, 1½" x 42"

8 binding strips, 2½" x 42"

From the blue print, cut:

7 border strips, 6" x 42"

Cutting from Scraps

If you prefer to use scraps, follow the instructions below. See "Cutting" above for instructions on cutting the borders and binding.

From the assorted dark prints, cut:

96 rectangles, 2½" x 4½"

219 squares, 2½" x 2½"

From the assorted light prints, cut:

82 rectangles, 2½" x 6½"

48 rectangles, 2½" x 4½"

114 squares, 2½" x 2½"

Piecing the Blocks

1 Sew a dark 2½" x 4½" rectangle to a light 2½" square. Press the seam allowances toward the dark rectangle. Make two.

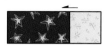

Make 2.

2 Sew a light 2½" x 4½" rectangle to a dark 2½" square. Press the seam allowances toward the light rectangle.

Make 1.

3 Sew the units from steps 1 and 2 together as shown to make the block. Press the seam allowances toward the unit from step 2. Make a total of 48 blocks.

Make 48.

Making the Sashing

1 Make a folded-corner unit as shown by sewing a dark 2½" square to a light 2½" x 6½" rectangle along the diagonal of the square. Trim the excess fabric from the corner, leaving a ¼" seam allowance, and press the unit open. Make 10.

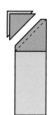 

Make 10.

2 Make a folded-corner unit as shown using a light 2½" x 6½" rectangle and two dark 2½" squares. Press. Make 72.

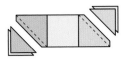

Make 72.

Assembling the Quilt Top

1 Arrange the blocks, pieced sashing units, and remaining light and dark 2½" squares in rows as shown. Sew the units together in horizontal rows, pressing the seam allowances as shown. Join the rows. Press the seam allowances toward the sashing rows.

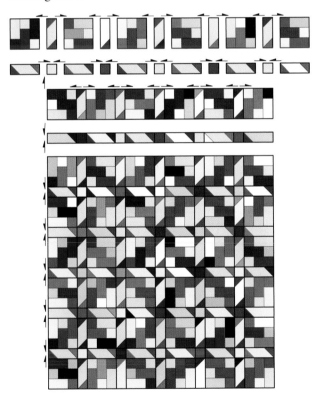

2 Join the brown 1½"-wide strips end to end. Measure the quilt top and cut two inner side borders to this length. Sew them to the quilt top. Measure the width of the quilt top, cut two border strips to this length, and add them to the top and bottom of the quilt top. Press all seam allowances toward the borders.

3 Repeat step 2 to add the blue 6"-wide outer border.

Finishing the Quilt

For help with any of the finishing steps, go to ShopMartingale.com/HowtoQuilt for free down-loadable information.

1 Layer, baste, and quilt your quilt, or take it to your favorite long-arm quilter for finishing.

2 Using the brown 2½"-wide strips, make and attach binding.

Whoo's Your Baby?

These little hoot owls will make a colorful addition to a nursery and will be just as popular with your baby when he or she is old enough to toddle around dragging along this lovable quilt. What's more, you're sure to have fun making this incredibly easy project.

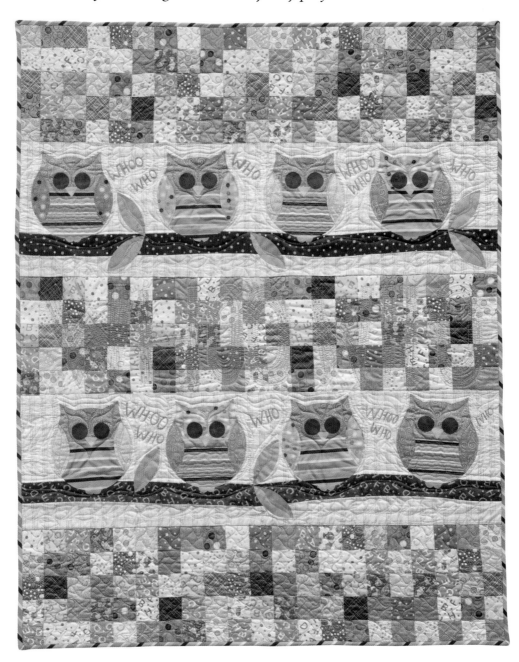

"Whoo's Your Baby?," designed, pieced, and machine appliquéd by Karen Costello Soltys; machine quilted by Karen Burns of Compulsive Quilting

FINISHED QUILT: 42" x 54"

Materials

Yardage is based on 42"-wide fabric, except where noted.

20 strips, 2½" x 42", of assorted light, medium, and dark prints for patchwork rows*

2 brown strips, 2½" x 42", for branches*

Assorted scraps for leaves, eyes, beaks, and feet*

¾ yard of light plaid for appliqué panels

¼ yard (or fat quarter) each of blue, red, green, and yellow fabrics for owl head and wing appliqués

¾ yard of striped fabric for owl body appliqués and bias binding

1½ yards of fabric for backing

48" x 60" piece of batting

1⅛ yards of 17"-wide fusible web**

Template plastic (optional)

Monofilament or threads to match appliqués for topstitching

You can substitute 1 Jelly Roll for all of these pieces.

**1⅛ yards of fusible web is sufficient if you mark and cut out smaller shapes such as wings and eyes from within the larger body and head shapes. If you prefer not to do that, you'll need 1½ yards of fusible web.*

Sorting the Precut Fabrics

This quilt is quite easy to piece and with the help of fusible web, the appliqué is easy, too. Even the planning is quite simple. First, set aside two of the Jelly Roll strips to use for the appliqué branches. Then set aside any others that you might want to use for other appliqué shapes. In the quilt shown, Karen set aside the solid-colored strips from her Jelly Roll as follows: green for leaves, orange for talons (feet), gold for beaks, brown for eyes.

From the remaining strips, select 20 assorted strips to use for the checkerboard panels.

Cutting

Appliqué patterns are on pages 246 and 247.

From the light plaid, cut:

2 strips, 12" x 42" (or as wide as your fabric)

From the striped fabric, cut:

206" of 2½"-wide bias strips

Piecing the Checkerboard Panels

1 Cut the 20 strips for checkerboards in half to make a total of 40 strips, 2½" x 21". This will enable you to create more variety in your strip sets and mix up the colors and prints a bit more easily in the patchwork panels.

2 Sew the strips together in sets of five to make a total of eight strip sets. Press all of the seam allowances in the same direction. Cut the strip sets into 2½"-wide segments. Each segment will have five squares in it. You should be able to cut eight or nine segments from each strip set, which will be more than you need, but will give you options when it comes to color placement. Make and cut all the strip sets before moving on to step 3 so that you'll have lots of variety to work with.

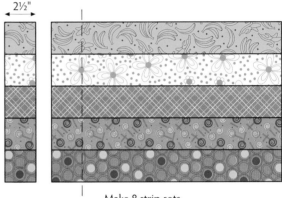

2½"

Make 8 strip sets.
Cut into 2½"-wide segments.

Mix 'em Up!

When sewing strip sets, make sure to not always have the same colors in the same positions, such as green always on the outer edge. You'll be sewing the strip-set segments to one another, and won't want all of the green squares to be on the outside and all of the lighter squares on the inside.

3 Sew the five-square segments together side by side to make three panels that are 21 squares wide and 5 squares deep. Mix and match the strips, turning them in either direction to position the colors or fabric patterns where you want them. You may need to press the seam allowances in the opposite direction on some of the segments so that you can abut the seams.

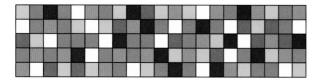

Make 3 checkerboard panels.

Preparing the Appliqués

1 Using the pattern pieces on pages 246 and 247, trace each shape onto template plastic and cut it out on the solid lines. (The dashed lines on the patterns indicate the placement of overlapping pieces.) Then trace around the plastic templates onto the paper side of fusible web, arranging like shapes together to conserve fabrics during the fusing process. Trace the smaller shapes inside the larger ones. You don't need to cover the entire owl body or head with fusible web; just around the perimeter will be sufficient.

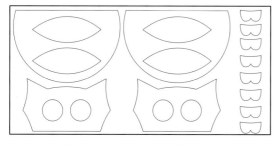

Trace wings inside of owl bodies
and eyes inside of owl heads.

2 Position the fusible web, adhesive side down, on the wrong side of your appliqué fabrics. In the quilt shown, the eyes, beaks, and feet were made from 2½"-wide strips, while the heads, wings, and bodies were cut from yardage. All eight owls have

striped bodies, but there are three red, three blue, and two green heads. Fuse the wings in pairs so that each owl will have a matching set of wings. In the quilt shown, there are three pairs of red wings, two pairs each of yellow and green wings, and one pair of blue wings. Fuse the feet, beaks, and eyes on orange, gold, and brown fabric, respectively, or on the colored fabrics of your choice. Prepare and fuse eight leaves (or as many as desired).

3 Cut out the prepared appliqué shapes on the solid lines. Do not add seam allowances to the patterns.

4 For the branches, do not use fusible web. Instead, press under a ¼" seam allowance along one long edge of each of the brown strips you've set aside for the branches.

Appliquéing the Owl Panels

1 Before you fuse anything, take the time to check the width of your appliqué panel background fabric. Compare the width of the appliqué panels to the width of your checkerboard panels. They need to be the same width. If you take a narrow seam allowance or your appliqué background fabric has less than 42½" of usable width after the selvages are trimmed, the appliqué panel may be shorter than your checkerboard panels. If the appliqué panel is shorter than the checkerboard panels, either adjust the seam allowance or remove one of the pieced strips on an end of each checkerboard panel. If the appliqué panel is too long, you can trim it after the appliqué pieces are edgestitched. Just be careful not to place the owls and leaves where they will be caught in the seam allowances.

2 Lay a prepared branch strip right side facing up on a light-plaid 12"-wide strip. Position the strip so that it's close to the bottom of the light strip and the folded edge is closest to the bottom of the panel. Machine stitch along the non-folded edge, sewing ¼" from the raw edge of the brown strip. To make a more realistic branch, you can make the strip gently undulate along the length of the cream strip; just take

care not to make it bend too far, as it's not cut on the bias and won't have more than a little bit of give.

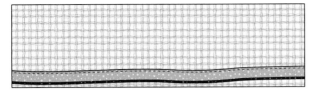

Stitch ¼" from top edge.

3 Press the seam to flatten the stitching. Then fold the branch up to cover the stitching and press in place. Using brown thread or monofilament, machine stitch the edge with the narrow hem using a narrow zigzag stitch. Press.

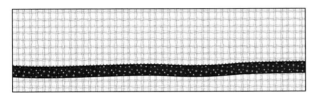

Press strip up. Machine topstitch in place.

4 Position the owl appliqués along the branch. Place the body first, and then overlap the head onto the body by roughly ¼". Place the wings on top to cover the gap at the sides of the body. When positioned correctly, the body, wings, and head will form a circle. Tuck the feet under the bottom of the body and fuse in place. Add the eyes and beak; fuse.

Go for Whimsy!

Karen admits she's never been one to mark appliqué placement precisely, and this juvenile quilt is not the place to start that! You can fit two owls on each side of the center of the panel, but if one owl is a bit closer to one neighbor than the other, that's fine. Some can be a bit higher than others, or tilted to one side or other. Make your owls whimsical. And then fill in any gaps in spacing with a few appliquéd leaves.

5 To secure all the appliqués, you'll want to add machine stitching of some sort, because baby quilts are bound to be washed. Repeatedly. And fusible web on its own won't stand up to all those washings. In the quilt shown, Karen used monofilament and a narrow zigzag (width set at 1) to stitch around all edges of body, head, wings, eyes, and beak. Stitch around the leaves, too. If you prefer not to use monofilament, you can use matching cotton threads and change the color as needed, or pick one color and make a statement.

Completing the Quilt Top

1 Measure the width of the checkerboard panels and, if necessary, trim the pressed appliqué panels to this length.

2 Sew a checkerboard panel to the bottom of each appliquéd panel. Press the seam allowances toward the appliqué. Sew these two units together, and then add the last checkerboard panel to the top of the quilt top. Press as before.

3 Before quilting, whether by hand or machine, machine stay stitch a scant ¼" from the edge, all the way around the quilt top to stabilize the edges. This is important since this quilt doesn't have borders to contain all those seam ends.

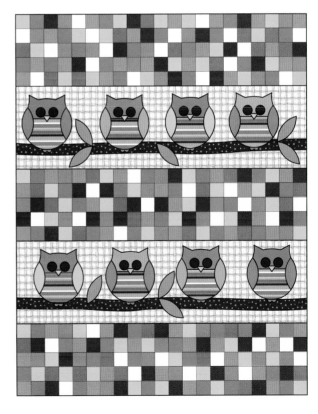

Finishing the Quilt

For help with any of the finishing steps, go to ShopMartingale.com/HowtoQuilt for free downloadable information.

1 Layer, baste, and quilt your quilt, or take it to your favorite long-arm quilter for finishing.

2 Using the striped 2½"-wide bias strips, make and attach binding.

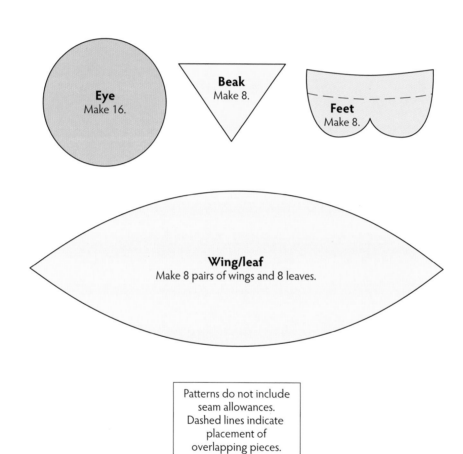

Eye
Make 16.

Beak
Make 8.

Feet
Make 8.

Wing/leaf
Make 8 pairs of wings and 8 leaves.

Patterns do not include
seam allowances.
Dashed lines indicate
placement of
overlapping pieces.

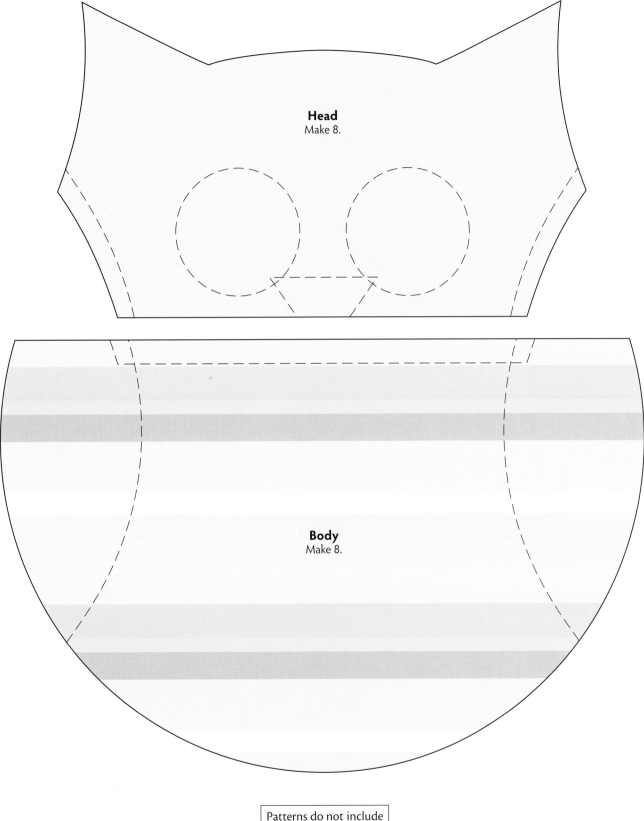

Head
Make 8.

Body
Make 8.

Patterns do not include
seam allowances.
Dashed lines indicate
placement of
overlapping pieces.

Peaks and Valleys

Embrace your wild side to make this fun quilt using lots of scraps. This quilt is guaranteed to put a dent in your stash. Use the All-in-One Ruler or make a cutting guide from the pattern provided to easily cut the trapezoid shapes, and piecing will be a breeze!

"Peaks and Valleys," designed, pieced, and quilted by Kim Brackett

FINISHED QUILT: 56½" x 64"

Materials

Yardage is based on 42"-wide fabric, except where noted.

30 strips, 2½" x 42", of assorted dark prints for braid pieces

27 strips, 2½" x 42", of assorted light prints for braid pieces

½ yard of yellow print for setting triangles

⅝ yard of red print for binding

4 yards of fabric for backing

61" x 68" piece of batting

All-in-One Ruler™ by That Patchwork Place or template plastic

Cutting

Refer to "Special Cutting" at right before you begin.

From *each* of the 30 dark print strips, cut:
6 rectangles, 2½" x 6½" (180 total; 4 are extra)

From *each* of the 27 light print strips, cut:
6 rectangles, 2½" x 6½" (162 total; 2 are extra)

From the yellow print, cut:
2 squares, 9¾" x 9¾"; cut into quarters diagonally to yield 8 quarter-square triangles

4 squares, 3¾" x 3¾"; cut in half diagonally to yield 8 half-square triangles

1 strip, 5⅛" x 42"; crosscut into 4 squares, 5⅛" x 5⅛". Cut the squares in half diagonally to yield 8 half-square triangles.

From the red print, cut:
7 binding strips, 2½" x 42"

Cutting from Scraps

If you prefer to use scraps, follow the instructions below. See "Cutting" above for instructions on cutting the setting triangles and binding. To cut the angled pieces for the braid, see "Special Cutting"; disregard step 1 of either option if you are not cutting the rectangles from strips.

From the assorted dark prints, cut:
176 rectangles, 2½" x 6½"

From the assorted light prints, cut:
160 rectangles, 2½" x 6½"

Special Cutting

There are two options for cutting the angled pieces that will create the braid units. Option 1 requires the All-in-One Ruler. Option 2 requires that you make a template from template plastic.

Option 1

1. Fold each of the 2½" x 42" strips in half, wrong sides together. From each strip, cut a total of six rectangles, 2½" x 6½" (three cuts, two layers).

2. Keep the pairs of rectangles wrong sides together. Place the bottom of the All-in-One Ruler along the long edge of the rectangle and the narrow, pointed edge of the ruler on the right edge of the rectangle as shown.

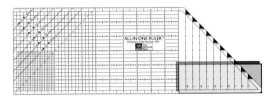

3. Trim the rectangles around the 45° edges of the ruler as shown. You'll have two mirror-image braid pieces.

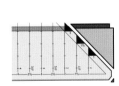 

Option 2

1. Follow step 1 of option 1 above to cut the 2½" x 6½" rectangles.

2. Make a template by tracing the pattern for the cutting guide on page 251 onto template plastic. Cut the template out on the traced lines using scissors.

3. Keep the pairs of rectangles wrong sides together and place the template on the top of the rectangles. Trim the rectangles by placing the edge of a rotary-cutting ruler along the 45° angles of the template. You'll have two mirror-image braid pieces.

Assembling the Rows

1 Sew a dark braid piece to the left side of a yellow 9¾" triangle as shown. Press the seam allowances away from the triangle. Make four. These will be the odd-numbered rows.

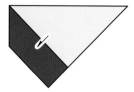

Make 4.

2 Sew a mirror-image dark braid piece to the right of each unit from step 1. Press the seam allowances away from the triangle. The triangle will be wider than the braid row. Just leave it for now; it will be trimmed later.

3 Add two light braid pieces, pressing seam allowances toward the piece just added. Continue to add two braid pieces, alternating two dark and two light pieces. Press seam allowances toward each newly added piece. End the rows with the eleventh dark pair of braid pieces.

4 Sew a yellow 5⅛" triangle to the left side of each row. Press seam allowances toward the triangle. Sew a yellow 3¾" triangle to the right side of the row. Press toward the triangle. Make four odd-numbered rows.

Make 4.

5 Trim the excess fabric from the triangles at the top of each row by placing the long edge of a ruler along the edge of the braid row. Trim away the excess triangle fabric.

6 Repeat steps 1–3 to make the even-numbered rows, but begin by sewing a braid segment to the right side of the triangle instead of the left side.

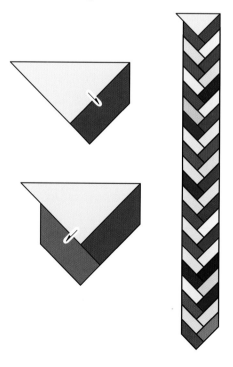

7 Sew a yellow 5⅛" triangle to the right side of
each row. Press the seam allowances toward
the triangle. Sew a yellow 3¾" triangle to the
left side. Press toward the triangle. Make four
even-numbered rows.

Make 4.

8 Trim the rows as you did in step 5.

Assembling the Quilt Top

1 Arrange the rows, alternating them as shown.
Join the rows. Press the seam allowances in
either direction.

2 Because this quilt doesn't have borders, all edges
of the quilt top have many seam intersections. To
stabilize them before quilting, stay stitch ⅛" around
the perimeter of the quilt.

Finishing the Quilt

For help with any of the finishing steps, go to
ShopMartingale.com/HowtoQuilt for free downloadable information.

1 Layer, baste, and quilt your quilt, or take it to
your favorite long-arm quilter for finishing.

2 Using the red 2½"-wide strips, make and attach
binding.

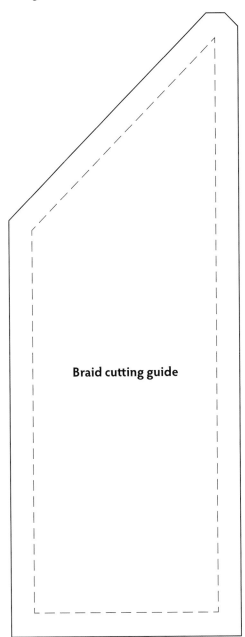

Braid cutting guide

Poinsettia

If you're like Kim Brackett and her friend Karen Williamson and have a collection of Christmas fabrics, show them off in this lovely Poinsettia quilt. This quilt is easier than it looks, made with a simple block and pieced sashings.

"Poinsettia," designed by Kim Brackett; pieced and quilted by Karen Williamson

FINISHED QUILT: 59½" x 59½" • FINISHED BLOCK: 6" x 6"

Materials

Yardage is based on 42"-wide fabric, except where noted.

28 strips, 2½" x 42", of assorted tan prints for blocks, sashing, and sashing posts

11 strips, 2½" x 42", of assorted red prints for blocks and sashing

1⅛ yards of large-scale floral for outer border

1 yard of green tone on tone for blocks, inner border, and binding

4¼ yards of fabric for backing

64" x 64" piece of batting

Cutting from Scraps

If you prefer to use scraps, follow the instructions here. See "Cutting" below for instructions on cutting the borders and binding.

From the assorted tan prints, cut:

44 rectangles, 2½" x 6½"

124 rectangles, 2½" x 4½"

97 squares, 2½" x 2½"

From the assorted red prints, cut:

52 rectangles, 2½" x 4½"

72 squares, 2½" x 2½"

From the assorted green prints, cut:

36 squares, 2½" x 2½"

Cutting

From *each of 16* assorted tan strips, cut:

2 rectangles, 2½" x 6½" (32 total)

4 rectangles, 2½" x 4½" (64 total)

3 squares, 2½" x 2½" (48 total)

From *each of 12* assorted tan strips, cut:

1 rectangle, 2½" x 6½" (12 total)

5 rectangles, 2½" x 4½" (60 total)

4 squares, 2½" x 2½"; cut 1 additional 2½" x 2½" square from scraps (49 total)

From *each of 8* red strips, cut:

5 rectangles, 2½" x 4½" (40 total)

6 squares, 2½" x 2½" (48 total)

From *each of 3* red strips, cut:

4 rectangles, 2½" x 4½" (12 total)

8 squares, 2½" x 2½" (24 total)

From the green tone on tone, cut:

10 strips, 2½" x 42"; crosscut 3 strips into 36 squares, 2½" x 2½". (Set aside the 7 remaining 2½" x 42" strips for binding.)

5 border strips, 1½" x 42"

From the large-scale floral, cut:

6 border strips, 6" x 42"

Piecing the Blocks

The blocks are scrappy, with no matching fabrics. Choose fabric pieces randomly from the assorted tan, red, and green prints.

1 Place a tan 2½" square right sides together with a red 2½" square. Sew them together diagonally, from corner to corner. Trim away one corner, leaving a ¼" seam allowance. Press the squares open, with seam allowances toward the red fabric. Repeat to make a total of 36 half-square-triangle units.

Make 36.

2 Sew a tan 2½" x 4½" rectangle to each half-square-triangle unit constructed in step 1. Press the seam allowances toward the rectangle. Make 36.

Make 36.

3 Make a folded-corner unit using a tan 2½" x 4½" rectangle and a green 2½" square, sewing diagonally from corner to corner of the square as shown. Press the seam allowances toward the green triangle. Make 36.

Make 36.

4 Sew a tan 2½" square to each folded-corner unit constructed in step 3 as shown. Press the seam allowances toward the light-tan square. Make 36.

Make 36.

5 Make a folded-corner unit using a tan 2½" x 6½" rectangle and a red 2½" square. Press the seam allowances toward the red triangle. Make 36.

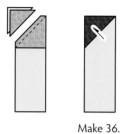

Make 36.

6 Sew together the units constructed in steps 2, 4, and 5 as shown to make the block. Press the seam allowances as shown. Make a total of 36 blocks.

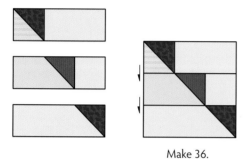

Make 36.

Piecing the Sashing Units

Place a tan 2½" x 4½" rectangle perpendicularly to a red 2½" x 4½" rectangle, with edges aligned at one corner. Sew diagonally from edge to edge where the rectangles intersect. Trim away the excess corner fabric, leaving a ¼" seam allowance. Press the seam allowances toward the light tan fabric. Make 52.

Make 52.

Assembling the Quilt Top

1 Arrange the blocks, the sashing units, and the remaining tan rectangles and squares in horizontal rows as shown. Sew the blocks and sashing pieces together in rows, pressing the seam allowances as shown. Join the rows. Press the seam allowances in the same direction.

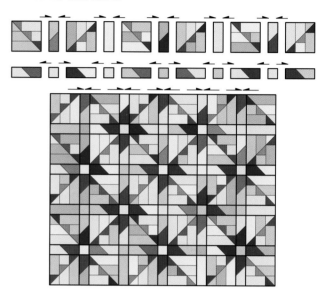

2 Using the green 1½"-wide inner-border strips and the floral 6"-wide outer-border strips, measure your quilt top and add the borders to fit.

Finishing the Quilt

For help with any of the finishing steps, go to ShopMartingale.com/HowtoQuilt for free downloadable information.

1 Layer, baste, and quilt your quilt, or take it to your favorite long-arm quilter for finishing.

2 Using the green 2½"-wide strips, make and attach binding.

THERE'S MORE ONLINE

We at Martingale and That Patchwork Place are happy to bring you this vast collection of quilts made from precut fabrics. To fit as many projects as possible into the book, we didn't include all of the basic how-to information for rotary cutting, piecing, pressing, adding borders, and more. If you need more information about any of these techniques, please go to ShopMartingale.com/HowtoQuilt to download illustrated instructions—for free!

And, if you like the projects in this book, we invite you to look for books by the project designers at your local quilt shop or at ShopMartingale.com. Below is a complete list of the books in which these projects originally appeared.

Another Bite of Schnibbles by Carrie Nelson

Back to Charm School by Mary Etherington and Connie Tesene

A Baker's Dozen by the Staff at That Patchwork Place

Charmed by Jodi Crowell

Charmed, I'm Sure by Lesley Chaisson

Clever Quarters, Too by Susan Teegarden Dissmore

Four-Patch Frolic by Barbara Groves and Mary Jacobson

Jelly Babies by the Staff at That Patchwork Place

Large-Block Quilts by Victoria L. Eapen

Loose Change by Claudia Plett and Le Ann Weaver

Modern Baby (various contributors)

Modern Quilts from the Blogging Universe (various contributors)

More Loose Change by Claudia Plett and Le Ann Weaver

Quilting with Fat Quarters by the Staff at That Patchwork Place

Quilting with Precuts and Shortcuts by Terry Martin

Quilts from Sweet Jane by Sue Pfau

Rolling Along by Nancy J. Martin

Schnibbles Times Two by Carrie Nelson

Scrap-Basket Beauties by Kim Brackett

Seamingly Scrappy by Rebecca Silbaugh

Simple Style by Sara Diepersloot

'Tis the Season by Jeanne Large and Shelley Wicks

Urban Country Quilts by Jeanne Large and Shelley Wicks

What's your creative passion?
Find it at ShopMartingale.com
books • eBooks • ePatterns • daily blog • free projects
videos • tutorials • inspiration • giveaways

Martingale
Create with Confidence